# Commercial Leases:
# Tenants' Amendments

**AUSTRALIA**
Law Book Co.
Sydney

**CANADA** and **USA**
Carswell
Toronto

**HONG KONG**
Sweet & Maxwell Asia

**NEW ZEALAND**
Brooker's
Wellington

**SINGAPORE** and **MALAYSIA**
Sweet & Maxwell Asia
Singapore and Kuala Lumpur

# Commercial Leases: Tenants' Amendments

*4th Edition*

## Robert Sweet

*LLM, Solicitor*
*Partner in KSB Law, Lincoln's Inn*

LONDON
SWEET & MAXWELL
2002

First edition 1992
Second edition 1995
Third edition 1998
Fourth edition 2002

*Published in 2002 by Sweet & Maxwell Limited of*
*100 Avenue Road*
*London NW3 3PF*
*Typeset by Servis Filmsetting Ltd*
*Printed in Great Britain by TJ International, Padstow, Cornwall*

No natural forests were destroyed to make this product; only farmed timber was used and replanted.

A CIP record for this book is available from the British Library

ISBN 0421 772 107

All rights reserved.
Crown copyright legislation is reproduced with the permission of the Controller of HMSO and the Queen's Printer for Scotland.

No part of this publication may be reproduced or transmitted in any form or by any means, or stored in any retrieval system of any nature without prior written permission, except for permitted fair dealing under the Copyright, Designs and Patents Act 1988, or in accordance with the terms of a licence issued by the Copyright Licensing Agency in respect of photocopying and/or reprographic reproduction. Application for permission for other use of copyright material including permission to reproduce extracts in other published works shall be made to the publishers. Full acknowledgment of author, publisher and source must be given.

©
Sweet & Maxwell Limited
2002

# Acknowledgment

The precedents and text from Volume 22 of the *Encyclopaedia of Forms & Precedents* (5th edition) reproduced herein are the copyright of Reed Elsevier (U.K.) Ltd and are reproduced with their kind permission.

# Contents

*Table of Cases* viii
*Table of Statutes* xii
*Table of Statutory Instruments* xiv

Introduction xv

1  Agreement for Lease 1
2  The Lease 49
3  Demise 71
4  Tenant's Covenants 75
5  Landlord's Covenants 112
6  Insurance 118
7  Guarantor's Covenants 140
8  Provisos 145
9  Execution of Deeds 163
10 The Premises 165
11 Rent Review Provisions 174
12 The Shop Covenants 200
13 Service Charges 215
14 Authorised Guarantee Agreement 241
15 Licence for Alterations 247

*Index* 267

# Table of Cases

Adami v. Lincoln Grange Management Ltd (1998) 30 H.L.R. 982; [1998] 1
   E.G.L.R. 58; [1998] 17 E.G. 148, CA..................................................................6.16
Addin Investments Ltd v. Secretary of State for the Environment [1997] 1 E.G.L.R.
   99; [1997] 14 E.G. 132; [1996] E.G.C.S. 195, Ch D.............................................11.12
Allied Dunbar Assurance Plc v. Homebase Ltd [2002] 1 P. & C.R. 1; [2002] L. &
   T.R. 1; [2001] 16 E.G.C.S. 146, Ch D....................................................................4.14
Anstruther Gough Calthorpe v. McOscar [1924] 1 K.B. 716, CA ...................................4.06
Ashworth Frazer Ltd v. Gloucester City Council (Consent to Assignment) [2001]
   UKHL 59; [2001] 1 W.L.R. 2180, HL ...................................................................4.14
B&Q Plc v. Liverpool and Lancashire Properties Ltd (2001) 81 P. & C.R. 20; [2001]
   1 E.G.L.R. 92; [2000] E.G.C.S. 101, Ch D...........................................................10.04
BHP Petroleum Great Britain Ltd v. Chesterfield Properties Ltd [2001] EWCA Civ
   1797, CA; reversing [2002] Ch. 12; [2001] 3 W.L.R. 277; [2001] 22 E.G. 155, Ch
   D..............................................................................................................................1.09
Balls Bros Ltd v. Sinclair [1931] 2 Ch. 325, Ch D .........................................................12.04
Barclays Bank Plc v. Savile Estates Ltd; sub nom. Barclays Bank Plc v. Saville
   Estates Ltd [2002] EWCA Civ 589; [2002] 18 E.G.C.S. 152; [2002] 18. E.G. 152,
   CA.........................................................................................................................11.12
Beacon Carpets v. Kirby [1985] Q.B. 755; [1984] 3 W.L.R. 489, CA ............................6.12
Becker v. Partridge [1966] 2 Q.B. 155; [1966] 2 W.L.R. 803, CA .................................1.20
Bernstein (Lord) v. Skyviews and General Ltd [1978] Q.B. 479; [1977] 3 W.L.R.
   136, QBD..............................................................................................................10.02
Boldmark v. Cohen (1987) 19 H.L.R. 135; [1986] 1 E.G.L.R. 47, CA .........................13.33
Boots the Chemists Ltd v. Pinkland [1992] 28 E.G. 118................................................11.11
Braddon Towers Ltd v. International Stores Ltd [1987] 1 E.G.L.R. 209......................12.06
Brett v. Brett Essex Golf Club Ltd (1986) 52 P. & C.R. 330; [1986] 1 E.G.L.R. 154,
   CA...........................................................................................................................2.08
Britel Corp. NV v. Orbach (1997) 29 H.L.R. 883, CA...................................................13.07
British Railways Board v. Ringbest Ltd [1996] 2 E.G.L.R. 82; [1996] 30 E.G. 94, Ch
   D............................................................................................................................11.09
Broomleigh Housing Association Ltd v. Hughes [1999] E.G.C.S. 134, Ch D ..............13.01
Burgess v. Purchase & Sons (Farms) Ltd [1983] Ch. 216; [1983] 2 W.L.R. 361, Ch
   D............................................................................................................................11.10
Cairnplace v. CBL (Property Investment) Co. [1984] 1 W.L.R. 696; [1984] 1 All
   E.R. 315, CA ..........................................................................................................4.34
Cellulose Acetate Silk Co. Ltd v. Widnes Foundry (1925) Ltd [1933] A.C. 20, HL.........2.03
Charles Hunt Ltd v. Palmer [1931] 2 Ch. 287; [1931] All E.R. Rep. 815, Ch D.............1.20
Claire's Accessories UK Ltd v. Kensington High Street Associates LLC [2001] ...........8.16
Cleve House Properties v. Schidlof, unreported, December 21, 1979, CC ...................13.24
Commercial Union Life Assurance Co. Ltd v. Label Ink Ltd [2001] L. & T.R. 29,
   Ch D .......................................................................................................................8.24

## Table of Cases ix

Concorde Graphics v. Andromeda Investments SA (1983) 265 E.G. 386 ...................... 13.08
Connaught Restaurants v. Indoor Leisure [1994] 1 W.L.R. 501; [1994] 4 All E.R.
 834, CA ............................................................................................................................ 3.02
Cooperative Insurance Society Ltd v. Argyll Stores (Holdings) Ltd [1998] A.C. 1;
 [1997] 2 W.L.R. 898; [1997] 23 E.G. 141, HL ........................................................... 12.06
Co-operative Wholesale Society Ltd v. National Westminster Bank Plc; Broadgate
 Square v. Lehman Bros; Scottish Amicable Life Assurance Society v. Middleton
 Potts & Co; Prudential Nominees v. Greenham Trading [1995] 1 E.G.L.R. 97;
 [1995] 01 E.G. 111; [1994] E.G.C.S. 184, CA ........................................................... 11.06
Costain Property Developments Ltd v. Finlay & Co. Ltd (1989) 57 P. & C.R. 345;
 [1989] 1 E.G.L.R. 237, QBD ....................................................................................... 12.06
Credit Suisse v. Beegas Nominees Ltd [1994] 4 All E.R. 803; (1995) 69 P. & C.R.
 177; [1994] 11 E.G. 151, Ch D ..................................................................................... 4.06
Curtis v. French [1929] 1 Ch. 253, Ch D ............................................................................ 1.22
Cynon Valley BC v. Secretary of State for Wales and Oi Mee Lam, 85 L.G.R. 36;
 (1987) 53 P. & C.R. 68, CA .......................................................................................... 4.20
Davenport v. Queen, The (1877–78) L.R. 3 App. Cas. 115, PC (Aus) ............................ 8.06
Davstone Estates Ltd's Leases, Re; *sub nom.* Manprop Ltd v. O'Dell [1969] 2 Ch.
 378; [1969] 2 W.L.R. 1287, Ch D ............................................................................... 13.08
Deerfield Travel Services v. Wardens and Society of the Mistery or Art of the
 Leather Sellers of the City of London (1983) 46 P. & C.R. 132, CA ........................ 14.00
Dennis and Robinson v. Kiossos Establishment (1987) 54 P. & C.R. 282; [1987] 1
 E.G.L.R. 133, CA ........................................................................................................ 11.03
Dunlop Pneumatic Tyre Co. Ltd v. New Garage & Motor Co. Ltd [1915] A.C. 79,
 HL ................................................................................................................................... 2.03
Durley House Ltd v. Cadogan [2000] 1 W.L.R. 246; [2000] L. & T.R. 255; [2000] 09
 E.G. 183, Ch D ............................................................................................................. 11.08
Earl of Chesterfield v. Duke of Bolton, 2 Com. 627 ......................................................... 4.06
Edge v. Boileau (1885-86) L.R. 16 Q.B.D. 117, QBD ..................................................... 5.02
English Exporters (London) Ltd v. Eldonwall Ltd [1973] Ch. 415; [1973] 2 W.L.R.
 435, Ch D ....................................................................................................................... 1.08
FW Woolworth & Co. Ltd v. Lambert. *See* Lambert v. FW Woolworth & Co. Ltd
 (No.1)
FW Woolworth Plc v. Charlwood Alliance Properties [1987] 1 E.G.L.R. 53; (1987)
 282 E.G. 585 ................................................................................................................ 12.06
Finchbourne Ltd v. Rodrigues [1976] 3 All E.R. 581, CA ................................. 13.06, 13.10
Fluor Daniel Properties Ltd v. Shortlands Investments Ltd [2001] 4 E.G.C.S. 145;
 (2001) 98(14) L.S.G. 39, Ch D ................................................................................... 13.09
Godbold v. Martin (The Newsagents) (1983) 268 E.G. 1202 ............................. 11.08, 12.02
Gran Gelato Ltd v. Richcliff (Group) Ltd [1992] Ch. 560; [1992] 2 W.L.R. 867,
 Ch D ............................................................................................................................... 1.22
Grossman v. Hooper [2001] EWCA Civ 615; [2001] 3 F.C.R. 662; [2001] 27 E.G.
 135, CA ........................................................................................................................... 1.28
Haedicke and Lipski's Contract, Re [1901] 2 Ch. 666, Ch D ........................................... 1.20
Halifax Building Society v. Keighley [1931] 2 K.B. 248, KBD ..................................... 6.14
Hamish Cathie Travel England v. Insight International Tours [1986] 1 E.G.L.R.
 244 ................................................................................................................................. 11.08
Harben Style Ltd v. Rhodes Trust [1995] 1 E.G.L.R. 118; [1995] 17 E.G. 125, Ch D ... 11.12
Harrison Ainslie & Co. v. Lord Muncaster [1891] 2 Q.B. 680, CA .............................. 5.02
Havenridge Ltd v. Boston Dyers Ltd [1994] 49 E.G. 111; [1994] E.G.C.S. 53, CA ........ 2.06
Hill v. Harris [1965] 2 Q.B. 601; [1965] 2 W.L.R. 1331, CA ......................................... 8.10
Hindcastle Ltd v. Barbara Attenborough Associates Ltd [1997] A.C. 70; [1996] 2
 W.L.R. 262; [1996] 1 All E.R. 737, HL ....................................................................... 7.04
Historic House Hotels Ltd v. Cadogan Estates Ltd [1995] 1 E.G.L.R. 117; [1995] 11
 E.G. 140, CA ............................................................................................................... 11.02
Holme v. Brunskill (1877-78) L.R. 3 Q.B.D. 495, CA ..................................................... 7.03

## Table of Cases

Howard de Walden Estates v. Pasta Place Ltd [1995] 1 E.G.L.R. 79; [1995] 22 E.G. 143, Ch D .................................................................................................................7.03
IBM United Kingdom Ltd v. Rockware Glass Ltd [1980] F.S.R. 335, CA .....................1.08
Javad v. Aqil [1991] 1 W.L.R. 1007; [1991] 1 All E.R. 243, CA....................................1.12
Jervis v. Harris [1996] Ch. 195; [1996] 2 W.L.R. 220; [1996] 1 All E.R. 303, CA..........4.10
Jones v. Sherwood Computer Services Plc [1992] 1 W.L.R. 277; [1992] 2 All E.R. 170, CA ..................................................................................................................13.08
Junction Estates v. Cope (1974) 27 P. & C.R. 482, QBD ................................................2.09
King, Robinson, Re v. Gray [1963] Ch. 459; [1963] 2 W.L.R. 629, CA .........................6.12
Kleinwort Benson Ltd v. Lincoln City Council [1999] 2 A.C. 349; [1998] 3 W.L.R. 1095; [1998] 4 All E.R. 513, HL........................................................................13.08
Koumoudouros & Marathon Realty Co., Re (1978) 89 D.L.R. (3d) 551, HC (Ont) ........4.18
Lambert v. FW Woolworth & Co. Ltd (No.1); *sub nom.* FW Woolworth & Co. Ltd v. Lambert [1937] Ch. 37; [1936] 2 All E.R. 1523, CA ..........................................12.04
Lambert v. FW Woolworth & Co. Ltd (No.2); *sub nom.* FW Woolworth & Co Ltd v Lambert [1938] Ch. 883; [1938] 2 All E.R. 664, CA .........................................14.00
Laura Investments v. Havering [1992] 1 E.G.L.R. 155; [1992] 24 E.G. 136..................11.08
Legal & General Assurance Society Ltd v. General Metal Agencies Ltd (1969) 20 P. & C.R. 953; 113 S.J. 876, QBD ..........................................................................8.06
London and Leeds Estates Ltd v. Paribas Ltd (1993) 66 P. & C.R. 218; [1993] 30 E.G. 89, CA ..........................................................................................................11.04
Lurcott v. Wakeley & Wheeler [1911] 1 K.B. 905; [1911-13] All E.R. Rep. 41, CA .......4.06
Mannai Investment Co. Ltd v. Eagle Star Life Assurance Co. Ltd [1997] A.C. 749; [1997] 2 W.L.R. 945; [1997] 1 E.G.L.R. 57, HL .................................................8.24
Manprop Ltd v. O'Dell. *See* Davstone Estates Ltd's Leases, Re
Mark Rowlands Ltd v. Berni Inns Ltd [1986] Q.B. 211; [1985] 3 W.L.R. 964, CA .........6.15
Mumford Hotels Ltd v. Wheeler [1964] Ch. 117; [1963] 3 W.L.R. 735, Ch D .......6.04, 6.10
National Westminster Bank Plc v. Arthur Young McCelland Moores & Co. [1985] 1 W.L.R. 1123; [1985] 2 All E.R. 817, CA ............................................................11.04
New England Properties v. Portsmouth New Shops [1993] 23 E.G. 130; [1993] 1 E.G.L.R. 84 ...........................................................................................................4.06
New Zealand Government Property Corp. v. HM&S Ltd (The New York Star) [1982] Q.B. 1145; [1982] 2 W.L.R. 837, CA ..................................................11.08, 11.09
99 Bishopsgate v. Prudential Assurance (1985) 273 E.G. 984; [1985] 1 E.G.L.R. 72, CA ...............................................................................................................11.03, 11.06
Norwich Union Life Insurance Society v. British Railways Board (1987) 283 E.G. 846; [1987] 2 E.G.L.R. 137 ..................................................................................4.06
Norwich Union Life Insurance Society v. Trustee Savings Bank Central Board [1986] 1 E.G.L.R. 136; (1985) 278 E.G. 162..........................................................11.04
Ocean Accident and Guarantee Corp. v. Next Plc; Commercial Union Assurance Co. Plc v. Next Plc [1996] 2 E.G.L.R. 84; [1996] 33 E.G. 91; [1995] E.G.C.S. 187, Ch D.............................................................................................................................11.03
O'May v. City of London Real Property Co. Ltd [1983] 2 A.C. 726; [1982] 2 W.L.R. 407, HL.......................................................................................................4.14, 11.02
Osbourne Assets Ltd v. Britannia Life Ltd [1997] ..........................................................8.24
Overbrooke Estates Ltd v. Glencombe Properties Ltd [1974] 1 W.L.R. 1335; [1974] 3 All E.R. 511, Ch D ............................................................................................1.22
Owen v. Gadd [1956] 2 Q.B. 99; [1956] 2 W.L.R. 945, CA..........................................10.14
P&A Swift Investments v. Combined English Stores Group Plc [1989] A.C. 632; [1988] 3 W.L.R. 313, HL......................................................................................7.03
P&O Property Holdings Ltd v. International Computers Ltd [2000] 2 All E.R. 1015; [1999] 2 E.G.L.R. 17; [1999] 18 E.G. 158, Ch D.................................................6.16
Paradine v. Jane (1647) Aleyn 26....................................................................................4.06
Pivot Properties Ltd v. Secretary of State for the Environment; *sub nom.* Secretary of State for the Environment v. Pivot Properties Ltd (1981) 41 P. & C.R. 248; (1980) 256 E.G. 1176, CA ..............................................................................................11.05

Ponsford v. HMS Aerosols Ltd [1979] A.C. 63; [1978] 3 W.L.R. 241; [1978] 2 All E.R. 837, HL ................................................................................................ 11.08, 14.00
Pontsarn Investments v. Kansallis-Osake-Pankki [1992] 1 E.G.L.R. 148; [1992] 22 E.G. 103, Ch D ..................................................................................................... 11.04
Portavon Cinema Co. Ltd v. Price (1939) 65 Ll. L. Rep. 161, KBD ............................... 6.04
Proudfoot v. Hart (1890) L.R. 25 Q.B.D. 42, CA ........................................................... 4.06
Redmond v. Dainton [1920] 2 K.B. 256 .......................................................................... 4.06
Rom Securities v. Rogers (Holdings) (1967) 205 E.G. 427 ............................................ 1.19
Rowlands (Mark) Ltd v. Berni Inns Ltd. *See* Mark Rowlands Ltd v. Berni Inns Ltd
Royal Bank of Scotland Plc v. Jennings (1998) 75 P. & C.R. 458, CA; affirming (1995) 70 P. & C.R. 459; [1995] 2 E.G.L.R. 87, Ch D ................................................ 11.12
Royal Insurance Property Services Ltd v. Cliffway Ltd [1996] E.G.C.S. 189, Ch D ..... 11.12
St Martins Property Investments Ltd v. CIB Properties Ltd; *sub nom.* St Martins Property Ltd v. Citicorp Investment Bank Properties Ltd [1999] L. & T.R. 1; [1998] E.G.C.S. 161, CA ................................................................................................ 11.09
St Martins Property Ltd v. Citicorp Investment Bank Properties Ltd. *See* St Martins Property Investments Ltd v. CIB Properties Ltd
Scottish & Newcastle Breweries v. Sir Richard Sutton's Settled Estates [1985] 2 E.G.L.R. 130; (1985) 276 E.G. 77 ............................................................................. 11.07
Scottish Mutual Assurance Plc v. Jardine Public Relations Ltd [1999] E.G.C.S. 43, QBD .............................................................................................................................. 13.09
Secretary of State for the Environment v. Pivot Properties Ltd. *See* Pivot Properties Ltd v. Secretary of State for the Environment
Secretary of State for the Environment v. Possfund (North West) Ltd [1997] 2 E.G.L.R. 56; [1997] 39 E.G. 179, Ch D ..................................................................... 13.34
Stacey v. Hill [1901] 1 Q.B. 660, CA ............................................................................. 7.04
Starmark Enterprises Ltd v. CPL Distribution Ltd [2001] EWCA Civ 1252; [2002] 2 W.L.R. 1009; [2001] 32 E.G. 89, CA ........................................................................ 11.11
Tea Trade Properties v. CIN Properties Ltd [1990] 22 E.G. 67 .................................... 12.03
Terrell v. Murray (1901) 17 T.L.R. 570 ........................................................................... 4.06
Terry and White's Contract, Re (1886) L.R. 32 Ch. D. 14, CA ..................................... 1.22
Tootal Clothing Ltd v. Guinea Properties Management Ltd (1992) 64 P. & C.R. 452; [1992] 41 E.G. 117, CA ............................................................................................... 1.28
Transworld Land Co. v. J Sainsbury Plc [1990] 2 E.G.L.R. 255 .................................. 12.06
Trow v. Ind Coope (West Midlands) Ltd [1967] 2 Q.B. 899; [1967] 3 W.L.R. 633, CA ............................................................................................................................... 2.02
United Scientific Holdings v. Burnley BC [1978] A.C. 904; [1977] 2 W.L.R. 806, HL ............................................................................................................................... 11.11
Universities Superannuation Scheme Ltd v. Marks & Spencer Plc [1999] L. & T.R. 237; [1999] 1 E.G.L.R. 13; [1999] 04 E.G. 158, CA ................................................. 13.08
Vyvyan v. Arthur [1814-23] All E.R. Rep. 352; (1823) 1 B & C 410, KBD .................. 3.02
Wallis Fashion Group Ltd v. CGU Life Assurance Ltd (2001) 81 P. & C.R. 28; [2000] L. & T.R. 520; [2000] 27 E.G. 145, Ch D ..................................................... 4.14
Walsh v. Greenwich London Borough Council [2000] 49 E.G. 118 ............................... 4.06
Watts v. Spence [1976] Ch. 165; [1975] 2 W.L.R. 1039, Ch D ...................................... 1.20
West Horndon Industrial Park Ltd v. Phoenix Timber Group Plc [1995] 1 E.G.L.R. 77; [1995] 20 E.G. 137; [1995] N.P.C. 42, Ch D ....................................................... 7.03
Williams v. Southwark London Borough Council (2001) 33 H.L.R. 22; [2000] B.L.G.R. 646; [2000] E.G.C.S. 44 Ch D ..................................................................... 2.06
Young v. Dalgety [1987] 1 E.G.L.R. 116; (1987) 281 E.G. 427, CA ........................... 11.03

# Table of Statutes

| | | |
|---|---|---|
| 1774 | Fires Prevention (Metropolis) Act (14 Geo.3, c.78) | |
| | s.83 | 6.04 |
| 1852 | Common Law Procedure Act (15 & 16 Vict., c.76) | 3.02, 4.26 |
| 1891 | Stamp Act (54 & 55 Vict., c.39) | |
| | s.56 | 3.03 |
| 1925 | Law of Property Act (15 & 16 Geo. 5, c.20) | |
| | s.38 | 8.03 |
| | s.44(2)-(4) | 1.20 |
| | s.62 | 8.07 |
| | s.140 | 7.03, 14.13 |
| | s.143 | 15.30 |
| | s.146 | 3.02, 4.18, 4.19, 4.26, 7.03, 8.02, 14.13 |
| | s.146(4) | 4.15 |
| | s.147 | 4.18, 4.19 |
| | s.196 | 8.16 |
| | s.196(4) | 8.16 |
| 1927 | Landlord and Tenant Act (17 & 18 Geo.5, c.36) | 15.40 |
| | Pt 1 | 15.40 |
| | s.19 | 4.34 |
| | s.19(1A) | 4.12, 4.13, 4.14 |
| | s.19(2) | 12.04, 15.23, 15.31 |
| 1938 | Leasehold Property (Repairs) Act (1 & 2 Geo. 6, c.34) | 4.10, 4.11 |
| 1954 | Landlord and Tenant Act (2 & 3 Eliz.2, c.56) | 2.01, 2.08, 4.09, 4.21, 4.25, 6.11. 8.09, 10.13, 11.02, 11.05 |
| | s.24 | 2.10, 4.23, 11.02 |
| | ss.24-28 | 4.14 |
| | s.34 | 11.03, 11.08 |
| | s.42 | 2.05, 4.13, 4.15 |
| 1958 | Costs of Leases Act (6 & 7 Eliz.2, c.52) | 4.34 |
| | s.1 | 1.25 |
| | s.2 | 1.25 |
| 1962 | Recorded Delivery Service Act (10 & 11 Eliz.2, c.27) | 8.16 |
| 1964 | Perpetuities and Accumulations Act (c.55) | 8.09 |
| 1969 | Law of Property Act (c.59) | 2.08 |
| 1970 | Taxes Management Act (c.9) | |
| | s.106(2) | 3.02 |
| 1972 | Defective Premises Act (c.35) | 4.30 |
| | s.4(4) | 4.10 |
| 1983 | Mental Health Act (c.20) | 4.31 |
| 1985 | Companies Act (c.6) | |
| | s.36A | 9.01 |

| | | |
|---|---|---|
| 1989 | Law of Property (Miscellaneous Provisions) Act (c.34) | |
| | s.1 | 9.01 |
| | s.2 | 1.28 |
| 1990 | Town and Country Planning Act (c.8) | 2.08, 15.05, 15.53 |
| | s.55 | 2.11 |
| | s.106 | 1.06 |
| 1990 | Planning (Listed Buildings and Conservation Areas) Act 1990 (c.9) | 2.08 |
| 1990 | Planning (Hazardous Substances) Act (c.10) | 2.08 |
| 1990 | Planning (Consequential Provisions) Act (c.11) | 2.08 |
| 1990 | Environmental Protection Act (c.43) | 13.03 |
| 1991 | Planning and Compensation Act 1991 (c.34) | 2.08 |
| 1992 | Access to Neighbouring Land Act (c.23) | 10.07 |
| 1993 | Reinsurance (Acts of Terrorism) Act 1993 (c.18) | 2.07 |
| | s.3(2) | 2.07 |
| 1994 | Finance Act (c.9) | |
| | s.240 | 9.01 |
| 1994 | Sunday Trading Act (c.20) | 2.04 |
| 1995 | Landlord and Tenant (Covenants) Act (c.30) | 2.08, 2.10, 4.13, 4.14, 7.01, 7.03, 8.21, 8.23, 14.19, 15.07 |
| | s.1 | 8.23 |
| | s.8 | 1.09, 4.34 |
| | s.11 | 4.12, 4.14 |
| | s.11(1) | 7.03, 14.06 |
| | s.16 | 14.00 |
| | s.24(2) | 7.01 |
| | s.25 | 14.17, 14.18 |
| | s.25(1) | 7.01 |
| | s.28(1) | 14.07 |
| 1995 | Disability Discrimination Act (c.50) | 4.09, 11.08, 12.02, 15.20 |
| 1996 | Arbitration Act (c.23) | 6.08, 6.11, 11.10 |
| 1998 | Human Rights Act (c.42) | 8.17 |
| 1999 | Contracts (Rights of Third Parties) Act (c.31) | 8.26 |
| | s.1 | 8.26 |
| 2000 | Terrorism Act | 2.07 |

# Table of Statutory Instruments

1987 Town and Country Planning (Use Classes) Order (S.I. 1987 No. 764) .................2.11
1994 Construction (Design and Management) Regulations (S.I. 1994 No. 3140)..........................................................................................1.06, 4.09, 4.12

# Introduction

As I said in the introduction to the previous editions, this book is not intended to be an authoritative textbook. It is merely to act as a guide to commercial conveyancers when amending and settling agreements for lease and leases. I have also added a chapter dealing with suggested amendments to a licence for alterations, which I hope will be of use to tenants and their advisers. It may possibly also be of interest to surveyors and others involved in commercial property as an insight into the often mysterious terminology of commercial property documentation.

There are several erudite and comprehensive authoritative textbooks available to guide the unwary through the maze that forms our property law and these should be looked to for a more detailed analysis. In particular: *Drafting and Negotiating Commercial Leases* by Murray J. Ross; *Drafting Business Leases* by Kim Lewison Q.C. and *Commercial Leases* by Stephen Tromans. All three textbooks have assisted me in compiling this book.

Once again, I am extremely grateful to Reed Elsevier (U.K.) Ltd for allowing me to reproduce precedents from Volume 22 of the *Encyclopaedia of Forms and Precedents* (5th ed.).

The format of the book is the setting out of a full precedent for both the agreement and lease, as well as the licence for alterations referred to above, so that readers can see the complete documentation and how I propose it should be amended. I have used Form 14 from Volume 22 of the *Encyclopaedia* for the agreement and Form 29 for the lease. These forms have in fact been updated in Volumes 22(2) and 22(4) of the 1997 reissue of that part of the *Encyclopaedia*, but the content of the forms has not varied enormously (apart, of course, from the introduction of provisions to accommodate changes in law, *e.g.* the Landlord and Tenant (Covenants) Act 1995) and I remain of the opinion that, despite the elaborate drafts that tumble onto my desk, the great majority of them are based on Forms 14 and 19, though obviously with some subtle and not-so-subtle corrections. All references to "the *Encyclopaedia*" and "the precedent" in the text refer to the *Encyclopaedia of Forms and Precedents*.

My amendments are not designed to cover every eventuality, which, of course, would be a practical impossibility, but are aimed at the provisions which tend to be common to most agreements and leases. Provisions are, however, phrased differently from agreement to agreement and lease to lease and the tenant's adviser will be expected to construe and amend the particular documentation accordingly, but perhaps considering the guidelines I have laid down in this book. Furthermore, there will naturally be many covenants and other provisions additional to those contained in the precedents, but the tenant's adviser will have to continue to tackle those himself, using his own judgment. I have added some clauses which I have included in recent years as part of my amendments to drafts in order to protect the tenant's interests.

As with the previous editions I have set out in bold type the precedents clause by clause interspersed with my own comments, followed, once again in bold type, by my suggested amendments to the particular parts of the precedents, where those amendments are not readily identifiable from my comments in the text. I have also tried to divide the particular provisions of the precedents into chapters, where appropriate, but I feel that the agreement does not lend itself to such a division and I have therefore dealt with that in a chapter by itself.

I should like to mention five areas of importance covered in this edition. First, the Landlord and Tenant (Covenants) Act 1995 has been effective since January 1, 1996 and the alienation provisions in the form of lease deal with this statute. Secondly, I remain of the opinion that insurance provisions in leases should be given careful consideration by tenants' advisers to try to counter both the expected and the unexpected. Thirdly, the tenant should pay close attention to service charge provisions, which are tending to give rise to service charges increasing at an alarming rate. The fourth area worthy of a special mention is environmental issues. As mentioned in previous editions, this area has not hitherto been given sufficient consideration by conveyancers and should not be sidestepped any longer. This could well be an area of expensive litigation in the future and should be taken seriously. Finally, the fifth area is terrorism, which regrettably will not go away. Advisers must, of course, also bear in mind the effect of the Code of Practice for Commercial Leases which was launched by the Government in April 2002. I have commented on this at the beginning of Chapter 2.

As I have mentioned in the previous editions, it must be appreciated that the amendments suggested in this book represent my opinion as to what is advisable in the tenant's best interests. I offer no warranty that they are conclusive and, if accepted by the landlord, produce ideal documentation from the tenant's standpoint. It may be that other commercial conveyancers would amend the documentation differently to me, or even disagree either with my amendments or my reasoning, and if so, I should be interested to hear from them.

*Robert Sweet*
*August 2002*

*Chapter 1*

# Agreement for Lease

## Introduction

In many instances, there is no necessity for an agreement for lease. For instance, a tenant may have agreed to take a lease from a landlord of premises which are free standing and are ready for immediate occupation by the tenant. In such circumstances, the lease and its counterpart can be exchanged immediately they have been settled by the parties' advisers, and any works to be carried out by the tenant can be dealt with in a licence for alterations. Where, however, there are conditions precedent to a lease being granted, *e.g.* the fact that the premises have not yet been constructed by the landlord, or the tenant is to carry out works before the lease is granted, or there is some other reason preventing the immediate completion of the lease, the parties will, or would be advised to, enter into an agreement for lease, perhaps along the following lines. **1.01**

**AN AGREEMENT** . . . (parties and commencement)

Where either party is a company it is advisable to insert its registered office as its address, as this is unlikely to alter regularly. The insertion of a company registration number aids identification, *e.g.* for company search purposes, and is unobjectionable.

## 1 Definitions and interpretation

1.1   "Architect" means _____ (name) of _____ (address) or such other person as the Landlord may from time to time appoint to perform the functions of the architect under the Building Contract and notify to the Tenant as having been so appointed   **1.02**

It may be that the landlord will entrust supervisory functions to a surveyor or some other suitably qualified person. There is no objection to this, but the tenant should ensure that the person so appointed is suitably qualified to enable him to carry out his functions in a proper and responsible manner. It may therefore be advisable to amend the clause slightly as follows:

**... or such other suitably qualified person as the Landlord ...**

**1.2** **"Building Contract" means a contract for the carrying out of the Works made the _____ day of _____ between (1) the Landlord as employer and (2) _____ (name) of _____ (address) as contractor**

Application should be made for sight of the building contract so that its provisions can be considered, although it is likely that the landlord will resist this. It would, for instance, be advisable for the tenant to check the defintion of "practical completion" in the building contract (amongst various other provisions) which has relevance for the purpose of clause 1.3. The tenant's understanding of "practical completion" may differ substantially from the definition contained in the building contract. Sometimes this clause is not included in an agreement for lease, because the landlord may not by then have entered into a building contract. In such circumstances the tenant would be sensible to try to ascertain the identity of the likely contractor so as to satisfy itself that the landlord's works will be done by a reputable concern in order to give the tenant some comfort against subsequent defects; though of course a reputable contractor does not necessarily mean a defect-free construction or, indeed, the completion of the landlord's works on time.

**1.3** **"Certificate" means a certificate by the Architect to the effect that in the opinion of the Architect practical completion of the Works has been achieved (and "Practical Completion" shall for the purposes of this agreement have the same meaning as in the Building Contract)**

The "opinion of the Architect" should be qualified to read "the reasonable opinion of the Architect", but it should be noted that practical completion can be certified even when some works under the building contract are still outstanding. All that is required is that sufficient of the works shall have been completed to enable the premises to be used for the purpose intended, and if the tenant has any particular concerns as to the completion of the works then it should ensure that express provision is made for those concerns in the agreement (see clause 2.8).

**1.4** **"Certificate Date" means the date on which the Certificate of Practical Completion is issued**

**1.5** **"Certificate of Practical Completion" means the Certificate issued by the Architect pursuant to clause _____ of the Building Contract**

The definitions in clauses 1.4 and 1.5 are self-explanatory.

**1.6** **"Completion Date" means whichever is the latest of:**
**1.6.1** **the date falling [twenty] working days after the Certificate Date and**
**1.6.2** **the date falling [five] working days after the date on which the Architect issues the Tenant's Certificate pursuant to clause 3.9 of this agreement and**
**1.6.3** **(if applicable) the date falling [ten] working days after the Landlord receives notification in accordance with clause 4.2.5 of this agreement**

It is better to err on the side of caution when agreeing time periods for the completion of the lease. There will be pre-completion searches to put in hand and in addition some corporate tenants in particular may require more than a few days in order to execute and return documentation. As such, the time periods in 1.6.2 and 1.6.3 seem a little tight and should be lengthened. Consider also the position where the landlord's works relate not only to the premises but also the construction of adjoining or neighbouring premises, *e.g.* a shopping centre. Another point worth mentioning is that the tenant should endeavour to ensure that the landlord has by the completion date obtained all necessary consents, from mortgagees, superior landlords (if applicable) or otherwise, to enable it to complete the lease.

**1.7** **"the Landlord" includes the successors in title of the Landlord to the Site and any other person who is at any time entitled to the reversion immediately expectant on the term agreed to be granted by this agreement**

Unless the agreement provides otherwise, the original parties will remain in a contractual relationship *inter se* to the extent of their obligations under the agreement. The landlord may, however, assign its reversion and there is no objection to clause 1.7 as drafted. In fact the definition will also include persons entitled to intermediate leasehold interests where created by the landlord between the date of the agreement and the grant of the lease.

**1.8** **"Landlord's solicitors" means _____ (specify firm) of _____ (address) or such other firm of solicitors as the Landlord may from time to time notify to the tenant as being the Landlord's solicitors for the purposes of this agreement**

**1.9** "Lease" means a lease of the Premises for a term of _____ years commencing on the Term Commencement Date reserving [a *or* an initial] rent of £_____ (_____ pounds) per year [exclusive of VAT] such lease to be in the form of the draft lease annexed and initialled by or on behalf of the parties with such modifications as may from time to time be agreed in writing by or on behalf of the parties or as may be made pursuant to clause 4 of this agreement

Subject to the comments in respect of clause 4.1, there is no objection to this clause in so far as it relates to modifications agreed by the parties, although in practice only minor modifications, if any at all, should be necessary. The reference to "an initial rent" is, of course, where the rent is reviewable. It is rare for the form of lease to be initialled and those words can be deleted if the parties' advisers so wish.

**1.10** "Possession Date" means the date on which the Architect serves on the Tenant a notice in accordance with clause 3.2 of this agreement

It may be that the possession date (which in most agreements is called the access date) will coincide with the issue of the certificate of practical completion. Many tenants would not want to take up possession of the premises until practical completion has been achieved because of the difficulties of having two teams of contractors working on the site at the same time. Also, where the premises form part of a new shopping centre, the tenant will not wish there to be a significant period of time between the possession date and practical completion of the shopping centre. There is no point in the tenant spending a vast sum in fitting out the premises only to see the premises remain closed because of delays to the remaining works. If, however, the tenant is prepared to accept possession in advance of the issue of the certificate of practical completion the suggested additional wording at the end of clause 2.8 should be added to clause 3.2, particularly as clause 1.12 provides for any rent-free period to commence to run from the possession date.

**1.11** "the Premises" means the part of the Site described in the second schedule together with such of the Works and the Tenant's Works as may from time to time have been carried out on the Premises

This describes the premises which are to be demised to the tenant and which will include the tenant's works and possibly also the landlord's works where alterations or refurbishment works have been carried out to the premises by the landlord. The problem with the premises being defined to include the tenant's works is that the tenant's works may be rentalised on rent review even though the tenant has paid for the works. This must be avoided.[1]

**1.12** **"Rent Commencement Date" means the date falling _____ after the Possession Date**

This provides for the tenant to be granted a rent-free period. This may be granted either for fitting out purposes or because the market is flat due to the economic climate. The length of the rent-free period will be a question of negotiation between the landlord and the tenant and should be settled prior to the drafting of the lease documentation. A problem can arise where the rent-free period runs from the possession date and that is in advance of the date of practical completion, *e.g.* where the premises are part of a shopping centre and the landlord's works relate to the whole site. The tenant will wish to safeguard itself against completing its own works but being unable to open for trade because the rest of the centre remains to be completed. In such a situation the tenant may consider the following provision in an endeavour to protect its position:

> **The Landlord shall procure that Practical Completion occurs no later than [    ] weeks after the Possession Date failing which there shall be granted to the Tenant [    ] additional days' rent-free period for each day that passes until Practical Completion occurs**

The number of additional days' rent-free period will again be for the landlord and tenant to negotiate, though it is advisable for this to be settled as one of the heads of terms. The tenant should bear in mind the cost of having employed and trained staff, etc. in calculating the daily loss. In any event it is vital for the tenant to ensure that, at the very least, it does not suffer the loss of the balance of a rent-free period in circumstances where it is ready to open for trade but is prevented from doing so.

It has been suggested by Customs and Excise that rent-free periods may be the subject of value added tax by virtue of their being treated as inducements. Fortunately the Government has now stated that rent-free periods are outside the scope of VAT unless services for the landlord are performed by the tenant in return. For example, where the tenant agrees to carry out work to the premises in return for a rent-free period, the tenant will be considered as having made a supply to the landlord equivalent to the amount of the rent foregone by the landlord, with the tenant being liable to account for the VAT thereon.[2] Therefore, the typical position where the landlord grants the tenant a rent-free period at the commencement of the term (not in return for works or another supply) would appear to be outside the scope of VAT, at least for the time being.

**1.04**  **1.13** "**Restrictions**" **means all matters affecting the Site or the Premises or their use that are registered or capable of registration as local land charges and all notices charges orders resolutions demands proposals requirements regulations restrictions agreements directions or other matters affecting the Site the Premises or their use or affecting the Works that are served or made by any local or other competent authority or otherwise arising under any statute or any regulation or order made under any statute**

**1.14** "**the Site**" **means the [building and adjoining] premises described in the first schedule**

The "Site" may be merely the site upon which the premises are to be constructed or may comprise the whole of the landlord's development. Whatever the site comprises it must obviously be clearly identifiable. Enquiries should be made of the landlord, its advisers and appropriate authorities, should there be any unusual structures or features that could affect the site or give rise to problems or expenditure for the tenant, *e.g.* the proximity of rivers, with the worry of intermittent flooding and the cost of bank shoring (via the service charge), public rights of way, etc. Flooding, in particular, has become an important consideration in the past few years and, apart from enquiries of relevant authorities in this regard, the tenant should include this in its enquiries of the landlord.

This is an appropriate juncture to mention contamination. The tenant should make enquiries of the landlord, the local authority and regulatory authorities as to whether the site has suffered any contamination. This is a subject which is going to have serious implications in the future, and it remains to be seen how the various statutory provisions relating to the cleaning-up of land will be enforced and interpreted. It is unclear at present as to whether a tenant would be liable to clean up a contaminated site under its repairing covenant contained in a lease. It has been suggested that the remedying of historical pollution to land may be outside the ambit of a tenant's repairing covenant but this is certainly not beyond doubt and even if this is correct, a tenant under a full repairing lease would probably be liable to repair damage to a building or other structure caused by contamination. Apart from this, there is, of course, the possibility of a tenant not being permitted to use premises until the contamination has been remedied, where contamination has created a health hazard or some other risk, *e.g.* the accumulation of methane gas emanating from landfill sites. There is also the possiblity of the tenant being liable for cleaning-up contamination under the tenant covenants to comply with the requirements of statutory or of any other authority. Where service charge provisions are drafted wide enough (as they usually are), the tenant may in any event find itself having to pay a proportion of any clean-up costs where the primary liability for clean-up rests with the landlord. The tenant should raise specific contamination enquiries of the landlord and require copies of any contamination reports or surveys to be supplied. If such enquiries, reports or surveys reveal the existence of contamination the tenant should endeavour to ensure that the landlord bears the cost of any immediate remedial works out of its own monies and try to include provisions in the lease to similar effect, should any de-contamination works subsequently be necessary. This is certainly a topic which will no doubt develop in the near future and, in the meantime, the tenant should treat this subject with the care it deserves.[3]

**1.15** **"the Tenant" does not include any successors in title of the Tenant**

Clause 1.15 is not acceptable as it is inadvisable to agree any unreasonable fetters on the tenant's right to assign the benefit of the agreement. There may for some reason be a substantial delay between the date of the agreement and the grant of the lease during which time the tenant may wish to assign its interest in it. The clause should therefore be amended to read:

**"the Tenant" includes the successors in title of the Tenant**

A landlord may nevertheless wish to ensure that the person with whom it is entering into the agreement will be the initial tenant under the lease, *e.g.* a substantial "anchor" tenant in a retail park. The tenant should, wherever possible, avoid such an obligation.[4]

**1.16** "Tenant's solicitors" means _____ (specify firm) of _____ (address) or such other firm of solicitors as the Tenant may from time to time notify to the Landlord as being the Tenant's solicitors for the purposes of this agreement
**1.17** "Tenant's Works" means the works which are to be carried out and completed by the Tenant on the Premises in accordance with clause 3 of this agreement consisting of:
**[1.17.1** the installation and fitting of a shop front
**1.17.2** the provision of floor covering and
**1.17.3** such other fitting-out works as the Tenant shall [reasonably] require]

The tenant's works may, of course, be far more extensive and the above works are given by way of illustration only. The details in this clause can either include a brief description of any more extensive works, or they can be set out in a separate schedule. Normally, in respect of shopping centres, the landlord will construct the premises to a "developer's shell", which will be handed over to the tenant on the possession date. The tenant will then carry out its fitting-out works, which can be extensive and often expensive.

Care should be taken to ensure that the tenant's works are not carried out under an obligation to the landlord or the tenant could be disadvantaged on next review.[5] The point is that the tenant should ensure that its works are disregarded on next reviews under the lease, in order to make certain that the works are not rentalised.

**1.05**  **1.18** **"Term Commencement Date" means:**
**1.18.1** **(if the Certificate Date falls on a usual quarter day) the Certificate Date and**
**1.18.2** **(in any other case) the usual quarter day immediately preceding the Certificate Date**

Landlords often insist that for management purposes the term of the lease should begin on a quarter day, particularly where the premises are part of a large development. This is also because rent reviews are usually geared to the term commencement date. This should be resisted by the tenant, as not only will the term be slightly diminished (by almost three months where, for instance, the certificate date is a few days before a quarter day) which could be relevant for a comparatively short-term lease, but also the first and subsequent rent review dates will be that much sooner, which at a rent of, say, £100,000 per year, increasing to, say, £140,000 per year (in an inflationary market) on the first rent review, would add £10,000 per quarter to the rent. This clause should therefore be amended to read:

**1.18** **"Term Commencement Date" means the Certificate Date**

It must be remembered, however, that if the landlord's works comprise the building of several properties, *e.g.* a shopping centre, and the certificate of practical completion is to be signed on completion of the development, but the tenant is allowed into possession of the premises on the possession date (as defined in clause 1.10), then it is unlikely that the landlord will agree that the term commencement date will be the certificate date. In such an event, the term commencement date will probably be the possession date, but, as mentioned, the tenant must be careful to make sure that there is no significant gap between the possession date and the date when practical completion of the landlord's works takes place.

Irrespective as to whether the premises can be accessed and serviced between the possession date and practical completion, there may be the problem that the planning permission may prevent opening the premises until various criteria are fulfilled, which may not be until practical completion.

**1.19** **"Working day" means any day on which clearing banks in the City of London are (or would be but for a strike lock-out or other stoppage affecting such banks generally) open during banking hours and "working days" shall be construed accordingly**

**1.20** **"Works" means the works [of alteration and refurbishment] which are being carried out on and to the Site by the Landlord and which are to be completed by the Landlord in accordance with clause 2 of this agreement**

The (landlord's) works can be the alteration and refurbishment of an existing building or can be the actual building of new premises or an entire development such as a shopping centre or retail park. In the majority of agreements for lease the definition is "Landlord's Works" as opposed to "Works". Where the landlord's works relate to the construction of other buildings in addition to the premises, *e.g.* in respect of a shopping centre, the tenant must ensure that there is an obligation on the landlord to carry out and complete the construction of such other buildings, service areas, car parks, etc., in accordance with all necessary "landlord's approvals" as soon as possible after the possession date (as defined in clause 1.10), and preferably by a specified date. There would be little advantage in the tenant's premises being available for occupation if the rest of the shopping centre remained to be constructed, even if the premises could be accessed and serviced.

**1.21** **Words importing one gender shall be construed as importing any other gender**
**1.22** **Words importing the singular shall be construed as importing the plural and vice versa**
**1.23** **Where any party comprises more than one person the obligations and liabilities of that party under this agreement shall be joint and several obligations and liabilities of those persons**
**1.24** **The clause and clause headings in the body of this agreement and in the schedules do not form part of this agreement and shall not be taken into account in its construction or interpretation**

## 2 Works

**1.06**  2.1 **In this clause:**

2.1.1 **"Landlord Approvals" means all approvals consents permissions and licences of any local or other competent authority that are from time to time necessary to enable the Landlord lawfully to carry out the Works**

The local authority may require the landlord to enter into an agreement under section 106 of the Town and Country Planning Act 1990. A section 106 agreement may contain various obligations and restrictions affecting the land, including purposes for which the land may be used. A section 106 agreement can be registered as a local land charge and can be enforced against estate owners of the land from time to time. A tenant should ensure that it is made aware of such an agreement so that it can consider the implications of it, particularly where the terms of it could result in unexpected expense for the tenant or have adverse consequences in respect of the tenant's business. Similarly, the planning permission for the site must be considered as it too could encompass provisions affecting such matters as hours of servicing, etc., which could result in added expense and inconvenience for a tenant.

2.1.2 **"Building Documents" means the plans drawings specifications and other documents relating to the Works which are listed in the third schedule**

The tenant should have sight of these as soon as possible to ensure that they are in accordance with its understanding of what has been agreed. They may also be relevant for the preparation of the tenant's own shopfitting drawings.

2.1.3 **"Surveyors" means _____ (Surveyors) of _____ (address) or such other firm of surveyors previously approved in writing by the Landlord [such approval not to be unreasonably withheld [or delayed]] as the Tenant may from time to time appoint to perform the functions of the Surveyors under this agreement**

It would be foolhardy for the tenant to put itself in a position whereby the landlord must approve the identity of its surveyors. It may also be that where the tenant is a company an in-house surveyor may perform the role. The clause should therefore be amended:

"Surveyors" means _____ (Surveyors) of _____ (address) or such other firm of Surveyors or suitably qualified individuals as the Tenant may from time to time appoint to perform the functions of the surveyors under this agreement

2.2 Subject to all Landlord's Approvals being obtained and continuing in force the Landlord shall at [its] own expense immediately proceed diligently to carry out the Works:

2.2.1 in a good and workmanlike manner and with sound materials of their respective kinds and

2.2.2 in accordance with the terms of all Landlord's Approvals and otherwise in compliance with all Restrictions and

2.2.3 (subject as provided in clauses 2.3 and 2.4) in accordance with the Building Documents

There must be an obligation on the landlord to make application for the approvals as soon as possible after the agreement has been entered into, assuming there is not a condition precedent which the tenant has agreed to accept. In addition to the landlord's approvals there may also be other consents (from superior landlords or mortgagees, for example) or covenants to be complied with in carrying out the works. Furthermore, care should be had in making the performance of the works subject to the landlord's approvals continuing in force and it is worthwhile ensuring, as in this clause, that the works will be carried out at the landlord's expense. The landlord should also be obliged, either specifically or under a general provision, to comply with the Construction (Design and Management) Regulations 1994. Clause 2.2 should preferably commence:

2.2 Subject to all Landlord's Approvals and all other consents being obtained (which the Landlord shall forthwith apply for and obtain with all due expedition) and continuing in force (which continuation in force the Landlord shall use its best endeavours to ensure is maintained) the Landlord shall entirely at its own expense in all respects immediately proceed diligently to carry out and complete the Works using reputable contractors.

Although the wording of clause 2.2.1 may possibly cover the point, it may be as well to include a separate provision:

the Landlord will not use or cause or permit or suffer to be used in or about the Works or any part or parts thereof high alumina cement woodwool slabs asbestos calcium chloride used as an accelerator urea formaldehyde or other harmful or deleterious substances

There are in fact many more substances that could be listed specifically if the tenant wishes, including polyisocynurate or polyurethane foam, dredged aggregates, ferrous wall tiles, iron pyrites based aggregate and Iberian peninsular roofing slates! The inclusion of the reference to "other harmful or deleterious substances" suggested above will hopefully help in keeping the list to a reasonable length.

The following additional clause could be added:

**2.2.4** **in compliance with the Construction (Design and Management) Regulations 1994**

It may also be advisable to insert an additional clause, either in clause 2 or towards the end of the agreement, along the following lines:

> **The Landlord shall procure that all conditions contained in any of the Landlord's Approvals shall have been complied with by no later than the date of Practical Completion**

This is not only to try to ensure that the conditions will be complied with but also to cover conditions that could possibly prevent the tenant from opening the premises for trading.

**1.07** **2.3** **If the Landlord is unable to obtain at a reasonable cost any of the materials referred to in the Building Documents the Landlord may [(subject to notifying promptly the Surveyors of its intention to do so)] in carrying out the Works substitute for them alternative materials as nearly as may be of the same quality**

There is probably no objection to this clause as it contains a reference to the alternative materials being as nearly as may be of the same quality. It may be advisable, however, to amend the clause slightly as follows:

> **... the Landlord may (subject to notifing promptly the Surveyors of its intention to do so and accepting such reasonable concerns they may make known) in carrying out the Works ...**

**2.4** **The Landlord may in carrying out the Works make such modification to the Building Documents and to the details of the Works contained in them:**

**2.4.1** **as may be required by any local or other competent authority as a condition of the grant or continuance in force of the Landlord's Approvals or any of them or**

**2.4.2** as may be [reasonably] required by the Architect provided that no modification shall be made pursuant to this clause 2.4.2 which would substantially alter the design layout nature capacity or standard of construction of the Premises as provided for in the Building Documents or substantially prejudice the use of the Premises for the purpose specified in the Lease

The problem is that while clause 2.4.1 does not seem unreasonable, and is indeed included in many agreements for lease, it is conceivable that the local or other competent authority could force upon the landlord modifications that could make the premises unviable for the tenant. A particular concern of some tenants is to try to ensure that the shopfront of their premises is not reduced, for rather obvious reasons. It is unlikely that the landlord would agree to a tenant's termination provision in the event of any modification being unacceptable to the tenant, although there is no harm in trying for this. An alternative is to amend clause 2.4.1 to read as follows:

**2.4.1** as may be required by any local or other competent authority as a condition of the grant or continuance in force of the Landlord's Approvals or any of them provided that the Landlord will use all reasonable endeavours to ensure that any such modification required by the local or other competent authority shall not materially alter the design layout width of the shopfront nature capacity or standard of construction of the Premises as provided for in the Building Documents or prejudice the use of the Premises for the purpose specified in the Lease

At the very least the tenant should substitute the word "materially" for the word "substantially" in clause 2.4.2, as the latter suggests that some alteration less than substantial may be permitted but which could result in not inconsequential prejudice occurring to the design or use of the premises. In fact, the word "substantially" in the pre-penultimate line should really be removed completely as the tenant should not be expected to countenance a modification by the architect that prejudices the use of the premises, whether substantially or materially. But the tenant should consider deleting the words

... or substantially prejudice the use of the Premises for the purpose specified in the Lease

and substituting them with:

... or reduce the area of the premises or affect their use or any ancillary services and facilities or increase the Tenant's liability under the Lease

The word "reasonably" should definitely be included in the first line of clause 2.4.2 and, as with clause 2.4.1 a reference to the width of the shopfront should be added.

**1.08**  2.5  The Surveyors may:
2.5.1 at any time on prior appointment with the Architect enter upon the Site and the Premises in order to view the state and progress of the Works but shall not interfere with the carrying out of the Works and
2.5.2 within [five] working days after any such entry serve on the Architect notice ("Defects Notice") specifying any respects in which they consider that the Works are not being or have not been carried out in accordance with this clause 2
2.6 The Landlord shall procure that the Architect shall have [due] regard to the contents of any Defects Notice

It is important for the tenant to ensure that the agreement contains provision for a right of inspection during or towards the end of the landlord's works (see clauses 2.10, 2.12) but while the five working day period in clause 2.5.2 is perhaps understandable from the landlord's point of view, clause 2.6 is too weak even with reference to "due" regard. In *English Exporters (London) Ltd v Eldonwall Ltd*[6] Megarry J. stated that the term "have regard" almost of necessity was bound to create difficulties, asking how much regard was to be had and what weight was to be attached to the regard when it has been had. Clause 2.6 should therefore read:

2.6 The Landlord shall forthwith investigate the matters contained in the Defects Notice and shall at its own expense remedy or procure the remedying of such matters within [seven] days of the service of the Defects Notice by the Tenant
2.7 If at any time any Works are carried out otherwise than in accordance with the Building Documents and this fact might [reasonably] have been expected to be apparent on visual inspection to the Surveyors on the first occasion following the carrying out of the relevant Works on which they actually inspected the same pursuant to clause 2.5 ("the Relevant Inspection") then unless within [five] working days after the date of the Relevant Inspection (time being of the essence) the Surveyors have served on the Architect a Defects Notice

in respect of such non-compliance the relevant Works shall be treated for all purposes of this agreement as having been carried out in accordance with the Building Documents

This provision should be deleted. It is not reasonable to expect a tenant to have to accept construction works which may differ from those in the building documents and accordingly be less beneficial to the tenant than it may be expecting as a result of what the surveyors may be perceived to notice on an inspection. The landlord should be responsible for ensuring that the works are carried out in accordance with the building documents and if there are any variations, it must either have them corrected or obtain the tenant's consent to their remaining.

2.8     Subject to the provisions of clause 2.9 the Landlord shall [use all reasonable endeavours to] carry out the Works to such a stage as would entitle the Architect to issue a Certificate in respect of all the Works not later than the _____ day of _____

It is essential that there is a specific date by which the certificate is to be issued, even though this may be weakened by the proviso at the beginning of this clause. The landlord must be given a specific date towards which to work (with time being of the essence), which will obviously also be important from the tenant's point of view as the tenant may be subject to seasonal trade variations in business and may wish, for example, to open the premises in time for the Christmas trade. Wherever possible, a tenant should endeavour to delete the opening proviso, namely:

**Subject to the provisions of clause 2.9**

but this is unlikely to be successful, in which case the tenant should amend to include a long stop date as mentioned under clause 5. The more important date for the tenant, however, may well be the possession date, if this falls before practical completion, particularly if the amendment to clause 3.5 is accepted, though the tenant will obviously need to ensure that practical completion is achieved soon after the possession date.

The tenant could consider adding the following clause (which would have to form part of the heads of terms) as a method of achieving as short a delay as possible between the possession date and practical completion, particularly where the presmises are part of a large complex:

**The landlord shall ensure that Practical Completion shall occur no later than [     ] months after the Possession Date failing which the Landlord shall pay to the Tenant as liquidated and ascertained damages for such delay the sum of**

[£ ] **per day for each whole day by which Practical Completion is delayed beyond [ ] weeks after the Possession Date together with interest on such damages at the [Interest Rate] for the period from and including the date when the damages become payable until the date of payment to the Tenant**

The words in square brackets should be deleted, or at the least the provisions should be amended to "best endeavours" to place a more stringent obligation on the landlord. Having said that, it has been suggested that the extent of the duty to use best endeavours depends upon the facts in each case and, pursuant to *IBM United Kingdom Ltd v. Rockware Glass Ltd*,[7] it may be that there is little practical difference between a covenant to use best endeavours, a covenant to use reasonable endeavours and a covenant to take all reasonable steps. But an obligation to use best endeavours does at least suggest something a little more strident than reasonable and could, for example, in the case of a refused application for planning permission, oblige an appeal to be pursued.

Consider adding the following words to this clause where the Possession Date coincides with the certificate Date. If, however, the Possession Date is earlier than the certificate Date, the following wording should more appropriately form part of clause 3.2 as the tenant would not want possession of the premises until these requirements have been satisfied:

> **by which date the Premises shall be clean watertight weatherproof defect free secure and in a fit state for fitting out with all service media forming part of the Works for incoming service supplies of water electricity [gas] and telephone installed and terminated in the Premises at the Landlord's expense (subject only to service connections which require the Tenant's application to be submitted to the relevant authorities) and the Landlord will ensure that all such services including drainage are available during the carrying out of the Tenant's Works**

The tenant also may wish to include other specific requirements, *e.g.* that the service area and necessary areas of the common parts are available for use by the tenant or that the floor slabs of the premises have been laid for a suffficient period to enable drying out to have been completed, as otherwise the tenant may be delayed in installing its flooring and thereby eating into a rent-free period.

2.9     If on one or more occasion the carrying out of the Works is delayed in consequence of any circumstance beyond the control of the Landlord which the Landlord could not [reasonably] have prevented or avoided then on each such occasion the Landlord shall be allowed such extension of time for carrying out the Works as may be certified by the Architect as being reasonable having regard to the delay in question and the date by which the Landlord is required to carry out the Works as provided in clause 2.8 shall be postponed accordingly     **1.09**

The problem here is the uncertainty from the tenant's point of view, hence the suggestion that there be inserted a long stop date (see clause 2.8). If the tenant is able to negotiate the inclusion of the damages provisions referred to under clause 2.8 or 3.2, the tenant should add the following words to this clause:

> **but the provisions of this clause shall be without prejudice to clauses [2.8] and [3.2]**

2.10     The Landlord shall procure that no Certificate shall be issued by the Architect unless the Architect has given to the Surveyors not less than [five] working days' notice that the Architect proposes on a date specified in such notice to carry out an inspection ("Inspection") of the Works with a view to issuing a Certificate

2.11     If the Inspection does not take place or if following the Inspection the relevant Certificate is not issued the Landlord shall procure that the same is not subsequently issued unless notice has again been given to the Surveyors in accordance with clause 2.10 (which procedure shall be repeated as often as necessary until the relevant Certificate is issued)

2.12     The Surveyors shall be entitled to attend every Inspection and the Landlord shall procure that the Architect shall have [due] regard[8] to any written representations made by the Surveyors to the Architect concerning the issue of the Certificate within [three] working days after the date of the Inspection but the issue or non-issue of any Certificate shall be in the sole professional discretion of the Architect

The time period referred to in this clause is tight of necessity, having regard to clause 2.10. If it is possible to add a few extra days to the period in clause 2.10 and in this clause, so much the better. The landlord may resist this, however, on the basis that there may still be a great deal of work to be done to the premises two weeks before the proposed issue of the certificate.

**2.13** **The Landlord shall procure that a copy of the Certificate of Practical Completion shall be supplied to the Tenant immediately following its issue**

Various provisions in the agreement stem from the issuing of the certificate of practical completion and it is therefore important that the tenant is informed of its issue without delay.

**2.14** **The Landlord shall procure that the obligations of the contractor under clause _____[9] of the Building Contract are complied with within the period applicable but (save as provided in clause 16.3 [of this agreement and in clause[s] _____ of the Lease] the Landlord shall with effect from the Certificate Date be under no liability to the Tenant in respect of any failure to carry out the Works in accordance with clauses 2.2.1 and 2.2.3 (save as regards matters specified in any Defects Notice which were not remedied to the Surveyor's [reasonable] satisfaction)**

The part of this clause commencing

> ... but (save as provided in clause 16.3 ...

to the end of the clause should be deleted, as a tenant may consider it unreasonable for a landlord to exempt itself from liability in this manner. A landlord should be responsible for the manner in which work at its instigation should be carried out and there is no reason why a tenant should suffer as a result of defects appearing within a reasonable time thereafter. The problem is that landlords are endeavouring to remove any contingent liability they may have in respect of defects, not only to avoid actions against themselves, but also to avoid the reversionary value being affected on a sale.[10] One is in fact tempted to amend the first two lines of the clause to read as follows:

> **The Landlord shall procure that the obligations of the contractor under the Building Contract are complied with**

In addition to this provision, or possibly in substitution for it, the tenant may wish to include a more positive obligation on the landlord in respect of defects such as:

> **The Landlord shall take such steps to enforce the rights and remedies it may have against the contractor in respect of any defects appearing in the Works as may be notified to the Landlord by the Tenant and shall use any monies recovered from the contractor in making good any such defects and the Landlord shall not assign or otherwise part with its rights under the Building Contract without first ensuring that its purchaser enters into a covenant with the Tenant in similar form to this provision [in respect of such rights and remedies as it may have against the contractor under the Building Contract]**

It may be appropriate also to include in the above clause all members of the landlord's professional "team" or to deal with their obligations by a separate clause. The tenant could also consider adding a clause along the following lines:

> **AND if the Landlord shall fail to take such proceedings as aforesaid and to have the defects remedied within [three] months of notification of them by the Tenant to the Landlord the Tenant may remedy such defects and all reasonable and proper costs and expenses in connection therewith shall be paid by the Landlord to the Tenant within [ten] working days of demand**

**1.10** It is now not unusual for warranties or duty of care deeds to be offered to a tenant by the landlord's professional "team". These generally comprise architects, structural engineers, main contractors, mechanical and electrical consultant, the landlord's project manager and surveyors, but if warranties from a wider range of persons can be procured, *e.g.* sub-contractors, then so much the better. Also, specific guarantees should not be ruled out, though in practice these seem to be seldom made available. Such warranties create contractual obligations with the result that a tenant should be able to maintain an action against the professional party in the event of a breach subsequently occurring, or occurring within the time specified in the warranty. There has in fact been a good deal of legal commentary as to the effectiveness of warranties, but it is now generally accepted that they are an effective weapon in the tenant's armoury (provided that they are properly and fairly drafted) and it would be advisable for a tenant to take up warranties (in a standard and acceptable form—ideally without a joint net contribution clause and definitely without a provision excluding "economic loss") if they are available. If possible, the tenant should also try to obtain copies of the documents of appointment of the professional team.

Where warranties are to be given, the following additional clause may be contained in the agreement:

> **The Landlord shall procure that prior to the issue of the Certificate of Practical Completion there shall be delivered to the Tenant collateral warranty agreements duly executed by the Architect the Landlord's structural engineers the Landlord's Contractors and the Landlord's Surveyors [etc] such collateral warranty agreements to be in the form of the drafts annexed hereto and the Landlord shall at the same time provide to the Tenant copies of the deeds of appointment of such warrantors**

The tenant will need to have sight of, and approve, the form of the warranties prior to the exchange of the agreement for lease. It is also essential that the landlord is obliged to procure delivery of the warranties to the tenant by a specified date. Once the lease has been completed the landlord may take a more relaxed attitude towards the issuing of the warranties, with the tenant left chasing them for months. Where no such warranties are to be given, or even in addition to such warranties, the tenant should consider including the following clause, even if subsequent negotiations with the landlord result in some watering down:

> **Notwithstanding anything herein contained or the completion of the Lease nothing in this agreement shall release the Landlord from any liability in respect of defects appearing in the Works due to bad or faulty workmanship or design or materials provided notice of the same shall have been given to the Landlord by the Tenant or its successors in title or assigns before the expiration of the period of [six] years from the date hereof and upon receipt of such notice the Landlord shall forthwith take such action as may be necessary to remedy the defects at its own expense with all possible expedition**

Where the landlord's works involve or include the actual building of the premises it may be necessary for the gross internal area of the premises to be measured in order to calculate the initial yearly next payable by the tenant under the lease. This occurs, for example, where the tenant has agreed to pay a rent at a rate per square foot (or square metre, for those metrically inclined). The measurement clause may read as follows, and the tenant should include the words in square brackets in respect of manifest error:

> **As soon as practical and in any event prior to the Possession Date the [Architect] and the Surveyors shall measure and agree the gross internal area of the Premises and if the same shall not have been agreed on or before the Possession Date either party may require the Premises to be measured by an independent chartered surveyor appointed on the application of either party by the President or other senior officer of the Royal Institution of Chartered Surveyors acting as an expert and not as an arbitrator and whose decision shall be final and binding upon the Landlord and the Tenant [except in the case of manifest error] and whose costs and expenses shall be borne [by the Landlord]**

From the tenant's point of view the costs of the expert should be borne by the landlord, but the landlord may try to insist on them being borne equally between the landlord and the tenant or otherwise as the expert shall determine.

The next question for the tenant to decide is as to whether it wants to have the right to terminate the agreement if the net internal area of the premises is outside agreed parameters, *e.g.* five per cent above or below an agreed area. This is something that would have to be set out in the heads of terms and, if agreed, the wording of the appropriate clause could be as follows:

> **If the gross internal are of the Premises as agreed or determined is less than [   ] square [metres/feet] or more than [   ] square [metres/feet] the Tenant may within [fourteen] days of the gross internal area of the Premises being agreed or determined serve not less than [seven] days notice on the Landlord terminating this agreement in which event this agreement shall terminate on the expiry of such notice but without prejudice to the rights of either party against the other for any antecedent breach of the terms hereof**

If the tenant accepts that the premises may be in excess of an agreed area, the tenant may want to "cap" the initial yearly rent by reference to the agreed area[11] and may not wish to pay rent on the excess area on rent reviews under the lease. If so, the tenant may consider inserting the following clause:

> **If the gross internal area of the Premises shall be more than [ ] square [metres/feet] there shall be included an assumption in paragraph 1.3 of the fourth schedule to the Lease to the effect that the gross internal area of the Premises shall be [ ] square [metres/feet] and that a willing tenant shall not be assumed to be willing to pay more rent for the Premises as a result of the actual gross internal area of the Premises exceeding [ ] square metres/feet]**[12]

**3   Tenant's Works**

**1.11**  3.1   **In this clause:**
3.1.1  **"Tenant's Approvals" means all (if any) approvals consents permissions and licences of any local or other competent authority which may from time to time be necessary to enable the Tenant lawfully to commence and to carry out the Tenant's Works**
3.1.2  **"Plans" means detailed plans drawings and specifications setting out the Tenant's proposals for the Tenant's Works and such other documentation and information as the Landlord may [reasonably] require in order to satisfy [itself] as to the nature and extent of the Tenant's Works**
3.2   **The Landlord shall procure that as soon as in the opinion of the Architect the Works on the Premises are sufficiently advanced to enable the Tenant to commence and carry out the Tenant's Works the Architect shall give notice to the Tenant to that effect**

The first line should be amended to refer to the "reasonable" opinion of the architect. See also the commentary on clause 1.3 and consider as to whether the notice should not be given until the position in respect of the premises as referred to in the suggested additional wording to clause 2.8 has been achieved.

Another point to be considered is that the tenant may require notice of the possession date in order to confirm its fitting out date to its contractors and to make other arrangements. If the proposed possession date is subsequently missed, the tenant may suffer financial loss for which it should expect to be compensated. The tenant should therefore consider adding the following clauses, which it would be wise to include as part of the heads of terms when negotiating the transaction:

> The Landlord shall give to the Tenant at least [three] months prior written notice of the Possession Date ("the Intended Possession Date")
>
> If the Possession Date occurs after the Intended Possession Date the Landlord shall pay to the Tenant as liquidated and ascertained damages for such delay the sum of [£   ] per day for each whole day by which the Possession Date is delayed beyond the Intended Possession Date together with interest on such damages at the [Interest Rate] for the period from and including the date when the damages become payable until the date of payment to the Tenant

3.3   The Tenant shall as soon as practicable after the date of this agreement at its own expense prepare the Plans and submit them to the Landlord for approval [such approval not to be unreasonably withheld [or delayed]]

The landlord's approval of the plans should not be unreasonably withheld or delayed and it would be advisable for the tenant to commence the preparation of the plans as soon as it may be practicable in order to avoid subsequent delay. Where the possession date is unlikely to occur for many months, *e.g.* where the premises are part of a shopping centre, the tenant may not want to prepare the plans until shortly before it has access to commence its works, particularly in view of the provisions of clause 3.4. In such circumstances, this clause should be amended as follows:

> The Tenant shall at its own expense no later than [eight] weeks before the Possession Date prepare the Plans ...

3.4   Immediately upon such approval being obtained the Tenant shall at its own expense apply for and use all reasonable endeavours to obtain without delay all Tenant's Approvals    **1.12**

The question of timing again arises and the tenant may prefer this provision to be watered down slightly as follows:

3.4   As soon as practicable after such approval has been obtained the Tenant shall at its own expense apply for and use all reasonable endeavours to obtain all Tenant's Approvals

3.5   With effect from the Possession Date or (if later) the date on which the Tenant has obtained all Tenant's Approvals the Tenant shall have licence and authority to enter upon the Premises for the purpose of carrying out the Tenant's Works in accordance with clause 3.7 but for no other purpose

The first point to note is that the rent free period, if any, is geared by clause 1.12 to run from the possession date and, therefore, the tenant's occupation of the premises should not be dependent upon obtaining all the tenant's approvals. Some approvals may not become available until after the tenant has commenced its works and as clause 3.4 contains an obligation on the tenant's part to obtain all tenant's approvals and clause 3.7.3 provides that the tenant's works must be carried out in accordance with the terms of all tenant's approvals, etc., the landlord would appear to be adequately protected. Furthermore, the words "but for no other purpose" could result in a period of non-user from the date of completion of the tenant's works and the date of the completion of the lease (see clause 1.6) and the clause should be amended as follows:

**3.5** **With effect from the Possession Date the Tenant shall have licence and authority to enter upon the Premises for the purpose of carrying out the Tenant's Works in accordance with clause 3.7 and thereafter to commence business at the Premises for the purpose permitted by the Lease**

**3.6** **To the extent that the Tenant has exclusive possession of the Premises at any time before completion of the Lease the Tenant shall hold the same as tenant at will of the Landlord**

The tenant may wish to delete this clause despite a footnote to the precedent to the effect that any purported determination of the tenancy at will by the landlord (other than where provided for in clause 5) would presumably constitute a breach of contract, *i.e.* for withdrawing the authority granted by clause 3.5. It is also suggested that determination by the tenant would give rise to a breach, *i.e.* failure to carry out the tenant's works. This may be a perfectly valid statement of the law but if a court decided otherwise the consequences for the tenant could be regrettable. *Javad v. Aqil*[13] confirms that the concept of a tenancy at will remains a reality and while the landlord may be concerned that the tenant should not become a periodic tenant until the grant of the lease, the tenant may wish to ensure that it has something more concrete than a tenancy at will.

There is also the point that circumstances beyond the control of the landlord or the tenant could prevent the lease being completed, or at least substantially delay its completion. In such an event, the tenant will wish to have something more than a tenancy at will, particularly where the tenant subsequently wishes to assign its interest in the premises before the lease is granted. A similar provision to clause 3.6 is that the tenant will have no greater interest in the premises than a licensee until completion of the lease.

*Agreement for Lease* 25

If the landlord refuses to agree to the deletion of this clause, a possible compromise would be that the tenant will have no greater interest than a licensee until the tenant's works have been completed.

**3.7 The Tenant shall at [its] own expense carry out and with due expedition complete the Tenant's Works:**

**3.7.1 in a good and workmanlike manner and with sound materials of their respective kinds**

**3.7.2 in accordance with the Plans approved by the Landlord pursuant to clause 3.3**

Add the following words to clause 3.7.2:

> **or as amended with the approval of the Landlord (such approval not to be unreasonably withheld or delayed)**

**3.7.3 in accordance with the terms of all Tenant's Approvals and otherwise in compliance with all requirements of the local and any other competent authority**

**3.7.4 in such a way as to cause no [material] obstruction to or interference with the carrying out of the Works**

See the commentary on clause 1.10 as to possession prior to the issue of the certificate of practical completion.

**3.7.5 to the [reasonable] satisfaction of the Architect in all respects**

The word in square brackets, or a similar qualification, is essential.

**3.8 The Tenant shall:**   1.13

**3.8.1 pay and indemnify the Landlord against all fees charges and other payments whatever which may at any time be payable to any local or other competent authority in respect of the Tenant's Works**

**3.8.2 be answerable for and indemnify the Landlord against all actions costs claims demands and liability whatever in relation to any failure by the Tenant to comply with [its] obligations under clause 3.7.3 or in relation to any claim made by any adjoining owner or occupier or member of the public or other person in connection with the carrying out of the Tenant's Works**

**3.8.3 with effect from the Possession Date pay and indemnify the Landlord against all rates taxes assessments duties charges impositions and outgoings from time to time charged upon the Premises or the owner or occupier of them**

Although unlikely to have such a construction placed on it, there is something to be said for inserting a similar exclusion into this clause to that inserted in clause 5.2.1 of the lease.

**3.9 The Landlord shall procure that as soon as practicable after the Tenant's Works have been [substantially] completed in accordance with clause 3.7 to the [reasonable] satisfaction of the Architect in all respects the Architect shall issue to the Landlord and the Tenant a certificate to that effect ("the Tenant's Certificate")**

The words in square brackets should be included as part of the clause.

In the normal situation, the tenant's works will comprise mainly fitting out works and it is unlikely that the landlord would require its architect (assuming it had one) to issue a certificate that the tenant's works have been completed, as proposed by this clause. It is more likely that the landlord's surveyors will confirm in writing, on the landlord's behalf, that he is satisfied that the tenant's works have been completed.

**3.10 Subject as provided in clause 5.5.3 all fixtures affixed to or installed in the Premises as part of the Tenant's Works (other than tenant's fixtures) shall become and remain the property of the Landlord notwithstanding that any of them may be affixed or installed after completion of the Lease**

The difficulty here is ensuring that both parties know what are tenant's fixtures, and it may be as well to include in a schedule the fixtures to which the landlord is referring.

It is also conceivable that the landlord has contributed towards the cost of the tenant's works and will therefore wish certain of the tenant's works to be taken into account on the rent reviews under the lease. If so, these should be clearly identifiable to avoid disputes at the time of the rent reviews, when evidence as to the true position may no longer be available.

The tenant may therefore decide either to replace this clause with the following provision, or add it as a separate clause:

> **The Tenant's Works shall be disregarded when calculating the rental value of the Premises on rent reviews under the Lease**

Either the landlord or the tenant may prefer for there to be a licence for alterations granted in respect of the tenant's works, which could also deal with the position on rent review. An example of a clause providing for this is as follows:

> The Tenant shall enter into a licence for alterations in respect of the Tenant's Works upon the grant of the Lease in the form of the draft licence annexed[14]

There may also be the following words added to this clause, to which there is no objection:

> ... and in the event that the Tenant shall carry out the Tenant's Works before the said licence for alterations is completed the Tenant shall comply with all the covenants on its part contained in the said licence for alterations as if the same had already been completed

As part of the heads of terms the tenant should ensure that it does not have to pay the landlord's costs for approvals and inspections in respect of the tenant's works. A possible clause to cover this is:

> **The Tenant shall not be liable for the cost of any approvals in respect of the Tenant's Works necessary to be obtained from the Landlord or Architect or for any supervision and/or inspections in respect thereof**

## 4　Form of Lease

[4.1]　The Landlord may at any time before the Certificate Date require the form of the Lease and the rights and obligations of the parties under it to be varied in such manner as the Landlord shall [reasonably] require to take account of any modifications made in accordance with clause 2.4 after the date of this agreement　**1.14**

There is limited scope in this clause for substantial amendment to the form of the lease and, as very few amendments are foreseeable, a tenant may be justified in deleting this provision, although clause 4.2 contains safeguards which make the clause tolerable if the landlord insists on its retention. Any clause containing the right for the landlord to vary the lease more substantially should be resisted strongly and the footnote to this clause contains the suggestion that in such circumstances the tenant should insist on a provision that no variation be made which would, *e.g.* reduce the area of the premises, or reduce the shopfront, or affect their use, or increase the tenant's liability under the lease.

[4.2　If by the Certificate Date the parties have been unable to agree whether any requirement of the Landlord made pursuant to clause 4.1 is reasonable the matter or matters in dispute shall be referred to a counsel to be agreed upon between the parties or failing agreement within [five] working days after the Certificate Date to one of the conveyancing counsel for the time being of the Chancery Division of the High Court of Justice ["Counsel"] to be nominated on the application of either party by the President for the time being of the Law Society (or his duly appointed deputy or any other person authorised by him to make appointments on his behalf) and Counsel shall:

4.2.1 act as an expert and not as an arbitrator

4.2.2 invite the parties to submit to him within such time limits as he may direct such written representations concerning the matter or matters in dispute as they may respectively wish

4.2.3 have such regard (if any) to any such representations as he shall consider appropriate

4.2.4 make such modifications to the form of the draft lease annexed as in the opinion of Counsel shall be necessary to incorporate any requirements of the Landlord made pursuant to clause 4.1 which in the opinion of Counsel are reasonable and

4.2.5 notify such modifications in writing to the Landlord and the Tenant

4.3 Counsel's fees and the costs of his appointment, including any VAT payable on them except where the VAT is recoverable or available by the Landlord as input tax, shall:

4.3.1 (if no modification is made by Counsel in accordance with clause 4.2.4) be borne by the Landlord

4.3.2 (if in Counsel's opinion all of the Landlord's requirements were reasonable) be borne by the Tenant and

4.3.3 (in any other case) be borne by the parties equally]

If clause 4.1 is included, there must obviously also be a machinery to cover the possibility of a dispute.

There is no real objection to any of the provisions in clauses 4.2 or 4.3 which seem sensible and fair from both parties' points of view, assuming of course that the tenant has been unsuccessful in having clause 4.1 deleted.

Where the tenant has to pay the VAT, the tenant should try to insist that a VAT invoice will be produced in the tenant's name so that it is able to recover the VAT payable. For example, where the landlord's solicitors' costs are payable by a tenant, the proper course is for the landlord's solicitors to issue a VAT invoice to the landlord as opposed to the tenant. If the landlord has opted to tax, the landlord will be able to recover the VAT and should accordingly issue its own VAT invoice to the tenant. If the landlord has not opted to tax, a VAT invoice cannot be issued to the tenant, who will be responsible for paying the whole account. The same principle applies in all cases where the tenant is liable under the lease to pay the landlord's solicitors' costs, *e.g.* in respect of a licence for alterations.

## 5 Termination

5.1 If at any time before completion of the Lease the Tenant (being an individual) dies or has a receiving order made against him or is adjudicated bankrupt or (being a company) has a petition presented for its winding up or goes into liquidation or (in either case) enters into a composition with his or its creditors then the provisions of clause 5.4 shall have effect immediately  **1.15**

5.2 If for any reason:

5.2.1 the Certificate of Practical Completion has not been issued by the expiry of the period of _____ immediately following the date of this agreement or

5.2.2 the Tenant's Certificate has not been issued by the expiry of the period of _____ immediately following the Possession Date

then the provisions of clause 5.4 shall have effect immediately upon the expiry of the relevant period (or upon the expiry of such extended period as the parties may within the relevant period agree in writing)

5.3 If at any time there has been any [material] non-compliance by the Landlord with any of [its] obligations under clause 2 or by the Tenant with any of [its] obligations under clause 3 and such default shall continue for or shall not be remedied to the [reasonable] satisfaction of the party not in default within [fifteen] working days (time being of the essence) after service on the party in default by the other party of a notice specifying the default and invoking the provisions of this clause then the provisions of clause 5.4 shall have effect immediately upon the expiry of the relevant period

5.4 In any of the circumstances specified in clauses 5.1, 5.2 and 5.3 or if the Tenant fails to comply with [its] obligations under clause 6.5 then and in any such case this agreement shall (save for clauses 3.8 and 5.5 and without prejudice to any pre-existing right of action of either party in respect of any breach by the other of [its] obligations under this agreement) immediately determine and cease to have effect and neither party shall be under any further liability to the other under this agreement

5.5 If this agreement determines in accordance with clause 5.4:

5.5.1 the Tenant shall immediately procure the cancellation of [any land charge registered at H.M. Land Charges Registry (or if the Landlord's title is registered) any notice or other entry registered against [the title referred to above (or as appropriate) titles referred to above or any of them]] in respect of this agreement[15]

5.5.2 the Tenant shall (if in occupation) immediately vacate the Premises and remove from the Premises all (if any) building and other materials and equipment on the Premises in connection with the Tenant's Works

5.5.3 the Landlord shall be entitled immediately or at any time subsequently to take and retain possession of all (if any) completed or partially completed Tenant's Works on the Premises which shall be forfeited and become the property of the Landlord and the Landlord shall not be liable to make to the Tenant any compensation or allowance in respect of them

This clause contains a number of matters of principal importance. Clause 5.1, for instance, could be of concern not only to the tenant but also to the tenant's mortgagees. Rather than for the agreement to determine automatically, it may be preferable for the landlord to be given the right to determine the agreement in such an event, and therefore line six could be amended to read:

> ... with his or its creditors the Landlord may determine this agreement by written notice served on the Tenant whereupon this agreement shall forthwith determine and cease to have effect

Some comfort may be had by adding the following words to the end of this clause, though their effectiveness is uncertain:

> ... provided that the Tenant shall have the same rights of relief against forfeiture as if the Lease had been completed

It is essential that some time limit be placed on the time within which the (landlord's) works are to be completed and the certificate of practical completion issued (see clause 2.8). In fact, because the tenant will presumably be commencing its works on the possession date, it will be this date rather than the certificate date which has the greater significance for the tenant. The tenant may therefore prefer to be given the right to determine the lease if the possession date has not occurred by a specified date as opposed to the certificate date (unless, of course, these fall on the same date) by which date the tenant may well have spent a good deal of time and money carrying out its works. As mentioned under clause 2.8, however, the tenant will wish to specify a critical date for the landlord to achieve practical completion, but if this falls after the possession date, the tenant may prefer to pursue a claim for compensation, etc., rather than determination. This period will, of course, depend upon the nature of the works being carried out and while the landlord will expect quite a long overrun period, it should be possible for the landlord and the tenant to agree a suitable long stop date.

Clause 5.2.1 could therefore be amended to read: **1.16**

**5.2.1 the Possession Date shall not have been attained by the _____ (time to be of the essence) the Tenant may at any time thereafter determine this Agreement by written notice served on the Landlord whereupon this Agreement shall forthwith determine and cease to have effect**

Obviously, if the tenant decides that it would be preferable to gear the possession date to the date of the certificate of practical completion (as to which see clause 1.10) the revised clause 5.2.1 should refer to the issue of the certificate of practical completion and not to the attainment of the possession date.

Similarly, it is understandable that a landlord will wish to ensure that the tenant's works are completed within a reasonable time. A tenant could argue that as rents will probably be geared to the issue of the certificate of practical completion or the possession date (as in this agreement—see clause 1.12), there may be no immediate financial disadvantage to the landlord. The landlord will nevertheless wish to ensure that the premises are occupied and trading as soon as possible, particularly if they are located in a parade or shopping centre or retail park, where the landlord's adjoining premises could benefit from customers to the premises.

The problem from the tenant's point of view is that a termination pursuant to 5.2.1 will not (at least in a normal market) result in the (landlord's) works being totally wasted unless carried out to a tenant's particular design specification, whereas the tenant may have expended a considerable sum of money not only on its works but also in preliminary arrangements. The tenant may discover that an unforeseen delay for which it is not responsible results in revocation of the agreement pursuant to clause 5.2.2, and if clause 5.5.3 remains unamended the tenant will receive no compensation for works carried out prior to such termination. The tenant should therefore initially attempt to delete clause 5.2.2, but if this is not accepted a sufficiently long date should be inserted in it and the clause should be amended to read as follows:

> **5.2.2** the Tenant's Works shall not have been substantially completed by the expiry of the period of _____ immediately following the Possession Date (or by the expiry of such extended period as the parties may within the relevant period agree in writing) unless prevented by any unforseeable or uncontrollable event or course of events the Landlord may determine this agreement by written notice served on the Tenant whereupon this agreement shall forthwith determine and cease to have effect.

It is stressed, however, that clause 5.2.2 should be resisted and deleted if at all possible.

Clause 5.3 is dangerous from both parties' points of view and the deletion of the clause may be advisable. The provisions of the clause are undeniably useful where the other party is in default, but as clauses 2 and 3 place an obligation on the landlord and the tenant, respectively, to complete their works in accordance with the provisions contained in those clauses, it may be as well to forego the provisions of clause 5.3 in case it backfires.

Clause 5.4 could therefore be redundant, but if it is wished (and if the relevant parts of the following amended clause are not included in clauses 5.2.1 and 5.2.2) it could remain and be amended as follows:

> **5.4** In the event that this agreement is determined pursuant to the provisions of clauses 5.2.1 or 5.2.2 this agreement shall (save for clauses 3.8 and 5.5 and without prejudice to any pre-existing right of action of either party in respect of any breach by the other of [its] obligations under this agreement) immediately cease to have effect and neither party shall be under any further liability to the other under this agreement

Clause 5.5.1 should refer also to the cancellation of any land charge registered at H.M. Land Charges Registry or any notice or caution registered at H.M. Land Registry[16] but the absence of such reference will be of no concern of the tenant.

Clause 5.5.3 is unreasonable and should be deleted. The tenant's works will probably include valuable fitting out items and, while a landlord will wish to reclaim vacant possession of the premises as soon as possible after determination in order to seek a reletting, the handing over of the tenant's works should be resisted. The following amendment is perhaps a fair compromise:

5.5 ... which shall be forfeited and become the property of the Landlord where the Tenant fails to remove them within ten working days of receipt from the Landlord of a notice in writing to do so

## 6 Grant of Lease

6.1 Subject to the above provisions of this agreement the Landlord shall grant the Lease and the Tenant shall accept the Lease and execute a counterpart of it  **1.17**

6.2 The Lease and the counterpart shall be prepared by the Landlord's solicitors and an engrossment of the counterpart shall be delivered to the offices of the Tenant's solicitors at least [five] working days before the Completion Date

Five working days is too short a time for most institutional tenants to execute and return documentation, particularly where the tenant's solicitor has to check the engrossment against the agreed form attached to the agreement for lease. Incidentally, it is imperative that the tenant's solicitor checks the engrossment or at least delegates it to some competent person in his office to do. Quite often leases are not granted until some years after the agreement for lease with the result that the fair copy has to be typed onto the landlord's solicitor's updated wordprocessing system. This can result in errors which can be costly if not picked up by the tenant's solicitor. Therefore, amend this clause to read:

... at least [fifteen] working days ...

to allow for pre-completion searches, etc., as well.

6.3 The Lease shall be completed on the Completion Date at the offices of the Landlord's solicitors or at such other place as the Landlord's solicitors shall [reasonably] require

The parties' solicitors will normally agree to complete without the necessity for personal attendance, but the tenant's solicitor may wish to amend this clause to provide for the agreed arrangements regarding completion, particularly where the landlord's solicitor's office is in Berwick-upon-Tweed and the tenant's solicitor is in Penzance.

**6.4** At any time on or after the Completion Date either the Landlord or the Tenant being ready and willing to complete the Lease and perform [its] other obligations under this agreement may (but without prejudice to any other available right or remedy) by notice to the other invoke the provisions of clause 6.5

**6.5** Within [fifteen] working days after service of such notice (excluding the day of service) the Lease shall be completed and time shall be of the essence of this provision

Advisable though this clause may be, the problem is that the agreement is liable to be brought to an end at the expiration of the notice, which could have dire consequences for a tenant who has expended a considerable sum of money on the tenant's works but is for some reason unable to complete. It is therefore sensible for a tenant who encounters such difficulties to advise the landlord of its position as early as possible in the hope of preventing the service of a completion notice. The alternative is for the tenant to refuse to accept this clause. The tenant's difficulty is to balance the possible disadvantage in allowing the clause to remain against the possible disadvantage of deleting it!

## 7 Rent Commencement [and trading]

**1.18** [7.1] If the Lease is completed rent shall be payable in accordance with the terms of the Lease with effect from the Rent Commencement Date

[7.2] The Tenant shall commence trading from the Premises not more than _____ after the Completion Date]

It is important to ascertain if any rent-free period is to include not only the rack rent but also service charges and/or insurance premiums. Usually, these will commence from the possession date, but this is not always the case and it may be that the tenant has negotiated as part of the heads of terms that the service charge should not commence to be payable until practical completion of the landlord's works. It is suggested that, unless the agreed form of lease makes it clear, liability with regard to service charges and insurance should be dealt with in this clause.

As regards clause 7.1 there is the possibility that the lease will not be completed until after the rent commencement date. The amendment suggested in clause 3.5 permits the tenant to have access to the premises with effect from the possession date and to commence business from the premises when the tenant's works have been completed. This is only reasonable, as the rent-free period will probably commence to run as from the possession date (as in clause 1.12). If, for some reason, the lease cannot be granted on the completion date and the amendment to clause 3.5 has been agreed, or the rent commencement date falls before the completion date, the landlord would still expect rent to be payable with effect from the rent commencement date, and therefore perhaps the following clause should be added:

7.3] **If the Rent Commencement Date is before the Lease is completed rent shall be payable from the Rent Commencement Date as if the Lease had been completed on the Rent Commencement Date provided that such rent [and other monies] as may be paid by the Tenant under the provisions of this clause shall be deemed to be payment for the period to which they relate of the yearly rent [and other monies] which would be payable under the Lease pursuant to the provisions of this agreement if the same had been granted on the Rent Commencement Date**

Clause 7.2 should be resisted. Various factors could prevent the tenant from commencing to trade within a specified period and where a tenant has fitted out the premises and is paying a full rent (or using up a rent-free period) the tenant would hopefully only delay opening for trade for a good reason.

There is also the point that the initial rent payable under the lease may not be an ascertained sum as at the date of the agreement for lease, eg where it is to be a sum per square foot/metre multiplied by the [gross] internal area of the premises when built, possibly also subject to a maximum sum. If so, there may be included in the agreement a definition (or calculation) clause along the following lines:

> **"the Initial Rent" means the [gross] internal area of the Premises multiplied by [£ ] per square foot/metre [or the sum of [£ ] whichever shall be the lower]**

Obviously, the agreement would also have to contain a definition of the gross internal area of the premises.

## 8  Damages, etc.

**No damage to or destruction of the Site or the Premises or any part of the Site or the Premises however occasioned shall in any way affect the obligations of the parties under this agreement**

1.19

First, it is suggested that the tenant should inspect the premises and the site (if, for instance, access to the premises is across other parts of the site) immediately before exchange. Secondly, although the doctrine of frustration applies to agreements for lease,[17] it would be only in quite exceptional circumstances that an agreement would be set aside on the grounds of frustration and it is suggested that the parties should provide in the agreement for either party to rescind the agreement in the event of substantial damage to the premises or the site prior to completion. It may, therefore, be advisable to delete this clause and substitute the following:

> **In the event of substantial damage to or destruction of the Site or the Premises or any part of the Site or the Premises however occasioned either party hereto may determine this agreement forthwith by serving notice to that effect on the other party and in such case this agreement shall (without prejudice to any pre-existing right of action of either party in respect of any breach by the other of its obligations under this agreement) immediately determine and cease to have effect and neither party shall be under any further liability to the other under this agreement and any dispute or difference between the parties as to what constitutes substantial damage or destruction for the purpose of this clause shall be decided by an independent surveyor who shall act as an expert and who shall be appointed by the President for the time being of the Royal Institution of Chartered Surveyors upon the application of either party**

## 9 Title

**1.20**  9.1  The Tenant shall assume the right of the Landlord to grant the Lease and shall not require any evidence of or raise any objection requisition or inquiry in respect of the Landlord's title to the Site [or the Premises]

9.2  The Premises shall be demised subject to the matters set out or referred to in clause _____ of the draft lease annexed and the Tenant or the Tenant's solicitors having been supplied with such information as the Landlord has concerning the same the Tenant has entered into this agreement with notice of and shall raise no objection requisition or inquiry in respect of such matters

Section 44(2)–(4) of the Law of Property Act 1925 prevents the tenant from investigating either the freehold or leasehold reversion when taking a lease of premises. It is suggested, however, that neither clause 9.1 nor 9.2 will offer any protection to a landlord who has misrepresented or misdescribed its title.[18] A misrepresentation or misdescription in respect of the title could result in the landlord being unable to enforce the terms of the agreement. See, for example, *Becker v. Partridge*,[19] where the seller of a sub-underlease whose title was defective was not able to enforce the contract in reliance on a provision that the buyer had accepted the title and would raise no requisition, as the seller had constructive notice of the defects.

In general terms, a landlord (like a vendor) should disclose to the prospective tenant any defects in title that may not be obvious to the tenant unless it was clear that the tenant knew of the defects when it entered into the agreement for lease. Nevertheless, clauses 9.1 and 9.2 are dangerous, as a tenant will prefer to know at the outset whether any defects affect the premises and the tenant's solicitor should amend them as follows:

**9.1** **The Landlord shall deduce its title to grant the Lease [including the production of the freehold title] and shall obtain all necessary consents for the grant of the Lease to the Tenant [and shall do all things necessary to enable the Tenant to obtain registration of the Lease at H.M. Land Registry with Title Absolute]**

This will include the provision by the landlord of all consents, mortgagee's or otherwise, necessary for the grant and registration of the lease. Where the term of the lease is more than 21 years from the date when the lease is granted, an application to register the lease must be made at H.M. Land Registry. If the landlord's title is registered, the tenant should ensure that the landlord's land or charge certificate is lodged at the Registry to enable registration of the lease to take place. If the landlord's title is unregistered, the tenant must ensure that the landlord's title is deduced and examined before completion of the lease, so that an examined epitome or abstract of title can be lodged, as otherwise the best title the tenant can expect may be good leasehold as opposed to absolute.

If the landlord's title is registered at H.M. Land Registry, the tenant should consider protecting the agreement by notice or caution. A notice is preferable as it imposes greater protection than a caution (which can be warned off) but requires the consent of the landlord as the land or charge certificate will need to be placed on deposit for the purpose of registration. It should, however, be remembered that a copy of the agreement will have to be supplied to the land registry in the case of a notice and anyone wishing to obtain a copy could do so on application. Concessionary terms offered to an anchor or other preferred tenant in a shopping centre may therefore fall within the knowledge of other prospective tenants.

In the case of registered land the following additional words should be included at the end of clause 9.1:

> **and the Landlord shall forthwith deposit its land or charge certificate in respect of the Site at H.M. Land Registry and inform the Tenant of the deposit number thereof within three working days of notice of the deposit number being given to the Landlord to enable the Tenant to register a notice of this agreement (to which the Landlord hereby grants consent)**
>
> **9.2 The Premises shall be demised subject to the matters set out in clause ... of the draft lease annexed**

Even with the latter part of this clause (as drafted) included it has been held that a landlord must still make full disclosure and not mislead the tenant[20] nor will these words protect the landlord from an action for misrepresentation or misdescription.[21]

## 10 Restrictions

1.21
- **10.1** The Premises shall be demised subject to all (if any) Restrictions affecting the Premises (whether in existence at the date of this agreement or arising at any later date)
- **10.2** No representation is made or warranty given by the Landlord as to whether any Restrictions exist or as to the permitted use of the Site or the Premises for planning purposes
- **10.3** The Tenant acknowledges that [its] obligations under this agreement and the Lease shall not be affected or lessened in any way by the fact that there may now or subsequently exist any Restrictions and the Tenant shall with effect from the Possession Date comply with and indemnify the Landlord in respect of any liability under any Restrictions (whether made before or after the Possession Date) except in so far as such liability arises from failure by the Landlord to comply with [its] obligations under clause 2.2.2

It need hardly be said that the tenant's solicitor should make all usual enquiries to ascertain whether any such restrictions exist at the date of the agreement, as some restrictions could be disastrous for the tenant's proposed use of the premises.

The following wording should be added to clause 10.1:

> **AND the Landlord hereby warrants to the Tenant that it has disclosed to the Tenant details of all Restrictions affecting the Premises known (or which ought reasonably be known) to the Landlord as at the date hereof**

Clause 10.2 should commence:

> **Save as provided in clause 10.1 ...**

and the tenant may attempt to delete the words:

> **or as to the permitted use of the Site or the Premises for planning purposes**

on the ground that the landlord will normally be responsible for obtaining the requisite planning permission, especially where the premises form part of a shopping centre. It is certainly worth arguing.

Clause 10.2 will not protect a landlord where there has been a warranty given, as in the amended clause 10.1 above, a misrepresentation made, or where there has been a misdescription of the site.

## 11  Representations, etc.

**11.1**  Save as provided in clause 11.2 no agent adviser or other person acting for the Landlord has at any time prior to the making of this agreement been authorised by the Landlord to make to the Tenant or to any agent adviser or other person acting for the Tenant any representation whatever (whether written oral or implied) in relation to the Site or the Premises or to any matter contained or referred to in this agreement  **1.22**

**11.2**  Any statement made in writing by the Landlord's solicitors to the Tenant's solicitors prior to the making of this agreement [in reply to an enquiry made in writing by the Tenant's solicitors] was made with the authority of the Landlord

**11.3**  No immaterial error omission or misstatement in this agreement or in any plan of the Site or the Premises referred to in this agreement or in any statement made by any person prior to the making of this agreement shall in any way affect the obligations of the parties under this agreement or entitle any party to damages or compensation

As the *Encyclopaedia* points out, there are a number of clauses in common use in leases attempting to place a limitation on the landlord's liability for misrepresentation, misdescription and non-disclosure, but fortunately (from the tenant's point of view) many such clauses are ineffective. Nevertheless, a landlord will be entitled to limit the authority of an agent to make representations[22] and clauses 11.1 and 11.2 have been drafted with this in mind.

It is suggested that the words in square brackets be deleted from clause 11.2 as the landlord's solicitors will doubtless make several statements in writing to the tenant's solicitors during a transaction and not always in reply to written enquiries. *Gran Gelato Ltd v Richcliff Group Ltd*[23] held that misstatements by a landlord's solicitors in replies to enquiries could not result in an action (of negligence) against the solicitors, but that such replies were given on behalf of the landlord. Any such action would therefore lie against the landlord, but the landlord may well have a claim against its solicitors for negligence. Clause 11.3 relates to misrepresentations and misdescriptions, the position as to the latter being similar to non-disclosure in that it can render the landlord liable in damages for breach of contract. If the misdescription is material the tenant would be able to rescind the agreement irrespective of whether or not the word "immaterial" is included in clause 11.3. If "immaterial" is excluded from clause 11.3 then, whatever the nature of the misdescription, a tenant seeking specific performance would not be entitled to compensation or damages.[24]

The tenant should consider deleting both clauses 11.1 and 11.2, though for the reasons given they could perhaps be tolerated if necessary.

## 12 Non-assignment

**1.23** **The Tenant shall not assign underlet charge or otherwise deal in any way with the benefit of this agreement in whole or in part and the Landlord shall not be obliged to grant the Lease to any person other than the Tenant**

This is not acceptable and must at least be qualified to allow the tenant to mortgage or charge the premises which might be vital to the tenant to fund the tenant's works or its business in general. It is also suggested that a company tenant which has already created a charge or debenture over future acquired property would be in breach of this clause upon exchange of agreements.

In addition, it is not unknown for a lease to be granted several years after the date of the agreement for lease, particularly where the landlord's own interest is leasehold and the completion of its lease is dependent upon various factors and conditions. The author is aware of an agreement for lease granted in 1965 purporting to grant a 21-year lease where the landlord was still not in a position to grant the lease by the expiration of the agreed term in 1986.

Landlords are often amenable to amendments permitting an assignment of an agreement for lease, usually after any tenant's works have been completed, but subject to the assignee covenanting with the landlord to be bound by the terms and conditions of the agreement, which is not unreasonable. Where there is a surety to the agreement and an assignment by the tenant is agreed by the landlord, it is advisable to ensure that while the surety may still be forced to be bound by the obligations on its part contained in the agreement, the surety should not be forced to be a party to the lease. Any provision for the original tenant under the agreement to be joined in the lease as surety for the assignee should be vehemently resisted.

Basic amendments to clause 12 could be the addition of the following provisos:

> **Provided that the Tenant shall be entitled to mortgage or charge its interest hereunder with the previous consent of the Landlord (such consent not to be unreasonably withheld or delayed)**

and

> **Provided that if the Lease shall not have been granted within a period of 12 months from the date hereof the Tenant shall be at liberty to assign underlet or otherwise deal with the benefit of this agreement subject to the same conditions as would be applicable to a corresponding transaction if the Lease had then been granted**

## 13  Notices

**13.1  In this clause:**  1.24
**13.1.1**  "the Landlord's Address" means the address of the Landlord shown on the first page of this agreement or such other address as the Landlord may from time to time notify to the Tenant as being [its] address for service for the purposes of this agreement
**13.1.2**  "the Tenant's Address" means the address of the Tenant shown on the first page of this agreement or such other

address as the Tenant may from time to time notify to the Landlord as being [its] address for service for the purposes of this agreement

13.2 Any notice or other communication given or made in accordance with this agreement shall be in writing and:

13.2.1 may (in addition to any other effective mode of service) be sent by registered or recorded delivery post and

13.2.2 shall (in the case of a notice or other communication to the Landlord but subject to clause 13.3.1) be served on the Landlord at the Landlord's Address

13.2.3 shall (in the case of a notice or other communication to the Tenant but subject to clause 13.3.2) be served on the Tenant at the Tenant's Address

13.3 Any notice or other communication given or made in accordance with this agreement:

13.3.1 by or to the Landlord may be given or made by or to the Landlord's solicitors on behalf of the Landlord

13.3.2 by or to the Tenant may be given or made by or to the Tenant's solicitors on behalf of the Tenant

The first point to make is that it is important to ensure that any notices to be served on the tenant will be certain to be received, which they may not be if served at the premises. The second point is that some solicitors or their clients may object to clause 13.3, preferring that notices or other communications are served directly on the landlord and the tenant. It is also a valid point that clause 13.3 may be inappropriate as it could lead to uncertainty due to difficulties that could arise where the landlord or the tenant change solicitors and fail to notify the other party.

## 14 Costs

**1.25** The Tenant shall on the making of this agreement pay to the Landlord the sum of £_____ (_____ pounds) exclusive of VAT as a contribution towards the legal and other professional costs incurred by the Landlord in relation to this agreement

Quite often, the landlord will seek to recover from the tenant not only the whole or a contribution towards legal and other professional costs incurred in relation to the agreement and the lease, but also in relation to the approval and supervision of the tenant's works. Obviously, the tenant should try to avoid paying the landlord's costs if possible, as the transaction is presumably to the equal benefit of both the landlord and the tenant. This clause should accordingly be deleted wherever possible. If not possible, however, a tenant should try to avoid paying VAT on the contribution.[25] If there is no such provision in the agreement, the tenant would not be liable to pay the landlord's legal costs in respect of the agreement (or the lease).[26]

## 15 Executory agreement

**15.1** **This agreement is an executory agreement only and shall not operate or be deemed to operate as a demise of the Premises**     **1.26**

An executory agreement is an agreement to be followed by a lease, usually after various preliminary matters have been dealt with or some future act has been done, *e.g.* works have been completed. If possible, this clause should be deleted.

**15.2** **Save as provided in clause 3 the Tenant shall not be entitled to occupation or possession of the Premises until the Lease is completed**

This clause should be deleted—see note to clause 3.5. The suggested amendment to clause 3.5, if accepted, should be a satisfactory compromise.

## 16 Non-merger, etc.

**16.1** **Subject as provided in clause 2.14 all the provisions of this agreement shall (to the extent that they remain to be observed and performed) continue in full force and effect notwithstanding completion of the Lease**     **1.27**

**16.2** **[Subject as provided in clause [s] _____ of the Lease[27] no *or* No] defect in the Works or the Premises at the date on which the Lease is granted shall in any way lessen or affect the obligations of the Tenant under the Lease**

**16.3** **On completion of the Lease the parties shall enter into a deed in the form of the draft deed annexed to this agreement marked _____ and initialled by or on behalf of the parties[28]**

Clause 16.2 gives great cause for concern and should be deleted. Defects can quite often appear after the lease has been granted and the tenant will not expect to have to repair defects as part of its own obligations under a full repairing lease or even through the service charge provisions of the lease, where the landlord covenants to repair and charge back. If any duty of care deeds are available from contractors, engineers, surveyors or other professional persons then they should be taken up. Also consider, as an alternative, requesting building defects insurance (premiums to be paid for by the landlord) such as 10-year latent defects insurance—but if not available, or in addition to such deeds, etc., the tenant should consider including the clause suggested at clause 2.14.

## 17 Entire understanding

**1.28**  17.1 This agreement embodies the entire understanding of the parties and there are no other arrangements between the parties relating to the subject-matter of this agreement

17.2 No amendment or modification of this agreement shall be valid or binding on any party unless the same:

17.2.1 is made in writing

17.2.2 refers expressly to this agreement and

17.2.3 is signed by the party concerned or [its] duly authorised representative

The problem with clause 17.1 is that it could prevent the parties from agreeing supplemental matters in side letters exchanged at the same time as the agreement. While this practice is not to be recommended, it does happen and, even without the wording of clause 17.1, section 2 of the Law of Property (Miscellaneous Provisions) Act 1989 could be instrumental. This section provides that the terms which the parties have agreed in respect of a disposition of an interest in land must be incorporated in a single document either by being set out in the document or by reference to another document. The position with regard to side letters (setting out supplemental agreements) is that they may not be binding as they probably will not have been referred to in the principal agreement. In fact, courts have tended to "save" such side letters wherever possible by taking a constructive rather than technical approach,[29] but the following amendment to clause 17.1 may assist:

17.1 This agreement embodies the entire understanding of the parties save as augmented by any side letter[s] [or other agreement[s]] exchanged contemporaneously with this agreement and signed by the parties hereto or by their duly authorised agents which side letter[s] [or agreement[s]] shall take effect either as [a] collateral agreement[s] to this agreement or if it [they] shall be incorporated by express reference all the terms and conditions of such side letter[s] [or other agreement[s]] shall be treated as being a single composite agreement with this agreement and subject thereto

> there are no other arrangements between the parties relating to the subject-matter of this agreement

It may be advisable to include an arbitration provision, either to deal with any particular point in the agreement or to attempt to resolve disputes in general. If this is thought advisable, the following additional clause could be added:

> **In the event of any dispute or difference between the parties hereto concerning any matter of thing arising under this agreement such dispute or difference shall be referred to an independent surveyor agreed between the parties hereto or in default of agreement to a surveyor appointed for the purpose on the application of either party by the President for the time being of the Royal Institution of Chartered Surveyors who shall act as an arbitrator pursuant to the Arbitration Acts 1950 to 1996 or any statutory re-enactment thereof for the time being in force**

The tenant may also wish to include various other clauses and these will be a matter for negotiation. For example, specific contamination provisions as mentioned under clause 1.14 and possibly giving the tenant the right to terminate the agreement in the event that significant contamination of the site is discovered during the carrying out of the landlord's works, or an agreement on the part of the landlord not to enter into agreements for lease or leases of adjoining or neighbouring premises in competition with the tenant, *i.e.* similar to clause 6.4 of the lease. Also, there may be certain times of the year when the tenant would not wish to open the premises for trading, resulting in the tenant not wanting possession for shopfitting during specified dates. A clause can be inserted to deal with this and to ensure that the lease term and rents and/or rent-free periods do not commence during these "window" periods. The wording of this clause could be as follows:

> **Notwithstanding any other provisions contained in this agreement if the Possession Date shall occur after [ (a) ] but on or before [ (b) ] then the Possession Date for the purposes of this agreement shall be deemed to be [ (b) ] and the provisions of this agreement shall be construed accordingly unless the Tenant shall at any time hereafter give written notice to the Landlord that it does not wish the provisions of this clause to apply**

> **[AS or IN] WITNESS, etc.**

There is no necessity for the agreement for lease to be under seal as the promise to grant and accept the lease will be adequate consideration, and although it is suggested that the agreement should be under seal if one or more of the parties is a company (to secure the presumption of due execution) in practice this is not usually done.

### FIRST SCHEDULE

#### The Site

[Describe the Site]

### SECOND SCHEDULE

#### The Premises

[Describe the Premises]

### THIRD SCHEDULE

#### Building Documents

[Insert details]

((signature and) seals of both parties)[30]

It may be appropriate to mention the stamp duty position as regards agreements for lease. Until May 5, 1994 agreements for lease were liable for stamp duty as if the lease had been granted. As from and including May 6, 1994, however, there is no necessity to stamp an agreement for lease until the completion of the lease. This is obviously advantageous, particularly where the lease is subsequently not completed for some reason. It had been feared that in order to register a notice of the agreement at H.M. Land Registry, it would still be necessary to have the agreement stamped, but it appears, however, that Land Registries are in fact prepared to accept unstamped agreements for noting.

1. See first schedule to the lease and fourth schedule to the lease, para. 1.4.3.
2. *Rigeons Bulk v. Commissioners of Customs and Excise* LON/1990/1702—see also [1992] 37 E.G. 97.
3. For an interesting review of this subject, see Murray Ross, *Drafting and Negotiating Commercial Leases* Division J.
4. See clause 12.
5. See fourth schedule to the lease, para. 1.4.3.
6. [1973] Ch. 415 at 426.
7. [1980] F.S.R. 335.
8. See clause 2.6, above.
9. The reference should be to the clause in the building contract dealing with defects during the defects liability period.
10. See the case of BHP *Petroleum Great Britain Ltd v. Chesterfield Properties Ltd* [2001] 22 E.G. 155 in which a landlord tried, but failed, to obtain release of its personal covenant to remedy defective refurbishment works under an agreement for lease by arguing that s. 8 of the Landlord and Tenant (Covenants) Act 1995 applied.
11. See clause 7.
12. See the suggested wording at the end of para. 1.3 of the fourth schedule to the lease.
13. [1991] All E.R. 243. A tenancy at will was held to exist where a person was allowed into possession of premises (and paid quarterly rent) while negotiations for the grant of a lease continued, the negotiations subsequently breaking down.
14. See the licence for alterations set out in Chapter 15.
15. *i.e.* to protect the tenant's interest in the premises.
16. See clause 9.1.
17. *Per* Goff J. in *Rom Securities Ltd v. Rogers (Holdings) Ltd* [1967] 205 E.G. 427, though the circumstances where frustration applies may be rare.
18. See also *Watts v. Spence* [1976] Ch. 165, where the court held that it was an implied term in an agreement for lease that the landlord had title to grant the lease.
19. [1966] 2 Q.B. 155.
20. *Re Haedicke and Lipski's Contract* [1901] 2 Ch. 666. The condition as to acceptance of title did not affect the general duty of disclosure.
21. *Charles Hunt Ltd v. Palmer* [1931] 2 Ch. 287. "Valuable business premises" had an absolute user clause.
22. *Overbrooke Estates Ltd v. Glencombe Properties Ltd* [1974] 3 All E.R. 511.
23. Noted in [1992] 4 E.G. 173.
24. See *Re Terry and White's Contract* (1886) 32 Ch. D. 14 and *Curtis v. French* [1929] 1 Ch. 253.
25. See [1992] *Law Society Gazette*, October 28, p. 42 with regard to the payment of VAT on a third party's legal costs, and also the comments under clause 9.18 of the lease.
26. Costs of Leases Act 1958, ss. 1 and 2.

[27] Where the lease makes specific provision for defects in the landlord's works.
[28] Where there is to be a deed between the landlord and the tenant whereby the landlord is to pursue remedies against third parties in respect of defects.
[29] See *Tootal Clothing Ltd v. Guinea Properties Management Ltd* [1992] 41 E.G. 117 in which it was held that s. 2 of the 1989 Act is of relevance only to executory contracts and has no relevance to executed contracts. It was therefore held that a supplementary agreement relating to payment for shopfittting works and entered into at the same time as the agreement for lease, was valid on the basis that it was not a land contract or, at least, if it was, by the incorporation therein of the terms of the agreement for lease, there was no issue because s. 2 only applied to executory contracts and there was no longer after completion of the lease any executory land contract in evidence to which s. 2 could apply. But now see *Grossman v. Hooper* [2001] 27 E.G. 135 which, rather regrettably, has cast some doubts on the collateral contract route to circumvent the strict interpretation of s. 2 on the basis that it is difficult to ascertain its existence composed with a composite contract. It is therefore vital to be careful with regard to the agreements or side letters unless, possibly, they are specifically referred to in the principal agreement, though avoiding them altogether is by far the safest course.
[30] See p. 46 as regards execution.

*Chapter 2*

# The Lease

## Introduction

The lease has been drafted for premises in a shopping centre and the suggested amendments are with that location in mind. It is not difficult, however, for the general nature of the amendments to be adapted to cater for a single property in a high street location or for a property in a retail park. **2.01**

When considering amendments to be made to Leases, one should bear in mind the Code of Practice for Commercial Leases in England and Wales which contains recommendations for landlords and tenants on the negotiation of a business lease and conduct during the Lease, to reflect best practice. This is a voluntary code but the government has made it clear that it will monitor the effectiveness of the Code and, if it be ignored, legislation could follow. The Code applies to new lettings and does not affect leases in place at the date of its implementation.

The principal requirements of the Code are as follows:

(a) Tenants should be offered a choice of lease term, including where appropriate break rights and a choice as to whether the lease should be protected by, or excluded from, the Landlord and Tenant Act 1954.

(b) If alternative commercial terms are offered to the tenant, different rents should apply for each set of terms.

(c) Rent reviews should be to open market levels, but, where possible, landlords should offer alternatives, including alternatives to upwards only review, *e.g.* upwards or downwards, with perhaps a minimum of the initial rent payable, or perhaps indexed linked.

(d) It is suggested that, unless there are particular circumstances justifying greater control, the only restriction on assignments or underlettings should be a requirement to obtain the landlord's consent which should not be unreasonably withheld. In addition, landlords will be encouraged not to require an authorised guarantee agreement unless, at the date of the assignment, the assignee is financially less sound than the assignor.

(e) Landlords should notify previous tenants and guarantors expeditiously if the current tenant defaults.
(f) Repair and service charge obligations should be appropriate to the term of the lease and the condition of the premises.
(g) The landlord's control over changes of use and alternatives should not be more restrictive than necessary to protect the reversionary value. Also, there should be no requirement on a tenant to reinstate unless such requirement is reasonable.
(h) Where a tenant occupies a whole building, in appropriate cases, the tenant should have the right to influence the choice of insurer. Additional insurance provisions are that tenants' interests should be endorsed on the policy and that if the premises are damaged or destroyed by an uninsured risk so as to prevent occupation, a tenant should be permitted to terminate the lease, unless the landlord agrees to reinstate at its own cost.
(i) Landlords should comply with good practice in respect of service charges.
(j) Both the landlord and the tenant should seek the consent of any guarantor to any proposed changes to the lease.
(k) Landlords and tenants are encouraged to settle disputes by agreement.
(l) Leasers will be encouraged not to impose on landlords their preferred form of lease.
(m) Landlords and tenants are to have regard to the Code when negotiating lease renewals, but not so as to fetter the court's jurisdiction.

Time will, of course, tell whether landlords adhere to the Code and what, in reality, will be the consequence of any non-compliance.

## Particulars Definitions and Interpretation

It is now common practice to commence a lease with particulars, definitions and interpretation, which are particularly useful as leases have become longer. The particulars in fact also act as a ready reference in certain respects.

**LEASE OF PART**
**Dated:**

**1  Particulars**

1.1.1   the Landlord   [AB *or* AB [Limited *or* plc]] (Landlord) [of (address, etc.) *or*

|   |   |   |
|---|---|---|
|   |   | whose registered office is at (address)] [Company Registration No.____ ] |
| 1.1.2 | the Tenant | [CD *or* CD [Limited *or* plc]] (Tenant) [of (address, etc.) *or* whose registered office is at (address)] [Company Registration No.____ ] |
| 1.1.3 | the Guarantor | [EF *or* EF [Limited *or* plc]] (guarantor) [of (address, etc.) *or* whose registered office is at (address)] [Company Registration No.____ ] |

The *Encyclopaedia* states that the definitions of "landlord" and "tenant" are preferable to "lessor" and "lessee" in order to make a clear distinction and avoid problems caused by carelessness. A tenant may not be in a position to determine which definitions are used, but it is a point worth noting.

Company registration numbers are sometimes included in the case of company landlords, tenants and guarantors to assist with the more positive identification of companies for search purposes at H.M. Land Registry, and are useful for searches at the Companies Registry.

| 1.2 | the Centre | ALL THAT (describe the Centre) shown [for the purpose of identification only] edged [with a thick black line] on the Plan |
|---|---|---|

There is no objection to including a definition of the centre in the particulars part of the lease, although it may more usually be included in clause 2 under the definitions section. Leases of premises within retail parks may refer to the estate (or the development) as opposed to the centre. The name is immaterial provided there is no confusion in the text of the lease. It is advisable for the precise extent of the centre to be readily identifiable and the tenant should take care to ensure that where there is a right for the landlord to extend or reduce the centre, such extension or reduction does not adversely affect the tenant's use or occupation of the premises and that there is provision for any specific service charge percentages to be varied accordingly. The tenant may prefer to delete a reference to the landlord being entitled to reduce the size of the centre, as a reduction in footfall could have a depreciating effect on business.

| | | | |
|---|---|---|---|
| | **1.3** | **the Premises** | Unit no. _____ of the Centre more particularly defined in the first schedule |

The premises must be readily identifiable and provision in the particulars is mainly for a unit or postal number to be inserted.

| | | | |
|---|---|---|---|
| | **1.4** | **Contractual Term** | _____ years from and including the _____ day of _____ |

See comments under clause 1.18 of the agreement for lease.

It is sensible for the term to be stated to be from and including a specific date to avoid the uncertainty caused by the general law that a term which is to commence "from" a certain date in fact commences at the beginning of the following day, with the term lasting during the whole anniversary of the day from which it is granted, unless there is some contra-indication in the lease. It appears that if the lease states that the term is to commence 'on' a specified date, the term will include that date.[1]

| | | | |
|---|---|---|---|
| **2.03** | **1.5** | **Rent Commencement Date** | the _____ day of _____ |

The rent commencement date will not always be the date of the lease, *e.g.* where there is a rent-free period or where the tenant has been in occupation of the premises prior to the date of the lease and is to pay rent from the date of occupation.

| | | | |
|---|---|---|---|
| | **1.6** | **Initial Rent** | £_____ (_____ pounds) per year |

The initial rent will be inserted and should be checked.

| | | | |
|---|---|---|---|
| | **1.7** | **Review Dates** | (insert review dates) and "Review Date" means any one of the Review Dates |

Many leases deal with rent review dates by stating that the initial rent will be subject to review on the _____ day of _____ and thereafter on every [fifth] anniversary of that date during the term. It is contended that, at least where the interpretation of "the term" includes not only the contractual term but also any period of holding over or extension or continuance of the contractual term, this could result in the landlord being entitled to review the rent on the day following the date of expiration of the contractual term. In an upwards market this would benefit the landlord, who could never hope to achieve a full market rent pursuant to an interim rent application, but would disadvantage the tenant, who would presumably prefer the old rent to continue during negotiations, thereby acting as a negotiating factor. The tenant should therefore press for the review dates to be set out in order to ensure that there is no end of term rent review.

To ensure certainty, the tenant shall not accept phrases such as "the expiration of every fifth year of the term". The following words should be added at the end of this definition:

> and "relevant Review Date" should be construed accordingly

as this definition is used in the rent reviews provisions.

**1.8  Interest Rate** \_\_\_\_\_**per cent per year above the base lending rate of XY Bank [Limited *or* plc] or such other bank [being a member of the Committee of London and Scottish Bankers] as the Landlord may from time to time nominate in writing**

The interest rate is a matter for negotiation. It is supposed to be a penal rate and tenants are expected to pay their rent (and other payments due under the lease) on time. Having said that, it is a comparatively recent imposition for rents to be payable in advance as opposed to in arrear and many tenants would argue that some account should be taken of the fact that landlords have had their money, and therefore presumably interest on it, in advance. The interest provision should in fact interrelate with the "period of grace" provision,[2] and a suggested formula is 2 per cent above base lending rate if payment is not made within 14 days after becoming due or 3 per cent above if not made within 21 days. The other point to mention is the identity of the bank, which should most certainly be a member of the Committee of London and Scottish Bankers. In addition, the landlord should not be entitled to switch banks as it may wish and the tenant should consider adding the following additional words at the end of this provision:

> **in the event that XY Bank [Limited *or* plc] subsequently fails to publish a base lending rate**

Some interest provisions attempt to insert a minimum rate, which should be avoided by both the landlord and the tenant. The landlord should beware, lest interest rates fall dramatically, leaving the minimum rate at a level substantially higher than the standard borrowing rate, in which case the interest may be void as amounting to a penalty[3]; and the tenant would be advised not to run the risk of having to pay interest at a substantially higher rate than the basic lending rate.

**1.9 Prohibited Users (specify prohibited users)**

This is self-explanatory and the tenant should be cautious of allowing the landlord to include various prohibited users, which may not affect the tenant's business but could restrict the persons to whom the tenant may wish to assign or sub-let the premises. In fact, the tenant's own business may alter during the term of the lease, eg the sale of items and provision of services by supermarkets that they would never have considered feasible 10 years ago.

**1.10 Permitted User (specify user) or such other user not being one of the Prohibited Users that falls within Class [A1] as referred to in Part A of the Schedule to the Town and Country Planning (Use Classes) Order 1987 as the Landlord shall from time to time approve [such approval not to be unreasonably withheld or [or delayed]]**

The permitted user will, of course, depend upon the use for which the tenant wishes to use the premises and will also be a matter of negotiation. The tenant will not wish to restrict himself to too narrow a use, for while this might be satisfactory in the short term, if the lease is for 25 years much can happen to the tenant's business, *e.g.* expansion or contraction resulting in the necessity for the tenant to assign or sub-let the premises, in which case the assignee or subtenant may wish to carry on a different use. The tenant will, however, need to ensure that too wide a use will not have adverse consequences on rent review.

It should be noted that the government is currently proposing changes to the Use Classes Order and the outcome of these proposals is awaited. In view of the comment made under clause 3.16 it may be as well to interpolate the following words after the reference to the 1987 Order:

**(to which the provisions of clause 3.16 shall not apply)**

**2.04 1.11 Decorating Years _____ (specify years)**

The tenant should ensure that these are not too frequent, and this will be a matter for negotiation.

| | | |
|---|---|---|
| **1.12** | **Shop Opening Hours** | **(specify hours) on Mondays to Saturdays (inclusive) other than Christmas Day Good Friday and any other statutory bank (or local) holiday** |

Leases quite often attempt to restrict the opening hours of premises, not only in respect of shops but also offices. There is no logical reason for this where premises stand alone, and in such circumstances these provisions should be deleted. It is understandable that leases of premises in shopping centres may contain restrictions on the opening hours of the premises either because of centralised heating and other services or because the main gates to the centre, or to the servicing facilities, are closed. If this provision is to apply, the tenant may wish to negotiate personal arrangements with the landlord for occupation outside these hours for special circumstances. In particular, if the shopping centre is closed outside these hours the tenant may need to be certain that it can have access for the purpose of servicing. In this regard, however, the tenant should check to ensure that there are no planning conditions restricting servicing outside specified hours.

The Sunday Trading Act 1994 should also be considered. This relaxed the previous prohibitions on Sunday trading and any restrictions on shop opening hours must be viewed in the light of this Act. The tenant should also be wary not to have to pay additional service charges incurred in respect of a shopping centre caused by Sunday opening, where that particular tenant prefers to remain closed. Any "keep open" covenant in the lease will also have to be considered, although the Act specifically renders "keep open" covenants unenforceable in respect of Sundays for existing leases and agreements unless they actually refer to Sundays.[4]

| | | |
|---|---|---|
| **1.13** | **Service Charge Percentage** | **\_\_\_\_\_per cent subject to the provsions for variation contained in the sixth schedule** |

See comments under sixth schedule, Part A, paragraph 5.

| | | |
|---|---|---|
| **1.14** | **Initial Provisional Service Charge** | **£\_\_\_\_\_ (\_\_\_\_\_ pounds) per year** |

This must be inserted and checked for accuracy.

| | | |
|---|---|---|
| **1.15** | **Insurance Rent Percentage** | **\_\_\_\_\_per cent** |

This must be inserted and checked for accuracy. In a shopping centre, or in other developments where premises are likely to be altered in size or scope, or new premises built (whether on newly acquired land or otherwise) there should be provision for the insurance rent percentage to be changed as occasion requires to reflect changes in circumstances. The tenant must ensure that its percentage is calculated on a fair and equitable basis. The problem is that other tenants at a shopping centre may have a higher fire risk than the tenant and it would be unreasonable to expect the tenant to pay a proportion of the cost of insuring such higher risk premises. The tenant should consider whether a more appropriate way of dealing with insurance rent is to provide for this to be:

> **... a fair and reasonable proportion to be determined by the Surveyor acting as an expert and not as an arbitrator**

## 2 Definitions

**2.05**   2.1   **For all purposes of this Lease the terms defined in clauses 1 and 2 and paragraph 1 of the fourth schedule and the sixth schedule have the meanings specified**

This is self-explanatory.

2.2   **"Accountant" means any person or firm appointed by the Landlord (including an employee of the Landlord or a Group Company) to perform any of the functions of the Accountant under this Lease**

The accountant, and for that matter any other professional persons, have very important roles to play in the lease and for this purpose alone the tenant will wish to ensure that they are suitably qualified. The minimum amendment that the tenant would expect is as follows:

> **... means any suitably qualified person or firm ...**

but the tenant should consider the following alternative suggested in the notes to the precedent:

> **"Accountant" means a chartered accountant acting as an expert and not as an arbitrator appointed by agreement between the parties or in default of agreement nominated by the President of the Institute of Chartered Accountants on the application of either the Landlord or the Tenant**

2.3   **"Adjoining Property" means any neighbouring or adjoining land or premises (excluding the remainder of the Centre) in which the Landlord or a Group Company has a freehold or leasehold interest or in which during the Term the Landlord or a Group Company shall have acquired a freehold or leasehold interest**

There is no objection to this, provided that the existence of any adjoining property does not have an adverse effect on the tenant's contribution towards service charges or other costs referred to in the lease and the tenant should therefore be vigilant in this regard when amending the lease.

**2.4** **"Common Parts" means any malls and other pedestrian ways concourses and circulation areas staircases escalators ramps and lifts service roads loading bays forecourts and other ways and areas in the Centre which are from time to time during the Term provided by the Landlord for common use by customers frequenting the Centre and by the tenants and the occupiers of the Centre or persons expressly or by implication authorised by them**

The third and fourth lines may benefit by amending them to read:

> **... ramps and lifts service roads service areas common loading areas forecourts car parking areas access ramps and other entrances fire escapes landscaped areas and other ways and areas in the Centre which are from time to time ...**

Although it is highly unlikely that the landlord would so amend or alter the common parts to make it impossible for the tenant to carry on its business, the following additional wording may be considered (or a separate landlord's covenant to the same effect, as suggested in the landlord's covenant contained in clause 6.7):

> **Provided that there shall at all times [during the Shop Opening Hours] be full and sufficient Common Parts and other joint facilities available for use in connection with the Permitted User of the Premises to enable the Tenant or any undertenant to carry on its or their normal business at the Premises**

Another point is that car parking at shopping centres and retail parks is of particular importance. Leases frequently include a specified definition of the car park and then include a reference to the car park in the definition of the common parts, *e.g.*

> **"Car Park" means that part of the Common Parts shown [edged green] on the Plan or such other area as the Landlord may specify**

The tenant must obviously ensure that the landlord does not subsequently reduce the car parking area to a level (by building additional units or otherwise) that could adversely affect the tenant's business. One option is to qualify the latter part of the definition to read:

> ... as the Landlord may reasonably specify

Another option is to amend the latter part as follows:

> ... or such additional area as the Landlord may from time to time reasonably specify.

**2.5** **"Group Company" means a company that is a member of the same group as the Landlord within the meaning of section 42 of the 1954 Act**

See clause 5.9.11. It is in fact surprising that landlords are prepared to allow occupation of premises by members of the same group of companies as the tenant without a formal assignment, but needless to say it may be in the tenant's best interests to try to include this provision if it is not initially incorporated in the lease.

**2.06** **2.6** **"Insurance Cost" means the sums that the Landlord shall from time to time pay by way of premium**

The case of *Havenridge Ltd v. Boston Dyers Ltd*[4] makes it clear that there will be no implication that premiums will be reasonable, but merely that the premium rate should be representative of the market rate, and that the insurance contract was negotiated at arm's length and in the market place. It is therefore vital that this provision be amended specifically to include a reference to reasonableness. There is also the point that the landlord may wish to place the insurance with an insurer where there is an agency or loyalty commission arrangement of which the landlord may seek to take advantage by retaining any discount or commission and charging the tenants the gross amount of the premium. Some leases actually provide for the landlord to retain discounts and commission, which can amount to a considerable sum. The case of *Williams v. Southwark London Borough Council*[5] involved a discount of 25 per cent, comprised of 20 per cent fee for services provided by the council for the insurer, which the court held should belong to the landlord, and 5 per cent loyalty or agency commission, which the court held should have been passed onto the tenants in the absence of an express provision in the lease to the contrary. To put the matter beyond doubt, landlords should perhaps provide specifically for the consideration for management services performed for the insurer to be retained by the landlord, but the tenant should try to have deducted from the insurance cost any commission the landlord may receive. Clause 2.6 could therefore be amended as follows:

2.6 "Insurance Cost" means such reasonable and competitive sums that the Landlord shall from time to time pay by way of premium after the deduction of all commission received by the Landlord

2.6.1 for insuring the Centre or (where such insurance includes the Centre and other premises) such proportion [reasonably] attributable to the Centre of the sums that the Landlord shall from time to time pay by way of premium for insuring the Centre and other premises to be determined from time to time by the Surveyor acting as an expert and not as an arbitrator

It is conceivable that the landlord may insure the centre with other premises in its ownership under a block policy. It is also essential that the tenant ascertains precisely what is being insured as part of the centre, *e.g.* the buildings alone or landlord's and tenant's fixtures and fittings as well? The tenant may wish to amend the lease to make the position clear, so that the tenant is not paying part of the premium for insuring other tenants' fixtures and fittings while insuring its own separately.

2.6.2 for insuring in such amount and on such terms as [the Landlord shall consider appropriate *or* shall be reasonable] against all liability of the Landlord to third parties arising out of or in connection with any matter involving or relating to the Centre

The option as to reasonableness is very much preferred, and this applies to both clauses 2.6.1 and 2.6.2.

2.7 "Insurance Rent" means:
2.7.1 the Insurance Rent Percentage of the Insurance Cost and
2.7.2 all of any increased premium payable by any act or omission of the Tenant

This is self-explanatory, but clause 2.7.2 should be carefully noted by the tenant. This provision, or another provision in the lease, may also make the tenant liable for the cost of insurance valuations as well as for all fees and expenses in connection with maintaining claims. The tenant should ideally resist such a provision, or at least stipulate that, in the case of insurance valuations, full valuations should not take place (at the expense of the tenant) more frequently than every [three] years.

2.8 "Insured Risks" means fire [lightning explosion aircraft (including articles dropped from aircraft) riot civil commotion malicious persons earthquake storm tempest flood

> **bursting and overflowing of water pipes tanks and other apparatus and impact by road vehicles] and such other risks as the Landlord from time to time in [its] absolute discretion may think fit to insure against**

It is essential to ensure that the risks to be covered by the insurance policy are sufficient to cover the main eventualities. This would normally be the position under current standard policies but there is no harm in setting out the principal risks. The tenant's repairing obligation will only be alleviated where there has been damage or destruction by any of the insured risks (see clause 5.4.1). The same applies in respect of the suspension of rent (see clause 7.5.2). It will therefore be seen that the tenant should insist on all usual risks to be covered, failing which the tenant should endeavour to cover the additional risks itself, which hopefully will leave the tenant exposed only to uninsurable risks.

One risk which must now be considered is terrorism. This has been defined as any act of any person acting on behalf of, or in connection with, any organisation with activities directed towards the overthrowing or influencing of any government *de jure* or *de facto* by force or violence.[7] This definition may, however, not be universal and may alter from insurer to insurer or from time to time. *E.g.* the definition now contained in the Terrorism Act 2000 is "the use or threat, for the purpose of advancing a political, religious or ideological course of action which (a) involves serious violence against a person, (b) involves serious damage to property, (c) endangers the life of a person, or (d) creates a serious risk to the health or safety of the public or a section of the public." This is much wider than the ABI standard exclusion used by Pool Re. Until January 1, 1993 terrorist activities would have fallen within the ambit of the other insured risks. *e.g.* fire or malicious damage. At the end of 1992, however, it was announced that the Association of British Insurers would not agree to provide cover against acts of terrorism as from January 1993. This would have had enormous implications for tenants, quite apart from landlords, but fortunately the Reinsurance (Acts of Terrorism) Act 1993 has done much to alleviate the concern caused by the Association's previous statement. The Act basically enables the government to stand in the place of the commercial reinsurers who withdrew from the market at the end of 1992.

The arrangements pursuant to the Act are that insurers wishing to offer property insurance, including cover for acts of terrorism, will become members of a mutual reinsurance company (Pool Reinsurance Company, known as Pool Re). That company will reinsure all terrorism risks situated in Great Britain borne by its insurer members, for which an additional insurance premium will have been paid by the insured. The government will then reinsure the insurance company. It is unlikely, however, that the government's involvement in the insurance market will be permanent and that it will withdraw as soon as adequate sources of commerical reinsurance are available.

In the meantime, it is a welcome lifeboat, but the tenant has to be wary that the landlord covenants to insure terrorism in the first place, and if not, or in addition to such a covenant, the tenant would be advised to ensure that the lease is amended to exclude damage or destruction by terrorism as referred to in this book in respect of various provisions of the lease. The point is that even if terrorism starts out as a specific "insured risk", exemptions in the landlord's insurance covenant may result in it not being an insured risk throughout the whole term of the lease. Furthermore, quite often the landlord will agree to insure terrorism while it can be covered "at reasonable premium rates" (or some similar wording). It may therefore subsequently not be covered. The amendment to this definition including terrorism as one of the insured risks is qualified to allow the tenant to object to terrorism being covered if it becomes too expensive to insure. Unfortunately, very few landlords will be likely to accept this qualification, particularly where they include it as one of the insured risks in the first place.

Another point to consider is whether the lease should be amended to contain a definition of terrorism. As mentioned above, however, the definition may change in the course of a fifteen-year term and the tenant may not wish to tie itself down to a definition which, in hindsight, could subsequently prove to be limited. Clearly, the tenant must decide whether it prefers the certainty of including a definition or the uncertainty of not having a specific definition and the hope that the word "terrorism" will include any subsequent alterations as opposed to running the risk of being void for uncertainty.

Some risks may not be appropriate or (quite apart from terrorism) may increase the premium unreasonably or unnecessarily. The tenant should nevertheless consider whether it wishes the specified risks to include subsidence, heave and landslip, the sprinkler system (if any), aerial devices in addition to aircraft and impact other than by road vehicles, among others. Also, perhaps the reference to "malicious persons" should more properly refer to "malicious damage". Unless the landlord is prepared to agree that the insurance should be in the joint names of the landlord and tenant, which is unlikely as the landlord will usually wish to keep control of the policy and proceeds, the tenant should ensure that either the landlord will act reasonably in deciding which other risks it may wish to insure against, or that the tenant will also have the right to nominate risks.

The reference to "or" such other risks should be amended to "and in addition to the foregoing", in order to make it clear that the landlord is not given the choice which of the stated risks it may choose to insure against—perhaps an obvious point but one worth making. Also, although perhaps not strictly necessary, the tenant could define "insured risk". The latter part of the clause should therefore be amended as follows:

> **terrorism (provided that cover against terrorism is available on terms reasonably acceptable to the Tenant) and in addition to the foregoing such other risks as the Landlord from time to time in its reasonable discretion may think fit to insure against or against which the Tenant may reasonably request the Landlord to insure and "Insured Risk" shall be construed accordingly**

**2.9** "Interest" means interest during the period from the date on which the payment is due to the date of payment both before and after any judgment at the Interest Rate then prevailing or should the base rate referred to in clause 1.8 cease to exist such other rate of interest as is most closely comparable with the Interest Rate to be agreed between the parties or in default of agreement to be determined by the Accountant acting as an expert and not as an arbitrator

This is not an unreasonable provision, and even though the accountant may be an appointee of the landlord, one would expect him to act fairly.

**2.08**    **2.10** "the 1954 Act" means the Landlord and Tenant Act 1954 [and all statutes regulations and orders included by virtue of clause 3.16]

It is as well to include the words in square brackets to ensure that subsequent amendments to the Act are taken into account, *e.g.* the Law of Property Act 1969[8] and, indeed, the likely replacement or substantial amendment of the 1954 Act.

**2.11** "the 1995 Act" means the Landlord and Tenant (Covenants) Act 1995 [and all statutes regulations and ordes included by virtue of clause 3.16]

The same comment as above applies in respect of the words in square brackets.

**2.12** "this Lease" (unless expressly stated to the contrary) includes any document supplemental to or collateral with this document or entered into in accordance with this document

This clause does not require comment.

**2.13** **"Pipes" means all pipes sewers drains mains ducts conduits gutters watercourses wires cables channels flues and all other conducting media and includes any fixings louvres cowls and any other ancillary apparatus**

This may require amendment depending upon the premises being demised.

**2.12** **"the Plan" means the plan annexed to this Lease**

In all cases the premises ought to be defined by reference to a plan, probably stated to be for identification purposes only unless the plan is supposed to take precedence over the verbal description of the premises.

**2.15** **"the Planning Acts" means the Town and Country Planning Act 1990 [and all statutes regulations and orders included by virtue of clause 3.16]**

It is likely that this definition will be extended to include any or all of the following Acts:

> **The Planning (Listed Building and Conservation Areas) Act 1990, the Planning (Consequential Provisions) Act 1990, the Planning (Hazardous Substances) Act 1990 and the Planning and Compensation Act 1991**

**2.16** **"Rent" means the Initial Rent and rent ascertained in accordance with the fourth schedule and such term includes neither the Insurance Rent nor the Service Charge but the term "rents" includes Rent the Insurance Rent and the Service Charge**

This definition should be amended to commence:

**2.16** **"Rent" means the Initial Rent until (but not including) the first Review Date and thereafter "Rent" means the rent ascertained in accordance with the fourth schedule ...**

See under clause 4 as to the reservation of the insurance rent and the service charge as rents.

**2.17** **"Retained Parts" means all parts of the Centre not let or constructed or adapted for letting including (but without prejudice to the generality of the above):**
**2.17.1** **the Common Parts**
**2.17.2** **office accommodation for the Centre manager and ancillary staff**

2.17.3   a central control station for any security system operating throughout the Centre
2.17.4   any nursery premises provided for the benefit of persons using the Centre generally
2.17.5   any public lavatories provided for the benefit of persons using the Centre generally
2.17.6   any staff rooms and storage premises used in connection with the provisions of services for the Centre
2.17.7   all Pipes equipment and apparatus used in the Centre (except such as are within and solely serve an individual unit which is let or constructed or adapted for letting)
2.17.8   the plant rooms ducts walkways channels and other areas which house or contain the items described in clause 2.17.7 and
2.17.9   such parts of the main structure walls foundations and roofs of the Centre that are not included in the Premises and that would not be included in the premises demised by the leases of all the other units in the Centre if let on the same terms as this Lease

This needs very careful consideration depending upon the composition of the centre. The tenant does not want to find itself paying a proportion of the service charge (which may include rates) of unlet units. The exclusion of parts of the centre "let or constructed or adapted for letting" is fair and reasonable, but quite often an exclusion will relate only to parts of the centre "not let on the same terms as this lease", which could result in the occupying tenants paying part of the service charges for unlet premises. Also, if there are nursery premises provided, as contemplated by clause 2.17.4, the tenant may wish to ensure that any fees charged should be brought into account to reduce the service charge.

**2.09**  2.18   "the Shop Covenants" means the covenants set out in the fifth schedule
2.19   "Surveyor" means any person or firm appointed by or acting for the Landlord (including an employee of the Landlord or a Group Company and including also the person or firm appointed by the Landlord to collect the rents) to perform any of the functions of the Surveyor under this Lease

As with the accountant the person performing the function of the surveyor should be professionally (or otherwise suitably) qualified and the following proviso should be added:

... provided that the person who purports to act as the Surveyor must be an Associate or Fellow of the Royal Institution of Chartered Surveyors or an Associate or Fellow of the Incorporated Society of Valuers and Auctioneers

If the tenant so wishes, it could insert a definition of "terrorism" at this juncture.[9]

**2.20** "VAT" means value added tax or other tax of a similar nature and unless otherwise expressly stated all references to rents or other sums payable by the Tenant are exclusive of VAT

This definition requires no comment.

## 3 Interpretation

**3.1** The expressions "the Landlord" and "the Tenant" wherever the context so admits include the person for the time being entitled to the reversion immediately expectant on the determination of the Term and the Tenant's successors in title respectively and any reference to a superior landlord includes the Landlord's immediate reversioner (and any superior landlords) at any time **2.10**

This is self-explanatory.

**3.2** Where the Landlord the Tenant or the Guarantor for the time being are two or more persons obligations expressed or implied to be made by or with such party are deemed to be by or with such persons jointly and severally

Quite often the landlord will attempt to avoid this provision applying to itself and this should be resisted.

**3.3** Words importing one gender include all other genders and words importing the singular include the plural and vice versa

This proviso is unobjectionable and requires no comment, but may be amended by adding the following wording where appropriate:

> ... and any reference to a person includes not only an individual but also a company whether limited or unlimited

**3.4** The expression "Guarantor" includes not only the person referred to in clause 1.1.3 (if any) but also any person who enters into covenants with the Landlord pursuant to clauses 5.9.5 or 5.23

If there is no initial guarantor the tenant may object to the inclusion of clause 8 despite the fact that guarantor's covenants may become necessary on an assignment. In such circumstances, it is possible to include the guarantor's covenants in a schedule. See, in general, the comments on guarantors in the introduction to clause 8. Also, see the comments under clause 5.23.

**3.5** **The expression "the Centre" where the context so admits includes any additional and adjoining land and buildings in which during the Term the Landlord or a Group Company shall have acquired the freehold or leasehold interest and which shall have been so constructed or acquired to form [an integral] part of the Centre**

It is important from the landlord's point of view to ensure that the centre does not expand where the tenant has been given a fixed service charge percentage, unless provisions are inserted in the lease to countenance this. Similarly, the tenant should ensure that its service charge percentage does not remain the same if the centre contracts, *e.g.* by the landlord selling off part.

**3.6** **Reference to "the Premises" in the absence of any provision to the contrary include any part of the Premises**

This is perhaps implied, but there is certainly no harm in spelling it out.

**3.7** **Any part of the Premises that faces onto any of the Common Parts shall be regarded as an external part of the Premises notwithstanding that such part of the Common Parts is covered in and "exterior" "external" and other words to similar effect shall be construed accordingly**

This will need to be considered more specifically having regard to the physical aspects of the premises, common parts and the centre.

**3.8** **The expression "the Term" includes the Contractual Term and any period of holding-over or extension or continuance of the Contractual Term whether by statute or common law**

It may be that the stated term runs on for some reason, *e.g.* the holding over by the tenant under the Landlord and Tenant Act 1954. The landlord will want to be certain that the tenant is still bound by the lease covenants and provisions during this period. There is accordingly no objection to this provision. A previous tenant's liability during this period is now, of course, subject to the Landlord and Tenant (Covenants) Act 1995. As regards guarantors, in the absence of any contrary indication in the lease, a guarantee does not extend to a period after the expiry of the term of the lease where the tenancy is being extended under section 24 of the Landlord and Tenant Act 1954.[10]

**3.9** **References to "the last year of the Term" include the last year of the Term if the Term shall determine otherwise than by effluxion of time and references to "the expiration of the Term" include such other determination of the Term**

This is self-explanatory and covers the situation where the lease is brought to an end earlier than the stated term by forfeiture, exercise of a break option, surrender or otherwise.

**3.10** **References to any right of the Landlord to have access to the Premises shall be construed as extending to any superior landlord and any mortgagee of the Premises and to all persons authorised by the Landlord and any superior landlord or mortgagee (including agents professional advisers contractors workmen and others) [where such superior lease or mortgage grants such rights of access to the superior landlord or mortgagee]**   **2.11**

The words in square brackets should most definitely be included and in addition, in order to avoid a continual stream of persons demanding access to the premises, the tenant may consider it advisable to add the following proviso at the end of this clause:

> ... **provided that such persons shall have sufficient reason to require access to the Premises**

It may also be advisable to provide that the persons requiring such rights of access should be authorised

> ... **in writing by the Landlord** ...

**3.11** **Any covenant by the Tenant not to do an act or thing shall be deemed to include an obligation [to use reasonable endeavours] not to permit or suffer such act or thing to be done by another person [where the Tenant is aware that such act or thing is being done]**

The words in square brackets should most definitely be included and although doubtless implied, it may be as well for the clause to commence:

Any covenant in this Lease by the Tenant ...

**3.12 Any provisions in this Lease referring to the consent or approval of the Landlord shall be construed as also requiring the consent or approval of any mortgagee of the Premises and any superior landlord where such consent shall be required but nothing in this Lease shall be construed as implying that any obligation is imposed upon any mortgagee or any superior landlord not unreasonably to refuse any such consent or approval**

Ideally, this provision should be deleted, or at the very least it should be amended so that it applies only to the consent of a mortgagee or superior landlord actually required under the terms of an existing mortgage or superior lease. The clause should be amended to read as follows:

**Any provisions in this Lease referring to the consent or approval of the Landlord shall be construed as also requiring the consent or approval of any existing mortgagee of the Premises and any superior landlord where such consent or approval shall be required under a mortgage or superior lease in existence at the date of this Lease and the Landlord shall use all reasonable endeavours to obtain such consent or approval with all due expedition**

The point is that without these words the landlord could subsequently grant a mortgage or superior lease containing provisions by which consent could be refused where it would otherwise be unreasonable, *e.g.* in respect of the tenant's right to assign or sub-let. The tenant should also request a copy of any existing mortgage or superior lease to check the rights relating to consent of the mortgagee or superior landlord.

**3.13 Reference to "consent of the Landlord" or words to similar effect mean a consent in writing signed by or on behalf of the Landlord and to "approved" and "authorised" or words to similar effect mean (as the case may be) approved or authorised in writing by or on behalf of the Landlord**

This is self-explanatory.

**3.14 The terms "the parties" or "party" means the Landlord and/or the Tenant but except where there is an express indication to the contrary exclude the Guarantor**

It is better to exclude the guarantor as one of the parties to the lease to avoid problems where the lease contains reference to "the consent of the parties" thereby including the guarantor.

**3.15** **"Development" has the meaning given by the Town and Country Planning Act 1990, section 55**

**3.16** **Any references to a specific statute include any statutory extension or modification amendment or re-enactment of such statute and any regulations or orders made under such statute and any general reference to "statute" or "statutes" includes any regulations or orders made under such statute or statutes**

The problem with this provision is that it could apply to orders such as the 1987 Order referred to in clause 1.10, which may subsequently be replaced or amended, thereby affecting the use to which the premises may be put, hence the suggested interpolation in that clause. A consultation paper has, in fact, been published on possible changes to the 1987 Order and temporary use provisions. The review forms part of the government's ongoing process of changes to the planning system.

**3.17** **Reference in this Lease to any clause sub-clause or schedule without further designation shall be construed as a reference to the clause sub-clause or schedule to this Lease so numbered**

This is self-explanatory.

**3.18** **The clause paragraph and schedule headings [and the table of contents] do not form part of this Lease and shall not be taken into account in its construction or interpretation**

**2.12**

This is normally inserted to avoid a badly worded clause heading from being construed against a landlord. It is unobjectionable from the tenant's point of view.

It may also be advisable to insert the following additional clause:

**3.19** **References in this Lease to any rights granted to the Tenant shall be construed as being granted to the Tenant and any undertenant or undertenants of the Tenant and all persons authorised by the Tenant or any undertenant or undertenants to exercise such rights**

**3.20** **Unless expressly stated to the contrary the expression "this Lease" includes any document supplemental to or collateral**

**with this document or entered into in accordance with this document**

This is self explanatory.

---

[1] *Trow v. Ind Coope (West Midlands) Ltd* [1967] 2 Q.B. 899.
[2] See clause 5.18.
[3] See *Dunlop Pneumatic Tyre Co. Ltd v. New Garage and Motor Co. Ltd* [1915] A.C. 79 and *Cellulose Acetate Silk Co. Ltd v. Widnes Foundry (1925) Ltd* [1933] A.C. 20.
[4] See fifth schedule, para. 5.
[5] [2000] E.G.C.S. 44.
[6] [1994] 49 E.G. 111.
[7] For the purpose of the standard exclusion in insurance policies and in section 3.2(2) of the Reinsurance (Acts of Terrorism) Act 1993.
[8] See *Brett v. Brett Essex Golf Club*, [1986]1 E.G.L.R. 154.
[9] See comment under "Insured Risks".
[10] See *Junction Estates Ltd v. Cope* (1974) 27 P.&C.R. 482.

*Chapter 3*

# Demise

## Introduction

This clause formally demises the premises to the tenant, referring to the rights to be granted with the demise and to the exceptions and reservations in favour of the landlord. It also sets out the term to be granted and the rents payable.  **3.01**

**4  Demise**

> The Landlord demises to the Tenant the Premises *Together* with the rights specified in the second schedule but *Excepting and reserving* to the Landlord the rights specified in the third schedule To *hold* the Premises to the Tenant for the Contractual Term *Subject* to all rights easements privileges restrictions covenants and stipulations of whatever nature affecting the Premises [including the matters contained or referred to in the seventh schedule] *Yielding and paying* to the Landlord: **3.02**

**4.1** the Rent payable without any deduction [or set-off] by equal quarterly payments in advance on the usual quarter days in every year and proportionately for any period of less than a year the first such payment being a proportionate sum in respect of the period from and including the Rent Commencement Date to and including the day before the quarter day next after the Rent Commencement Date to be paid on the date of this Lease and

**4.2** by way of further rent the Insurance Rent payable on demand in accordance with clause 7 and the Service Charge payable in accordance with the sixth schedule

Comments on the rights, exceptions and reservations are included under the second and third schedules.

The words

> **of whatever nature affecting the Premises including the matters**

should be deleted so that, in the words of the note to the precedent, the schedule becomes comprehensive rather than illustrative.

An interesting point is that the words "yielding and paying" actually imply a covenant to pay the rent,[1] but it is more usual to have a specific tenant's covenant in this regard.

The reference to the rent being payable without any deduction (or set off) is to avoid the tenant attempting to set off expenses or payments due from the landlord against the rent. The words "set-off" were not in fact included in the precedent, but are now invariably added since it was held that a covenant to pay rent "without any deduction" would not exclude the tenant's right of set-off.[2] The tenant may, however, try to retain this useful right and endeavour to exclude any reference to the payment of rent "without deduction or set-off" or similar wording. There may, however, be instances where the tenant is obliged to make deductions, *e.g.* tax payable to the Inland Revenue where the landlord is non-resident, and the following amendment to clause 4.1 may therefore be advisable[3]:

> **without any deduction (except where lawfully made pursuant to statute)**

The tenant should always ensure that the words "and proportionately for any period of less than a year", or similar words to the same effect, are included. Present-day rent-free periods can be up to a year or even longer, and the tenant will not wish to make the first payment of rent on the date of the lease where the Rent Commencement Date is 12 months hence. This clause should be amended to provide that the first rent payment will be due and payable on the Rent Commencement Date.

It is a question of negotiation as to whether the insurance rent and the service charge, and any other payments for that matter, are reserved by way of rent, and the tenant may initially wish to challenge this. The landlord will usually prefer such a reservation in order to utilise the remedy of distress for arrears, and to forfeit the lease without the necessity to serve a notice under section 146 of the Law of Property Act 1925, which would otherwise apply if these payments were merely tenant's covenants. Having said that, the landlord may accept that there is more certainty in serving a section 146 notice with a short period of notice, leading to re-entry, rather than to run the risk that the tenant may subsequently utilise the Common Law Procedure Act 1852 which permits the tenant to apply for relief for up to six months after judgment in respect of forfeiture for arrears of rent. A compromise that can frequently be reached is that while insurance premiums and "on account" service charge payments should be reserved as rent, the balancing service charge should not be. This is because balancing service charges can sometimes be subject to dispute and the tenant does not want to be forced to pay the balancing charge, for fear of the consequences of not doing so, when it feels that it has a genuine grievance. The latter part of clause 4.2 could therefore be amended to read:

> **. . . and the provisional sum payable pursuant to the sixth schedule Part B paragraph 7.3**

One further comment that should be made on the reservation of rents is that there has been the suggestion that section 56 of the Stamp Act 1891 could be utilised by the Inland Revenue to charge stamp duty on the accumulated VAT payable on rent for the duration of the term granted by the lease.[4] Section 56 applies where monies, other than rent, are paid periodically under a lease (or other conveyance) and results in *ad valorem* duty being charged on the total amount which would, or may, be payable during the period of 20 years following the date of the lease. It should be stated that section 56 would only apply in respect of VAT where the landlord has either elected to waive the exemption in respect of VAT or there is no agreement by the landlord not to elect to waive the exemption during the term granted by the lease.

**3.03**

The effect of section 56 in respect of a rent of £100,000 per annum is to increase the stamp duty payable thereon from £2,350 to £9,000 (at a current VAT rate of 17.5 per cent) and is, therefore, not to be taken lightly.

The Inland Revenue issued a Statement of Practice in September 1991 stating that if a lease provides for payment of VAT on the rent otherwise than as rent, duty will be charged on the VAT element as consideration payable periodically, *i.e.* as referred to in section 56. The suggestion that has been made by certain commentators, therefore, is that it is important to ensure that the lease reserves VAT as additional rent due to the landlord. Unfortunately, this would result in a downside to the tenant (see above with regard to distress, etc.) and it would be preferable not to proceed along this line unless necessary.

It seems highly unlikely that the Inland Revenue would ever try to implement section 56 except where a lease specifically states that any VAT payment on rent is not reserved as rent, and the author has been in correspondence with the Inland Revenue who have confirmed that it is not their intention to implement section 56 except as aforementioned. Nevertheless, in view of the possible adverse consequences so far as the tenant is concerned, and the fact that the Inland Revenue would presumably not be bound by the correspondence with the author, it may be as well for the tenant to ensure that VAT is reserved as additional rent, at least until the position is clarified. It may therefore be as well to include the following additional provision:

**4.3 where VAT is payable on the Rent (whether as a result of an election by the Landlord or otherwise) the amount of that VAT**

---

[1] See *Vyvyan v. Arthur* (1823) 1 B. & C. 410.
[2] See *Connaught Restaurants Ltd v. Indoor Leisure Ltd* [1994] All E.R. 834; [1994] 1 W.L.R. 501, CA.
[3] Despite such exclusions as aforesaid being ineffective where statute provides that the right to deduct cannot be excluded, *e.g.* s. 106(2) of the Taxes Management Act 1970.
[4] See Marsh [1991] 42 E.G. 94.

*Chapter 4*

# Tenant's Covenants

## Introduction

As landlords' solicitors become ever wary that they should leave nothing to chance, the number of individual tenant's covenants appear to be increasing, with heavyweight commercial leases quite often having comfortably in excess of 30 covenants and not far short of 50. It is therefore quite impossible to suggest amendments to all permutations of the obligations currently being imposed on tenants, but the tenant's adviser should be watchful for new variations on an old theme and, indeed, for innovative covenants which could cause the tenant a good deal of anxiety.  **4.01**

The problem is that most tenant's covenants appear at the outset to be quite reasonable and innocuous, but if a week is a long time in politics then 15 years is a lifetime in property, during which time circumstances can and will change with the result that a previously innocent-looking covenant could become highly restrictive and troublesome.

The following comments and suggested amendments are offered in respect of the precedent:

## 5 The Tenant's covenants

The Tenant covenants with the Landlord: **4.02**

### 5.1 Rent

5.1.1 to pay the rents on the days and in the manner set out in this Lease and not to exercise or seek to exercise any right or claim to withhold rent or any right or claim to legal or equitable set-off **4.03**

5.1.2 if so required in writing by the Landlord to make such payments by banker's order or credit transfer to any bank and account [in the United Kingdom] that the Landlord may from time to time nominate

There may be occasions where the tenant would wish to withhold rent or claim a set-off[1] and while the point is worth negotiating, clause 5.1.1 is otherwise not unreasonable.

Any reference to payment of rent by banker's order or credit transfer should be vigorously contested. The landlord's argument will be that the rent should be paid on time, but the tenant could respond that it is a fairly recent innovation in legal terms for rent to be paid in advance as opposed to in arrears and, furthermore, that the landlord has the benefit of three months' rent in advance, despite the fact that it may not arrive on the actual quarter day. In addition, most company tenants will have a standard mechanism for payment of rent and will not be geared up to make exceptions to cover these particular lease arrangements. It is in fact also suggested that there are dangers for a landlord in this clause in that the acceptance of rent by the bank after a breach of covenant by the tenant could waive the breach.

Clause 5.1.2 should therefore be deleted.

**5.2 Outgoings and VAT**

**4.04**

**To pay and indemnify the Landlord against:**

**5.2.1** **all rates taxes assessments duties charges impositions and outgoings which are now or during the Term shall be charged assessed or imposed upon the Premises or upon the owner or occupier of them [excluding any payable by the Landlord occasioned by receipt of the rents or by any disposition of dealing with or ownership of any interest reversionary to the interest created by this Lease] [and if the Landlord shall suffer any loss of rating relief which may be applicable to empty premises after the end of the Term by reason of such relief being allowed to the Tenant in respect of any period before the end of the Term to make good such loss to the Landlord] and**

**5.2.2** **VAT (or any tax of a similar nature that may be substituted for it or levied in addition to it) chargeable in respect of any payment made by the Tenant under any of the terms of or in connection with this Lease or in respect of any payment made by the Landlord where the Tenant agrees in this Lease to reimburse the Landlord for such payment**

The tenant should ensure that there is excluded from the tenant's liability any taxes properly payable by the landlord both in respect of rents received and the landlord's dealings with the reversionary interest. In the case of an under-lease there should also be excluded rents and outgoings payable by the landlord under its own lease.

Reference to the loss of rating relief should be deleted. This arises where the tenant has closed the premises prior to the end of the term and has used up the full entitlement to rating relief. In most cases the tenant will only close the premises if the tenant's business is unprofitable, and therefore the last thing the tenant wants is then to have to reimburse the landlord for the landlord's loss of rating relief.

The lease may also contain a tenant's covenant dealing with outgoings assessed on the premises and other property, *e.g.*

**5.2.3** **the proportion reasonably attributable to the Premises (to be properly and reasonably determined by the Surveyor) of all rates taxes assessments duties charges impositions and outgoings which are now or during the Term shall be charged assessed or imposed on the Premises and any other property including the rest of the Centre and any adjoining property of the Landlord or on their owners or occupiers**

This is acceptable, but subject to the same exclusions as referred to in the first square brackets in clause 5.2.1 and in the first paragraph above.

See comments post with regard to VAT.

**5.3** **Electricity gas and other services consumed**

**To pay to the suppliers and to indemnify the Landlord against all charges for electricity gas and other services consumed or used at or in relation to the Premises (including meter rents)**   **4.05**

In a footnote to the precedent it is stated that this clause is possibly superfluous in the case of a separate building, as the tenant would make arrangements for a separate supply to be provided to the premises, but there is no objection to its inclusion. The covenant may also refer to the compliance by the tenant with the lawful requirements and regulations of the suppliers. It is, of course, difficult to resist this.

**5.4** **Repair and cleaning**

**5.4.1** **To repair the Premises and keep them in repair excepting damage caused by an Insured Risk other than where the insurance money is irrecoverable in consequence of any act or default of the Tenant or anyone at the Premises expressly**   **4.06**

or by implication with the Tenant's authority [and under the Tenant's control]

5.4.2 To replace from time to time the Landlord's fixtures and fittings in the Premises which may be or become beyond repair at any time during or at the expiration of the Term

5.4.3 To clean the Premises and keep them in a clean neat and tidy condition and (without prejudice to the generality of the above) to clean both sides of all windows and window frames in the Premises [at least [once] every [week] or as often as is [reasonably] necessary]

It is quite easy to devote a whole chapter to the subject of repair and the Law Commission has published a consultation paper on the state and condition of leasehold property with a view to considering existing obligations and how the law can be improved with regard to them. Perhaps the best definition of repair was that given by Buckley L.J. in *Lurcott v Wakely & Wheeler*[2]: "Repair is restoration by renewal or replacement of subsidiary parts of a whole. Renewal, as distinguished from repair, is reconstruction of the entirety, meaning by the entirety not necessarily the whole but substantially the whole.' The suggestion is, therefore, that while repair may necessitate the renewal of subsidiary parts, it does not require the renewal of the whole except, curiously, where the premises are damaged or destroyed by fire, tempest or enemy bomb.[3] It is, of course, possible for a covenant to go beyond a standard repairing obligation by the use of clear and precise wording, *e.g.* "to keep the demised premises in good and substantial repair and condition and when necessary to rebuild reconstruct or replace the same"[4] or "keep . . . in good and substantial repair . . . and to renew or replace the same or any part or parts thereof whenever . . . necessary."[5] It need hardly be said that the tenant should be alert to provisions like these.

The case of *Walsh v. Greenwich London Borough Council*[6] is also of significance. In that case the obligation was to maintain the premises in good condition and repair. The court concluded that the word "condition" added something to the meaning of the word "repair" and, as such, the presence of condensation in the premises (caused by lack of insulation) was a feature of the condition of the premises and had to be rectified under the covenant, despite the fact that the premises were not in disrepair. It should be noted, however, that the case related to a short form residential tenancy agreement and may possibly not be applicable to a standard commercial lease, but one cannot be sure of that.

It is also worthwhile to bear in mind the standard of repair which it was stated in *Proudfoot v. Hart*[7] would have to take into account the age, character and locality of property. The case is also authority for the fact that if the premises are out of repair at the commencement of the term then the tenant would be under an obligation to repair them.

"To put in repair" is sometimes used and imposes no greater obligation than "to repair" any more than to keep "in repair", "in good repair", "in sufficient repair" or "in tenantable repair" (*Anstruther-Gough-Calthorpe v. McOscar.*[8]) Consideration must, however, be given to the case of *Credit Suisse v. Beegas Nominees Ltd*[9] where the obligation was "to repair and otherwise keep in good condition". It was held that in order to put and keep premises in a specified condition of good and tenantable repair, the work required may not be a repair strictly so called. In such cases the required condition is not by reference to the state of the actual building at the date of the demise, but the requirements as to condition of reasonably minded tenants of the class likely to take the premises at that date.

The tenant may wish to limit its liability to the state and condition of the premises at the commencement of the term, in which case it would need to include a provision that it will:

**keep the Premises in no worse condition than they are in at the commencement of the Term as evidenced by the Schedule of Condition annexed hereto**

A schedule of condition would then, of course, have to be settled including, if possible, a portfolio of photographs.

There should be excepted from the tenant's repairing obligation damage or destruction caused by any of the insured risks (as defined). In fact, it would be preferable, from the tenant's point of view, to exclude damage or destruction by uninsured as well as insured risks, particularly as the landlord will almost invariably be in control of what is insured. It is therefore worth the tenant trying to cover this position, but it is unlikely to be accepted by the landlord, in which case the tenant will remain liable if damage results from an uninsured risk. An amendment to endeavour to deal with this is suggested below in the amended clause 5.4.1 but will probably be resisted by the landlord. The tenant may wish to reduce the number of people for whom the tenant may be vicariously liable. The precedent suggests a reference to persons

**under the Tenant's control**

in order to exclude certain categories of "visitors", but where the clause refers to servants of the tenant (which some precedents do, despite the archaic nature of the expression) it may be as well to qualify this with the words

### in the course of employment

in case it is claimed that a servant will, by the nature of the expression, always be under the tenant's control. The reference to "by implication" is designed to include callers at the premises, *e.g.* tradesmen. The tenant could try to resist this.

Despite the fact that terrorism may be stated to be one of the insured risks (see clause 2.8) it would be as well to amend the tenant's repairing covenant specifically to state that damage or destruction caused by terrorism is excepted where terrorism is for any reason not one of the insured risks. It could transpire that even where terrorism is within the definition of the insured risks at the commencement of the lease, limitations and exclusions may subsequently result in it not being insured. In order to avoid argument and possible litigation as to whether or not, in such circumstances, terrorism would be excepted, it would be preferable to spell it out. If the premises are damaged or destroyed by terrorism, where the latter is not covered as an insured risk and where there is no specific exclusion, the tenant would be liable to reinstate out of its own monies. This would be in respect of the "premises" as defined in the lease, but the tenant would also have to contribute to the reinstatement of any "common parts", including structure, etc., through the service charge provisions in the lease.[10]

The tenant may wish to avoid responsibility for structural or inherent defects, *i.e.* the rectification of faults in the design or construction of a building which may otherwise be passed on to the tenant by virtue of the general effect of a tenant's covenant to repair. An exclusion of

### structural or inherent defects

may be a starting point, although it could be suggested that the expression "inherent defect" has no clear meaning and that the exemption of the tenant from such liability may, from the landlord's point of view, make serious inroads into a full repairing liability. The exception may nevertheless be worthwhile making to see what the landlord will offer as a compromise.

Although rarely seen (and unlikely to be accepted) in a lease of commercial premises, the tenant may consider inserting an exception in respect of damage (or disrepair) by fair wear and tear.[11] This may give the tenant some protection when taking a lease of an older property and, in any event, could be a useful negotiating point.

The tenant should in addition endeavour to obtain collateral warranties/duty of care agreements from, *inter alia*, the designers and constructors of the premises.[12]

There is no objection to the replacement of the landlord's fixtures and fittings from time to time or to cleaning the premises and the windows, provided that the latter is not too frequent.

It must be remembered that not all of the insurance monies may be irrecoverable as a result of default, hence the suggested additional words below, namely "to the extent that" and the proviso.

Clause 5.4.1 could therefore be amended as follows:

**5.4.1 To repair the Premises and keep them in repair excepting damage or destruction caused by fair wear and tear or by structural or inherent defects or by any of the Insured Risks (or by terrorism (whether or not at any time one of the Insured Risks) or by any other risks against which the Landlord (acting reasonably) ought to have insured) other than to the extent that the insurance money is irrecoverable in consequence of any act or default of the Tenant or anyone at the Premises with the Tenant's authority and under the Tenant's control *Provided that* where the insurance money is not wholly irrecoverable such sums as are recoverable shall be made available to the Tenant as soon as possible to apply to the repair of the Premises**

**5.5 Decoration**

**[As often as may in the [reasonable] opinion of the Surveyor be necessary in order to maintain a high standard of decorative finish and attractiveness and to preserve the Premises *or* In each of the Decorating Years] and in the last year of the Term to redecorate the Premises in a good and workmanlike manner and with appropriate materials of good quality [to the [reasonable] satisfaction of the Surveyor] the tints and colours and patterns of such decoration to be approved by the Landlord [provided that the covenants relating to the last year of the Term shall not apply where the Tenant shall have redecorated the Premises less than [18] months prior to the expiry of the Term]**

**4.07**

The tenant should not accept the provisions contained in the first three lines of this clause as these could impose an obligation on the tenant to redecorate on a frequently recurring basis. The tenant should therefore choose the certainty of the second option.

Most tenants would not wish to be under an obligation to redecorate the interior or exterior of the premises more frequently than every five years, although this is a matter for negotiation.

The landlord may wish to have some control over the external colour scheme, but the tenant should resist a provision for the landlord's consent to the internal colour scheme, except perhaps in the last year of the term where the tenant does not propose to seek a renewal. The tenant should, however, attempt to delete the reference to the tints and colours and patterns being approved by the landlord. At the very least, a major retailer would wish to exclude its "house" colours from this position. The tenant should also resist the reference to the redecoration being carried out to the reasonable satisfaction of the surveyor. The majority of substantial tenants would regard that provision as an intrusion.

It is also important to ensure that the tenant should not have to redecorate more than once in any one year and that while there is no objection to paints and materials being of "good quality" they should not be of the "best" quality. Also, a small point, but one worth making, is that two coats of paint should suffice with today's quality of paint.

Some tenants also amend this clause to exclude damage or destruction by the insured risks, etc., but this will depend upon what is covered by the insured risks.

### 5.6 Aerials signs and advertisements

**4.08** **Not to erect any pole mast or wire (whether in connection with telegraphic telephonic radio or television communication or otherwise) upon the Premises**

It may be that the nature of the tenant's business necessitates an aerial or satellite dish being erected, and therefore the following amendment should be made:

> **Not without the previous consent in writing of the Landlord (such consent not to be unreasonably withheld or delayed) to erect any pole mast wire aerial satellite dish or other telecommunications receiving equipment upon the Premises (whether in connection with telegraphic telephonic radio or television communication or otherwise)**

### 5.7 Statutory obligations

**4.09** 5.7.1 **At the Tenant's own expense to execute all works and provide and maintain all arrangements upon or in respect of the Premises or the use to which the Premises are being put that are required in order to comply with the requirements of any statute (already or in the future to be passed) or any**

government department local authority other public or competent authority or court of competent jurisdiction regardless of whether such requirements are imposed on the lessor the lessee or the occupier

5.7.2 Not to do in or near the Premises any act or thing by reason of which the Landlord may under any statute incur have imposed upon [it] or become liable to pay any penalty damages compensation costs charges or expenses

5.7.3 Without prejudice to the generality of the above to comply in all respects with the provisions of any statutes and other obligations imposed by law or by any byelaws applicable to the Premises or in regard to carrying on the trade or business for the time being carried on at the Premises

It may be that clause 5.7.1 should, in certain circumstances, have the following proviso added:

**except where such compliance is within the ambit of the Landlord's obligations contained in this Lease**

Almost all leases will contain a tenant's covenant to comply with statutory obligations, which could involve fairly substantial capital expenditure. An example would be the installation of a sprinkler system that was forced on the tenant by the local fire authority. The interrelationship of this clause with the rent review clause should be considered. The point is that there may not be disregarded on rent review under the lease the cost to the tenant of carrying out work under this clause, as it will have been effected pursuant to an obligation to the landlord. It is possible, and indeed advisable, to stipulate in the rent review clause for such works to be disregarded—see fourth schedule, paragraph 1.4.3—but the works will not be disregarded on a renewal under the Landlord and Tenant Act 1954. A more serious consideration is whether clause 5.7 places on the tenant an obligation to remedy contamination. Landlords may be tempted to include wording to put the point beyond doubt, through some commentators feel that the typical wording of statutory obligation provisions is wide enough already to cover outgoings and requirements under environmental legislation. An incoming tenant should seriously consider having an environmental survey carried out and, if there is cause for concern, should try to include a suitable provision in the lease to place the burden of remedying any contamination problems on the landlord.[13]

It has been suggested that where a tenant has had to make substantial alterations the court may force the landlord to make a contribution, but this is not to be relied upon.

A particular area of concern in this regard is likely to be the impact of the Disability Discrimination Act 1995 which is due to take effect in 2004. Many tenants are already carrying out works in order to comply with the Act and would expect the works to be disregarded on rent review, despite being carried out pursuant to a statutory obligation.

There may also be included a covenant that the tenant will comply with the Construction (Design and Management) Regulations 1994 as the landlord will wish to avoid the liabilities placed on a client under these regulations where the works are being carried out for the tenant. A typical clause may be as follows:

**5.7.4.1** **Without prejudice to the generality of clause 5.7.1 to comply with the provisions of the Construction (Design and Management) Regulations 1994 ("the CDM Regulations") and to be the only client as defined in the provisions of the CDM Regulations and to fulfil in relation to all and any works all the obligations of the client as set out in or reasonably to be inferred from the CDM Regulations and to make a declaration to that effect to the Health and Safety Executive in accordance with the Approved Code of Practice published from time to time by the Health and Safety Executive in relation to the CDM Regulations**

**5.7.4.2** **At the end of the Term to deliver to the Landlord any and all health and safety files relating to the Premises in accordance with the CDM Regulations**

Anything more stringent should be resisted by the tenant.

### 5.8 Access of Landlord and notice to repair

**4.10**  **5.8.1** To permit the Landlord:

**5.8.1.1** to enter upon the Premises for the purpose of ascertaining that the covenants and conditions of this Lease have been observed and performed

**5.8.1.2** to view (and to open up floors and other parts of the Premises where such opening-up is required in order to view) the state of repair and condition of the Premises and

**5.8.1.3** to give to the Tenant (or leave upon the Premises) a notice specifying any repairs cleaning maintenance or painting that the Tenant has failed to execute in breach of the terms of this Lease and to request the Tenant immediately to execute the same including the making good of such opening-up (if any)

|  | provided that any such opening-up shall be made good by and at the cost of the Landlord where such opening up reveals no breaches of the terms of this Lease |
|---|---|
| 5.8.2 | Immediately to repair cleanse maintain and paint the Premises as required by such notice |
| [5.8.3 | If within [one month] of the service of such a notice the Tenant shall not have commenced and be proceeding diligently with the execution of the work referred to in the notice or shall fail to complete the work within [two] months [or if in the Landlord's [Surveyor's] [reasonable] opinion the Tenant is unlikely to have completed the work within such period] to permit the Landlord to enter the Premises to execute such work as may be necessary to comply with the notice and to pay to the Landlord the cost of so doing and all expenses incurred by the Landlord (including legal costs and surveyor's fees) within [14] days of a written demand] |

While it is recognised that the landlord should have the right to enter the premises from time to time to ensure that the tenant's covenants have been complied with, this clause could cause severe disruption to the tenant's business and should be amended accordingly. The tenant will wish to have prior notice of such entry and the draftsman of the precedent has suggested an amendment to the commencement of the clause to cover this.

The landlord may indeed wish to open up floors and other parts of the premises in connection with inspections, but such works would have a quite catastrophic effect on the tenant's business and should therefore be resisted. If the landlord insists on the provision remaining then he should be prepared to pay compensation to the tenant for loss of business if the opening up reveals nothing untoward. Initially, however, the tenant should insist on deletion of the provision.

The tenant should be careful also not to agree a too restrictive period of time in which to carry out remedial works. The draftsman of the precedent suggests the substitution of:

**within a reasonable period**

for

**two months**

which seems a fair compromise. The point is that the tenant will need to satisfy itself that the works are necessary to be carried out and, if so, the tenant may, depending on the nature and extent of the works, then need a period of time to employ a contractor to carry these out.

By reserving a right for the landlord to carry out the works in the event of the tenant's default, the landlord does in fact run a slight risk pursuant to section 4(4) of the Defective Premises Act 1972,[14] but the risk is small compared to the relative advantage of the re-entry provision. It should be noted that, pursuant to the case of *Jervis v. Harris*,[15] a claim for the recovery of costs by the landlord is to be treated as a claim for the recovery of a debt as opposed to damages and can be enforced without the necessity of the landlord having to obtain the leave of the court under the Leasehold Property (Repairs) Act 1938. In an effort to try to put the point beyond doubt the landlord may include an express provision that such costs are recoverable as "rent" or "as a debt", and the tenant should endeavour to protect itself from the consequences of this case. Clause 5.8 should be amended to read as follows:

### 5.8 Access of Landlord and notice to repair

**4.11**
- **5.8.1** To permit the Landlord upon reasonable notice during normal business hours except in the case of emergency:
- **5.8.1.1** to enter upon the Premises for the purpose of ascertaining that the covenants and conditions of this Lease have been observed and performed
- **5.8.1.2** to view the state of repair and condition of the Premises and
- **5.8.1.3** to give to the Tenant (or leave upon the Premises) a notice specifying any repairs cleaning maintenance or painting that the Tenant has failed to execute in breach of the terms of this Lease and to request the Tenant to execute the same
- **5.8.2** As soon as reasonably practicable (or immediately in the case of emergency) to repair cleanse maintain and paint the Premises as required by such notice (except in the case of manifest error or genuine dispute)
- **5.8.3** If within two months of the service of such a notice the Tenant shall not have commenced and be proceeding diligently with the execution of the work referred to in the notice or shall fail to complete the work within a reasonable period to permit the Landlord to enter the Premises to execute such work as may be necessary to comply with the notice and to pay to the Landlord as damages (and not so as to exclude the provisions of the Leashold Property (Repairs) Act 1938) the proper and reasonable cost of so doing and all necessary expenses incurred by the Landlord (including proper and reasonable legal costs and surveyor's fees) within 28 days of a written demand

5.9 Alienation

5.9.1 Not to hold on trust for another or (save pursuant to a transaction permitted by and effected in accordance with the provisions of this Lease) part with the possession of the whole or any part of the Premises or permit another to occupy the whole or any part of the Premises  **4.12**

5.9.2 Not to assign [underlet] or charge part only of the Premises [and not to underlet the whole or any part of the Premises]

5.9.3 Not to assign [underlet] or charge the whole of the Premises without the prior consent of the Landlord such consent not to be unreasonably withheld or delayed

5.9.4 If any of the following circumstances (which are specified for the purposes of the Landlord and Tenant Act 1927, section 19 (1A)) applies either at the date when application for consent to assign is made to the Landlord or after that date but before the Landlord's consent is given the Landlord may withhold its consent and if after the Landlord's consent has been given but before the assignment has taken place any such circumstances apply the Landlord may revoke its consent whether its consent is expressly subject to a condition as referred to in sub-clause 5.9.5 or not. The circumstances are:

5.9.4.1 that any sum due from the Tenant under this Lease remains unpaid

5.9.4.2 that in the Landlord's [reasonable] opinion the assignee is not likely to be able to comply with the tenant covenants of this Lease and to continue to be able to comply with them following the assignment

5.9.4.3 that without prejudice to sub-clause 5.9.4.2 in the case of an assignment to a Group Company in the Landlord's [reasonable] opinion the assignee is or may become less likely to be able to comply with the tenant covenants of this Lease than the Tenant requesting consent to assign which likelihood is judged by reference in particular to the financial strength of that Tenant aggregated with that of any guarantor of the obligations of that Tenant and the value of any other security for the performance of the tenant covenants of this Lease when assessed at the date of grant or where the Tenant is not the [original Tenant] the date of the assignment of this Lease to that Tenant or

## Tenant's Covenants

5.9.4.4  that the assignee or any guarantor for the assignee other than any guarantor under an authorised guarantee agreement is a corporation registered or otherwise resident in a jurisdiction in which the order of a court obtained in England and Wales will not necessarily be enforced against the assignee or guarantor without any consideration of the merits of the case

5.9.5  The Landlord may impose any or all of the following conditions (which are specified for the purposes of the Landlord and Tenant Act 1927, section 19 (1A)) on giving any consent for an assignment by the Tenant and any such consent is to be treated as being subject to each of the following:

5.9.5.1  a condition that on or before any assignment and before giving occupation to the assignee the Tenant requesting consent to assign together with any former tenant who by virtue of the 1995 Act, section 11 was not released on an earlier assignment of this Lease must enter into an authorised guarantee agreement in favour of the Landlord in the terms set out in the ninth schedule

5.9.5.2  a condition that if reasonably so required by the Landlord on an assignment to a limited company the assignee must ensure that at least [two] directors of the company or some other guarantor or guarantors [reasonably] acceptable to the Landlord enter into direct covenants with the Landlord in the form of the guarantor's covenants contained in this Lease with "the Assignee" substituted for "the Tenant"

5.9.5.3  a condition that on or before any assignment the Tenant making the request for consent to assign must give to the Landlord a copy of the health and safety file required to be maintained under the Construction (Design and Management) Regulations 1994 containing full details of all works undertaken to the Premises by that Tenant and

5.9.5.4  a condition that if at any time before the assignment the circumstances specified in clause 5.9.4 or any of them apply the Landlord may revoke the consent by written notice to the Tenant

[5.9.6  That each and every permitted underlease shall be granted without any fine or premium at a rent not less than the then open market rental value of the Premises [to be approved by the Landlord prior to any such underlease] [and to be determined by the Surveyor acting as an expert and not as an arbitrator] or the Rent then being paid (whichever shall be the greater) such rent being payable in advance on the days on which Rent is payable under this Lease and shall contain provisions approved by the Landlord:

5.9.6.1 for the upwards only review of the rent reserved by such underlease on the basis and on the dates on which the Rent is to be reviewed in this Lease

4.13

5.9.6.2 prohibiting the undertenant from doing or allowing any act or thing in relation to the underlet premises inconsistent with or in breach of the provisions of this Lease

5.9.6.3 for re-entry by the underlandlord on breach of any covenants by the undertenant

5.9.6.4 imposing an absolute prohibition against all dispositions of or other dealings whatever with the Premises other than an assignment [underletting] [or charge] of the whole

5.9.6.5 prohibiting any assignment [underletting] [or charge] of the whole without the prior consent of the Landlord under this Lease

5.9.6.6 prohibiting the undertenant from permitting another to occupy the whole or any part of the Premises

5.9.6.7 imposing in relation to any permitted assignment [underletting] [or charge] the same obligations for registration with the Landlord as are contained in this Lease in relation to dispositions by the Tenant and

5.9.6.8 imposing in relation to any permitted underletting the same obligations as contained in clause 5.9.6 and in clause[s] 5.9.7 [5.9.8 and 5.9.9]]

[5.9.7 Prior to any permitted underletting to procure that the undertenant enters into a direct covenant with the Landlord that during the period when the undertenant is bound by the tenant covenants of the underlease together with any additional period during which the undertenant is bound by an authorised guarantee agreement the undertenant will observe and perform the tenant covenants contained in the Lease—except the covenant to pay the rent reserved by this Lease—and in that underlease]

[5.9.8 To enforce the performance and observance by every such undertenant of the provisions of the underlease and not at any time either expressly or by implication to waive any breach of the covenants or conditions on the part of any undertenant or assignee of any underlease nor (without the consent of the Landlord such consent not to be unreasonably withheld or delayed) vary the terms or accept a surrender of any permitted underlease]

[5.9.9 In relation to any permitted underlease:
5.9.9.1 to ensure that the rent is reviewed in accordance with the terms of the underlease
5.9.9.2 not to agree the reviewed rent with the undertenant without the approval of the Landlord
5.9.9.3 where the underlease provides such an option not to agree that the third party determining the rent in default of agreement shall act as an arbitrator or as an expert without the approval of the Landlord
5.9.9.4 not to agree upon the appointment of a person to act as the third party determining the rent in default of agreement without the approval of the Landlord
5.9.9.5 to incorporate as part of [its] submissions or representations to that third party such submissions or representations as the Landlord shall [reasonably] require
5.9.9.6 to give notice to the Landlord of the details of the determination of every rent review within [28] days
provided that the Landlord's approval specified above shall not be unreasonably withheld [or delayed]]
5.9.10 Within [28] days of any assignment charge underlease or sub-underlease or any transmission or other devolution relating to the Premises to produce for registration with the Landlord's solicitor such deed or document [or a certified copy of it] and to pay the Landlord's solicitor's charges of [£20 (twenty pounds)] for the registration of every such document *or* reasonable charges for the registration of every such document such charges not being less than [£20 (twenty pounds)]
[5.9.11 Notwithstanding clause 5.9.1 the Tenant may share the occupation of the whole or any part of the Premises with a company which is a member of the same group as the Tenant (within the meaning of Section 42 of the 1954 Act) for so long as both companies shall remain members of that group and otherwise than in a manner that transfers or creates a legal estate]

On the one hand, the tenant will wish to deal with the premises in the most cost-effective manner, even if this means subletting parts and, on the other hand, the landlord will wish to exercise fairly strict control over alienation, first by ensuring that any assignee is able to pay the rents reserved by the lease and perform the tenant's obligations under it, and secondly by ensuring that at the end of the term the landlord is not left with an undertenant of a small part of the premises, which could affect the value of the landlord's interest in the whole.

In the unlikely event that there are no restrictions in the lease prohibiting alienation, the tenant will be free to deal with the premises as it so wishes, whether by means of assignment, underletting, charge or otherwise. It should also be remembered that section 19(l)(a) of the Landlord and Tenant Act 1927 provides that where there is a covenant, condition or agreement against assigning, underletting, charging or parting with possession of the premises or any part thereof without licence or consent, this is deemed to be subject to a proviso to the effect that such licence or consent is not to be unreasonably withheld. This is a most useful provision that has come to the assistance of many tenants over the years, but is now affected by the provisions of the Landlord and Tenant (Covenants) Act 1995 and the tenant should be wary of any restrictions introduced into the alienation provision as a result of this Act.[16]

**4.14** Some alienation provisions contain surrender-back clauses which should be strongly resisted by the tenant, as they lead to uncertainty as to whether the tenant will be permitted to assign the lease to the person of its choosing, and unless carefully worded, could result in the tenant obtaining less from the landlord on surrender than it would have done from the assignee.

The following provisions should be noted in particular:

As regards clause 5.9.1, many company tenants do not like a restriction on holding on trust for another as this may interfere with their internal arrangements, but the landlord's concerns are understood in this regard.

Some premises are not given to be divided and therefore an absolute prohibition on underletting or charging of part may be appropriate and acceptable, but a restriction against underletting the whole should be resisted. It is, of course, not surprising that it is standard to prohibit an assignment of part of the premises and a right to assign part is extremely rare. While a provision that sections 24–28 of the Landlord and Tenant Act 1954 should be excluded from an underletting of part may be understandable (though resisted wherever possible), a provision that those sections should be excluded from an underletting of the whole of the premises should be vigorously resisted. An undertenant taking on an underlease five years before the expiration of the lease term, and spending a considerable sum on fitting out the premises, would doubtless expect to be able to continue trading at the end of the term and to have a new lease granted to it.

Clauses 5.9.4 and 5.9.5 have been drafted to accommodate the provisions of the Landlord and Tenant (Covenants) Act 1995. These clauses set out the circumstances and conditions which are proposed should be satisfied by the tenant and the assignee as pre-requisites to an assignment being permitted by the landlord. As stated in the precedent, they are specified for the purposes of section 19(1A) of the Landlord and Tenant Act 1927 (as inserted by the 1995 Act), but it should not be forgotten that the Landlord can still withhold consent to an assignment on other reasonable grounds. An example of this is where the landlord, in its reasonable judgment, considers that the assignment will lead to a breach of covenant.[17] The circumstances enable the Landlord to refuse consent to an assignment and the conditions are conditions precedent to an assignment.

Clause 5.9.4.1 should be amended to refer only to the yearly rent, as service charges and insurance premiums and, indeed, other payments demanded of the tenant may possibly be in dispute. It should therefore read:

**5.9.4.1 that the Rent that has become due from the Tenant under this Lease remains unpaid**

Clause 5.9.4.2 is not unreasonable but clause 5.9.4.3 should be resisted. It may be that a group company assignee will be less likely to be able to comply with the tenant covenants of the lease than the outgoing tenant even with a guarantor but, provided that the circumstance set out in clause 5.9.4.2 is satisfied, that is no reason for the landlord to withhold consent. It is accepted that the landlord will wish to avoid an assignment to a weak group member, but clause 5.9.4.2 should help to prevent that happening. The landlord will, of course, also have the benefit of an authorised guarantee agreement from the outgoing tenant, though he will point out that this will fall away when the group member assigns.

Clause 5.9.4.4 is understandable from the landlord's standpoint, but should be resisted wherever possible as being a further fetter on the tenant's ability to assign.

The circumstances may also include financial and profits tests which should be vigorously resisted by the tenant.

Clause 5.9.5.1 is an absolute provision requiring the outgoing tenant, and any former tenant who has not been released from liability pursuant to the excluded assignments provisions detailed in section 11 of the 1995 Act, to enter into an authorised guarantee agreement. The tenant should amend this to provide that the guarantee should only be imposed if reasonable to do so as, otherwise, the landlord will almost invariably insist on its implementation, which may be pointless if one substantial tenant is assigning to another. The clause could therefore commence:

**5.9.5.1 a condition that if reasonably so required by the Landlord on any assignment ...**

It is fair to say that in a new development situation, *i.e.* where the tenant is not renewing a pre-1995 Act tenancy, the landlord may well insist on an obligatory authorised guarantee agreement ("AGA") on an assignment, but the case of *Wallis Fashion Group Ltd v. CGU Life Assurance Ltd*[18] provides that on a renewal of a lease that is not already subject to an obligatory AGA (*e.g.* a pre-1995 Act tenancy) the *O'May* case[19] makes it clear that there has to be a good reason for imposing a new term in the renewed lease against the wishes of one of the parties. In *Wallis Fashion*, the tenant had suggested that the landlord could only require an AGA "where reasonable", and the court agreed with that position.

Despite the provisions of clause 5.9.5.1, a landlord may also require a guarantor or guarantors for an assignee. This may work in the outgoing tenant's best interests where it is entering into an authorised guarantee agreement and where the assignee is not as sound as the outgoing tenant would wish, assuming of course that the assignee is able and willing to provide a guarantor. In such circumstances, the guarantor should give covenants not only to the landlord but also to the outgoing tenant. It may be that, often, with a rent well into six figures it is unrealistic to expect directors to give guarantees and therefore the following amendment may be considered appropriate:

**5.9.5.2  a condition that if reasonably so required by the Landlord on an assignment to a private limited company the assignee will ensure that a suitable guarantor reasonably acceptable to the Landlord enters into direct covenants with the Landlord in the form of the guarantor's covenants contained in this Lease with "the Assignee" substituted for "the Tenant".**

It is not unusual for a lease to provide that, on an assignment, any guarantor or guarantors of the tenant's covenants will join in the AGA to guarantee the obligations of the incoming tenant, on the basis that the landlord required the tenant's obligations to be guaranteed because of the status of the tenant and therefore the landlord should not be forced to rely upon an AGA by the outgoing tenant alone. This should be resisted by the tenant, although it has to be accepted that the landlord has a valid point and the tenant may be forced to concede. If so, the tenant will have to make certain that it will be in a position to ensure that the guarantor or guarantors will join in the AGA at the appropriate time or the assignment could be jeopardised.

Clauses 5.9.5.3 and 5.9.5.4 do not seem unreasonable.

There are various matters to be considered in connection with a permitted underlease (not the least of which being as to whether the tenant should be allowed to underlet part or parts of the premises as well as the whole), *e.g.*:

**4.15**

(1) In respect of any permitted underlease it is better to remove reference to the landlord's approval of the rent reserved by it, and if possible (particularly in a falling market) to remove reference to the rent being not less than the passing rent under the lease, although the landlord will normally object to this on the basis that a low underlease rent could be used as a comparable on any subsequent rent review under the lease or in respect of other premises within the centre.[20] The landlord may also express concern that on a forfeiture of the lease the undertenant may try to seek relief from forfeiture under section 146(4) of the Law of Property Act 1925 at a rent less than the lease rent.

(2) The tenant may contemplate more frequent rent reviews under the underlease than those in the lease, although it is accepted that the rent review dates should otherwise coincide.

(3) The tenant should resist a provision not to agree the reviewed rent under the underlease without the landlord's approval, as the time it could take to obtain such approval could result in the undertenant changing its mind. Similarly the tenant should resist the landlord's interference in the appointment of the independent valuer, either as to the capacity or identity of the valuer.

(4) Sub-clause 5.9.9.5 should also be resisted for obvious reasons, as too should 5.9.9.6, if possible, as that sub-clause places yet another obligation on the tenant.

(5) The registration of dealings clause should be amended to ensure that the original disposition does not have to be produced to the landlord; a certified copy is perfectly adequate. Furthermore, while nobody would deny the landlord's solicitor a reasonable fee for the registration of dealings, care should be had to ensure that the registration charge is kept within reason.

Clauses 5.9.6 to 5.9.11 could be amended as follows:

**[5.9.6 That each and every permitted underlease shall be granted without any fine or premium at a rent not less than the then open market rental value of [the Premises] [that part of the Premises to be underlet] such rent being payable in advance on the days on which Rent is payable under this Lease and shall contain provisions:**

**5.9.6.1 for the [upwards only] review of the rent reserved by such underlease on the basis and at least on the dates on which the Rent is to be reviewed in this Lease (but having regard to the length of the proposed term of the underlease)**

The words "upwards only" should be deleted as the rent will be reviewed on the same basis as the lease (presumably not upwards/downwards) and the rent on review may, of course, remain unaltered if reviewed in a falling market.

5.9.6.2 prohibiting the undertenant from doing or allowing any act or thing in relation to the underlet premises inconsistent with or in breach of the provisions of this Lease

5.9.6.3 for re-entry by the underlandlord on breach of any covenants by the undertenant

5.9.6.4 imposing an absolute prohibition against all dispositions of or other dealings whatever with the Premises other than an assignment [or underletting] of the whole

(This is, of course, subject to negotiation and it may be appropriate for an undertenant of large premises to be given the right to sub-underlet part or parts of them.)

5.9.6.5 prohibiting any assignment [or underletting] of the whole [or underletting of part] without the prior consent of the Landlord under this Lease (such consent not to be unreasonably withheld or delayed)

5.9.6.6 prohibiting the undertenant from permitting another to occupy the whole or any part of the Premises (otherwise than as permitted in this clause 5.9)

5.9.6.7 imposing in relation to any permitted assignment [or underletting] the same obligations for registration with the Landlord as are contained in this Lease in relation to dispositions by the Tenant and

5.9.6.8 imposing in relation to any permitted underletting the same obligations in clause 5.9.6 and in clause[s] 5.9.7 [5.9.8 and 5.9.9]]

[5.9.7 Prior to any permitted underletting to procure that the undertenant enters into a direct covenant with the Landlord that during the period when the undertenant is bound by the tenant covenants of the underlease together with any additional period during which the undertenant is bound by an authorised guarantee agreement the undertenant will observe and perform the tenant covenants contained in the underlease]

[5.9.8 To enforce the performance and observance by every such undertenant of the provisions of the underlease and not at any time either expressly or by implication to waive any breach of the covenants or conditions on the part of any undertenant or assignee of any underlease nor (without the consent of the

> Landlord such consent not to be unreasonably withheld or delayed) vary the terms of any permitted underlease]
> 
> [5.9.9 In relation to any permitted underlease to ensure that the rent is reviewed in accordance with the terms of the underlease]
> 
> 5.9.10 Within [28] days of any assignment charge underlease or sub-underlease or any transmission or other devolution relating to the Premises to produce for registration with the Landlord's solicitor such deed or document [or a certified copy of it] and to pay the Landlord's solicitor's charges of [£20 (twenty pounds)] for the registration of every such document *or* reasonable charges for the registration of every such document such charges not being less than [£20 (twenty pounds)]
> 
> [5.9.11 Notwithstanding clause 5.9.1 the Tenant may share the occupation of the whole or any part of the Premises with a company which is a member of the same group as the Tenant (within the meaning of section 42 of the 1954 Act) for so long as both companies shall remain members of that group and otherwise than in a manner that transfers or creates a legal estate]

**4.16** As well as a joint occupation clause, the tenant should consider including a provision permitting the tenant to share the premises with franchisees or concessionaires where the premises are sufficiently large and the tenant's business could accommodate such trading operations, *e.g.*:

> 5.9.12 Notwithstanding clause 5.9.1 the Tenant may share the occupation of the whole or any part of the Premises with franchisees or concessionaires on terms which do not result in security of tenure between the Tenant and such franchisees or concessionaires provided that the Tenant shall give written notice to the Landlord within 21 days of the commencement and termination of such arrangements

It may be, however, that the landlord will wish to place a limitation on the area of the premises that may be occupied by franchises or concessionaires, but this will be for a matter of negotiation.

### 5.10 Nuisance, etc., and residential restrictions

**4.17**
> 5.10.1 Not to do nor allow to remain upon the Premises anything which may be or become or cause a nuisance annoyance

|  |  |
|---|---|
| | disturbance inconvenience injury or damage to the Landlord or [its] tenants or the owners or occupiers of adjacent or neighbouring premises |
| 5.10.2 | Not to use the Premises for a sale by auction or for any dangerous noxious noisy or offensive trade business manufacture or occupation nor for any illegal or immoral act or purpose |
| 5.10.3 | Not to use the Premises as sleeping accommodation or for residential purposes nor keep any animal fish reptile or bird anywhere on the Premises |

A tenant would find it difficult to resist a covenant against nuisance. although the references in clause 5.10.1 to annoyance and inconvenience seem a little superfluous. Having said that, there is now a more serious implication as a result of the usual nuisance covenant, and that is whether the landlord will be able to use the covenant to require the tenant to carry out clean-up works where the site of the premises is contaminated. In addition to carrying out a contamination survey, the tenant should either try to exclude liability for contamination not caused by itself, or try to include the suggested additional clause 6.6. There is also no definite legal meaning of "offensive" which should be read in the context of the lease.[21] Another objection to this clause is whether there should be a restriction against using the premises for a sale by auction. This seems quite antiquated and unnecessary but it seems to appear in virtually all commercial leases and landlords' solicitors seem reluctant to start a new trend by agreeing to its deletion.

Clause 5.10.3 may have to be amended where the premises comprise part business, part residential accommodation, *e.g. a* high street shop with flats above.

## 5.11 Landlord's costs

| | | |
|---|---|---|
| | To pay to the Landlord on an indemnity basis all costs fees charges disbursements and expenses (including without prejudice to the generality of the above those payable to counsel solicitors surveyors and bailiffs)[22] [properly and reasonably] incurred by the Landlord in relation to or incidental to: | **4.18** |
| 5.11.1 | every application made by the Tenant for a consent or licence required by the provisions of this Lease whether such consent or licence is granted or refused or proffered subject to any [lawful] qualification or condition or whether the | |

application is withdrawn [unless such refusal qualification or condition is unlawful whether because it is unreasonable or otherwise]

5.11.2 the preparation and service of a notice under the Law of Property Act 1925 section 146 or incurred by or in contemplation of proceedings under sections 146 or 147 of that Act notwithstanding that forfeiture is avoided otherwise than by relief granted by the court

5.11.3 the recovery or attempted recovery of arrears of rent or other sums due from the Tenant and

5.11.4 any steps taken in [contemplation of or in] [direct] connection with the preparation and service of a schedule of dilapidations during or after the expiration of the Term

The costs charged to the tenant should be qualified by the word "reasonable". It is important to try to contain the scope of the costs that may be recoverable, *e.g.* whereas a surveyor's fees may be reasonable to seek to recover, it is arguable that it may not be reasonable for the landlord to instruct an architect in respect of the matters contemplated by this clause. This is a fairly standard tenant's covenant and basically acceptable, although the following comments are worth noting:

Despite the landlord's common law right to distress, some tenants object to the sight of a reference to bailiffs in leases and prefer it to be deleted.

There may also be good reason for deleting reference to the contemplation of proceedings under sections 146 or 147 of the Law of Property Act 1925, as the costs recoverable under such a provision may not be easy for the tenant to assess and counter.

It may also be advisable to try to amend clause 5.11.4 as detailed below. It is important to try to place a limitation on the time during which a terminal schedule may be served.

The clause could be amended as follows:

5.11 Landlord's costs

**4.19**     To pay to the Landlord all reasonable costs fees charges disbursements and expenses (including without prejudice to the generality of the above those payable to solicitors and surveyors) properly and reasonably incurred by the Landlord in relation to or incidental to:

5.11.1 every application made by the Tenant for consent or licence required by the provisions of this Lease whether such consent or licence is granted or refused or proffered subject to any

|  |  |
|---|---|
| 5.11.2 | lawful qualification or condition or whether the application is withdrawn unless such refusal qualification or condition is unlawful whether because it is unreasonable or otherwise and unless such consent or licence is unreasonably refused |
| | the preparation and service of a notice under the Law of Property Act 1925 section 146 or incurred in proceedings under sections 146 and 147 of that Act notwithstanding that forfeiture is avoided otherwise than by relief granted by the court |
| 5.11.3 | the recovery or attempted recovery of arrears of rent or other sums due under this Lease from the Tenant and |
| 5.11.4 | any steps taken in direct connection with the preparation and service of a schedule of dilapidations during or after the expiration of the Term but if after the expiration of the Term only in respect of wants of repair occurring during the Term and where served within one month after the expiration of the Term |

5.12  The Planning Acts

5.12.1  Not to commit in relation to the Premises any breach of planning control (such term to be construed in the way in which it is used in the Planning Acts)  **4.20**

5.12.2  Not without the consent in writing of the Landlord to apply for planning permission to carry out any development in or upon the Premises and at the expense of the Tenant to supply the Landlord with a copy of any application for planning permission together with such plans and other documents as the Landlord may [reasonably] require and to supply prior to the commencement of any development a copy of any planning permission granted to the Tenant

5.12.3  To pay and satisfy any charge that may be imposed upon any breach by the Tenant of planning control or otherwise under the Planning Acts

5.12.4  Unless the Landlord shall otherwise direct to carry out and complete before the expiry of the Term any works required to be carried out to or in the Premises as a condition of any planning permission which may have been granted during the Term irrespective of the date by which such works were required to be carried out

It is understandable that a landlord will wish to ensure that the tenant not only complies with planning legislation but also does not make application for planning permission without the landlord's consent. An application for a change of use for instance could, if successful, saddle the landlord with a detrimental use which may only be reconverted by another planning permission.[23] The tenant, however, will wish to make certain that the landlord's consent for an application for planning permission cannot be unreasonably withheld at least for certain specified matters, having regard to the nature and situation of the premises. It may be a question of compromise between the landlord and the tenant but a general qualification is suggested as an initial amendment.

The other point in this regard is that a requirement for the tenant to obtain the landlord's consent prior to making an application for planning permission could result in a considerable delay in the application being made in circumstances where the tenant requires the planning permission rather urgently, *e.g.* in connection with its shopfront or signage, hence the amendment suggested below.

**5.12.2** **Not without the consent in writing of the Landlord (such consent not to be unreasonably withheld or delayed and which consent shall not be required in relation to applications in respect of the shopfront or signage or aerials or other telecommunications equipment at the Premises) to apply for planning permission ...**

The landlord will probably insist on the retention of clause 5.12.4 in order to avoid the problem of a limited planning permission being issued containing a reinstatement provision becoming effective after the lease term has expired. Some Planning Act covenants also include a provision for the tenant to provide security for compliance with planning permission conditions, which should be resisted wherever possible. Large commercial tenants would not be greatly impressed by its inclusion and smaller tenants may have difficulty in providing the "security" required. A qualification that security need only be provided if the landlord reasonably so requires would be inadequate having regard to the non-immunity from failure of "solid" commercial tenants in periods of recession.

In addition, any covenant requiring the tenant to appeal against a refusal of planning permission (particularly at the cost of the tenant) should be resisted as the tenant could find itself paying for the cost of appealing against a refusal of planning permission applied for by the landlord for the redevelopment of the premises at the end of term, where the tenant may wish to take a renewal of the lease.

There may also be a covenant that the tenant should not implement any planning permission before it has been produced to and approved by the

*Tenant's Covenants* 101

landlord. The tenant should endeavour to resist a covenant of this nature, but if the landlord insists on its retention, it should be qualified so that the landlord's approval is not unreasonably withheld or delayed.

### 5.13 Plans documents and information

5.13.1    If called upon to do so to produce to the Landlord or the Surveyor all plans documents and other evidence as the Landlord may [reasonably] require in order to satisfy [itself] that the provisions of this Lease have been complied with    **4.21**

5.13.2    If called upon to do so to furnish to the Landlord the Surveyor or any person acting as the third party determining the Rent in default of agreement between the parties under any provisions for rent review contained in this Lease such information as may [reasonably] be requested in writing in relation to any pending or intended step under the 1954 Act or the implementation of any provisions for rent review

This seems quite innocuous but an unreasonable landlord could become a nuisance and, apart from ensuring that "reasonably" is included, the tenant should also begin each sub-clause as follows:

> If called upon to do so (but not more frequently than may be reasonable)

### 5.14 Indemnities

To be responsible for and to keep the Landlord fully indemnified against all damage damages losses costs expenses actions demands proceedings claims and liabilities made against or suffered or incurred by the Landlord arising directly or indirectly out of:    **4.22**

5.14.1    any act omission or negligence of the Tenant or any persons at the Premises expressly or impliedly with the Tenant's authority [and under the Tenant's control] or

5.14.2    any breach or non-observance by the Tenant of the covenants conditions or other provisions of this Lease or any of the matters to which this demise is subject

The same point applies as above with regard to persons on the premises under the tenant's control.

It is suggested that the tenant should in fact attempt to delete this clause on the ground that the landlord is already protected by the other covenants contained in the lease and can take such action as may be necessary either for breach of contract or in tort. This clause, it is suggested, could unfairly extend the tenant's liability. If the clause is deleted, however, the landlord may argue for a covenant by the tenant to observe such restrictions to which the premises may be subject, with an indemnity for any breach. It is probably better to retain the covenant, subject to the slight amendment referred to above and subject also to the deletion of the word "losses" in line 2.

### 5.15 Re-letting boards

**4.23** To permit the Landlord at any time during the last [six] months of the Contractual Term and at any time thereafter [unless the Tenant shall have made a valid court application under section 24 of the 1954 Act or otherwise be entitled in law to remain in occupation or to a new tenancy of the Premises] [(or sooner if the rents or any part of them shall be in arrear and unpaid for longer than [28] days)] to enter upon the Premises and affix and retain anywhere upon the Premises a notice for re-letting the Premises and during such period to permit persons with the written authority of the Landlord or [its] agent at reasonable times of the day to view the Premises

It is not unreasonable for the landlord to be entitled to erect a re-letting board at the premises within a reasonable period prior to the termination of the term unless the tenant proposes to apply for a new tenancy of the premises, provided that the board is in a position so as not to interfere with the tenant's or any undertenant's business being carried on at the premises. The tenant should not, however, accept the reference to rents being in arrear and unpaid. The clause could be amended as follows:

To permit the Landlord at any time during the last [6] months of the Contractual Term and at any time thereafter unless the Tenant shall have made a valid court application under section 24 of the 1954 Act or otherwise be entitled in law to remain in occupation or to a new tenancy of the Premises to enter upon the Premises and affix and retain upon the Premises in a position so as not to interfere with the Tenant's or any undertenant's business being carried on at the Premises a notice for re-letting the Premises and during such period to permit persons with the written authority of the Landlord or its agent at reasonable times of the day on reasonable notice to view the Premises

### 5.16 Encroachments

5.16.1 Not to stop up darken or obstruct any windows or light belonging to the Premises  **4.24**

5.16.2 To take all [reasonable] steps to prevent any new window light opening doorway path passage pipe or other encroachment or easement being made or acquired in against out of or upon the Premises and to notify the Landlord immediately if any such encroachment or easement shall be made or acquired (or attempted to be made or acquired) and at the request of the Landlord to adopt such means as shall [reasonably] be required to prevent such encroachment or the acquisition of any such easement

The landlord will wish to ensure that encroachments are prevented. This clause is neither unusual nor unreasonable, provided, of course, that the references to "reasonable" and "reasonably" are included.

The tenant should also consider amending line 6 of clause 5.16.2 to read:

> ... acquired (or attempted to be made or acquired) and which shall come to the knowledge of the Tenant and at the ...

The tenant may amend the sub-clause further by trying to make the landlord responsible for the cost of the means required, or at least to provide that the cost be shared.

### 5.17 Yield up

At the expiration of the Term:  **4.25**

5.17.1 to yield up the Premises in repair and in accordance with the terms of this Lease

5.17.2 to give up all keys of the Premises to the Landlord and

5.17.3 to remove all signs erected by the Tenant in upon or near the Premises and immediately to make good any damage caused by such removal

It is advisable (at least for the purpose of this clause) for the tenant to ensure that the term includes any period of holding over or continuation of the contractual term (as it does in this lease by virtue of clause 3.8), although it must be considered highly unlikely that the tenant would be forced to yield up the premises to the landlord during a continuation under the Landlord and Tenant Act 1954.

This clause may also contain an obligation by the tenant specifically to remove tenant's fixtures and fittings which the tenant may do in any event. The tenant should, however, be careful to ensure that the landlord cannot retain items that the tenant wishes to remove. In the case of a fixed term tenancy, tenant's fixtures and fittings must, in the absence of agreement allowing removal, be removed by the termination date of the tenancy, or the right to remove them will be lost when possession of the premises is given up.

There may also be a provision, either in this clause or elsewhere in the lease, that the tenant will pay to the landlord loss of rent that the landlord may suffer, where the landlord is unable to relet premises forthwith on the expiration of the term because of existing breaches of covenant by the outgoing tenant, *e.g.* repairing and reinstatement obligations.[24] The tenant should resist a provision of this nature on the basis that the landlord should serve any schedule of dilapidations on time and because a dilatory landlord could take several months to remedy a minor breach, particularly if the outgoing tenant was still paying rent in a recessed market.

Finally, any provision in this clause that the tenant should deliver vacant possession of the premises on yielding up should, of course, be deleted. A tenant who has underlet the whole or part of the premises inside the 1954 Act certainly could not comply with such a provision.

### 5.18 Interest on arrears

**4.26**  5.18.1 **If the Tenant shall fail to pay the rents or any other sum due under this Lease [within [14] days of the date due] whether formally demanded or not the Tenant shall pay to the Landlord Interest on the rents or other sum from the date when they were due to the date on which they are paid [and such Interest shall be deemed to be rents due to the Landlord]**

5.18.2 **Nothing in the preceding clause shall entitle the Tenant to withhold or delay any payment of the rents or any other sum due under this Lease after the date upon which they fall due or in any way prejudice affect or derogate from the rights of the Landlord in relation to such non-payment including (but without prejudice to the generality of the above) under the proviso for re-entry contained in this Lease**

The period of grace before interest bites will be a matter of negotiation between the landlord and the tenant. Fourteen days seems to be a fair and reasonable period, although a landlord will argue that the rent should be paid on the due date. The author has handled a matter for a tenant where the landlord was endeavouring to have cleared funds by the due date! The tenant should resist a provision that interest should be deemed to be rent due to the landlord as this will have the effect of making available the remedy of distress as well as that of forfeiture without the necessity to serve a section 146 notice. Relief will, however, be available for six months after judgment under the Common Law Procedure Act 1852 should this line be adopted.

Clause 5.18.2 is self-explanatory and while tenants would doubtless wish to have it deleted, they are unlikely to succeed.

There is also the point that, as drafted, the reference to "or any other sum due under this Lease" will include payments that may have been successfully excluded from the definition of "rents", *e.g.* balancing service charge payments and, for that reason, those words are best deleted.

### 5.19 Statutory notices, etc.

> To give full particulars to the Landlord of any notice direction order or proposal for the Premises made given or issued to the Tenant by any local or public authority within [seven] days of receipt and if so required by the Landlord to produce it to the Landlord and without delay to take all necessary steps to comply with the notice direction or order and at the request of the Landlord but at the cost of the Tenant to make or join with the Landlord in making such objections or representations against or in respect of any notice direction order or proposal as the Landlord shall deem expedient

**4.27**

Seven days may be too short a period, particularly if the notice is served at the premises and not forwarded to the appropriate officer of a tenant company with any great alacrity. Fourteen days would seem to be a more reasonable period, though the landlord may be concerned that this could leave little time for it to make a considered response where the notice is subject to a time restriction.

It may not be in the tenant's best interests to make objections or representations and an amendment in this regard is suggested below. The tenant should also endeavour to ensure that the cost of the landlord's objections or representations is borne by the landlord.

... and at the request and cost of the Landlord to make or join with the Landlord in making such objections or representations against or in respect of any notice direction order or proposal as the Landlord shall reasonably deem expedient except where the Tenant reasonably considers that any such objections or representations are against its best interests or those of any undertenant or other lawful occupier

5.20 Keyholders

**4.28** To ensure that at all times the Landlord has [and the local police force has] written notice of the name home address and home telephone number of at least [two] keyholder[s] of the Premises

While this is not necessarily objectionable it is a provision that is easily overlooked and imposes an obligation on the tenant which may not be appropriate in the circumstances. It may be a clause that a particular tenant may prefer to delete unless other factors necessitate its inclusion. It may, for example, not be advisable for too many people to know the home address of keyholders for fear that they could be put in danger where valuables are kept at the premises.

5.21 Sale of reversion, etc.

**4.29** To permit [upon reasonable notice] at any time during the Term prospective purchasers of or agents instructed in connection with the sale of the Landlord's reversion or of any other interest superior to the Term to view the Premises without interruption provided they are authorised in writing by the Landlord or its agents

This is a normal provision and the only comment to make is that it could be disruptive to a tenant's business, although one would hope that the frequency of a sale of the reversion would be limited. The words

**at reasonable times of the day**

should be inserted after the words

**to view the Premises**

5.22 Defective premises

**4.30** To give notice to the Landlord of any defect in the Premises which might give rise to an obligation on the Landlord to do or refrain from doing any act or thing in order to comply with the provisions of this Lease or the duty of care imposed on the Landlord pursuant to the Defective Premises Act 1972 or otherwise and at all times to display and maintain all notices which the Landlord may from time to time [reasonably] require to be displayed at the Premises

The difficulty here is that this covenant could impose an unfair obligation on the tenant and it should therefore be amended as follows:

> To give notice to the Landlord upon becoming aware of any defect...

### 5.23 New guarantor

> Within [14] days of the death during the Term of any Guarantor or of such person becoming bankrupt or having a receiving order made against him or having a receiver appointed under the Mental Health Act 1983 or being a company passing a resolution to wind up or entering into liquidation or having a receiver appointed to give notice of this to the Landlord and if so required by the Landlord at the expense of the Tenant within [28] days to procure some other person acceptable to the Landlord [such acceptance not to be unreasonably withheld] to execute a guarantee in respect of the Tenant's obligations contained in this Lease in the form of the Guarantor's covenants contained in this Lease

**4.31**

Although this may be perfectly fair and reasonable in that a guarantor's covenants are expected to last during the period for which they are given, many tenants try to resist this covenant on the basis that it may be extremely difficult for the tenant to produce an alternative guarantor. At present day commercial rents, directors would be foolhardy to stand as guarantors. Therefore, the guarantor may more usually be a holding company or substantial "sister" company. A replacement guarantor may accordingly be extremely difficult to find and if it is not possible to find a replacement the tenant will accordingly be in breach of covenant and risk forfeiture of the lease. If the provision is included in the lease and is exercised, the tenant should not forget to obtain a release of the original guarantor on the execution of the guarantee by the new guarantor. There should also be a limitation on the time during which the landlord can require the tenant to procure a new guarantor and the following amendment is suggested:

> ... and if so required by the Landlord by notice to the Tenant given within 28 days of receipt of the Tenant's notice at the expense of the Tenant within 56 days to procure some other person reasonably acceptable to the Landlord such acceptance not to be unreasonably withheld or delayed...

The preferred view, however, is to insist that this clause is deleted for the reason stated above.

### 5.24 Landlord's rights

**4.32** To permit the Landlord at all times during the Term to exercise without interruption or interference any of the rights granted to [it] by virtue of the provisions of this Lease

The point here is to ensure that the landlord's rights contained in the lease are not such as to cause unreasonable interference with the business being carried on at the premises. The extended meaning given to the 'landlord' by clause 3.10 should also be noted.

### 5.25 The Shop Covenants

**4.33** 5.25.1 To observe and perform the Shop Covenants
5.25.2 To observe and perform [its] obligations contained in the fifth schedule

See the fifth schedule.

### [5.26 Landlord's costs on grant, etc.

**4.34** [To pay the fees and disbursements of the Landlord's solicitors agents and surveyors and all other costs and expenses incurred by the Landlord in relation to the negotiation preparation execution and grant of this Lease and the stamp duty on the counterpart]

Any proposal that the tenant should pay the landlord's costs incurred in connection with the grant of the lease should be vigorously rejected and the tenant's adviser should encourage the tenant to ensure that this aspect is dealt with during negotiations. The Costs of Leases Act 1958 provides that, in the absence of agreement in writing to the contrary, each party to a lease bears its own solicitor's costs, and this should be the position. In *Cairnplace Ltd v. CBL (Property Investment) Co. Ltd*[25] it was held that there should not be inserted in a renewal of a lease a provision that the tenant should pay the landlord's costs despite the fact that there was a similar provision contained in the previous lease. The fact remains that the landlord litigated the point and perhaps this is the justification for trying to ensure that the tenant's interests are fully protected in leases wherever possible.

Pursuant to the Landlord and Tenant (Covenants) Act 1995[26] the landlord may include the following covenant on the part of the tenant:

> **Not unreasonably to withhold consent to a request made by the Landlord under the Landlord and Tenant (Covenants) Act 1995, section 8 for a release from all or any of the landlord covenants of this Lease**

This looks quite innocuous, but the tenant should realise this covenant is seeking a right of action for loss where the tenant unreasonably withholds consent to an application by the landlord for a release. The tenant may decide to delete this covenant and suggest that the landlord should fall back on the provisions contained in the Act, much the same as the tenant.

---

[1] See comments on clause 4.1.
[2] [1911] 1 K.B. 905.
[3] See *Earl of Chesterfield v. Duke of Bolton* 2 Com. 627; *Paradine v. Jane* (1647) Aleyn 26 and *Redmond v. Dainton* [1920] 2 K.B. 256.
[4] *Norwich Union Life Insurance Society v. British Railways Board* [1987] 2 E.G.L.R. 137.
[5] *New England Properties v. Portsmouth New Shops* [1993] 1 E.G.L.R. 84.
[6] [2000] 49 E.G. 118.
[7] (1890) 25 Q.B. 42.
[8] [1924] 1 K.B. 716.
[9] [1994] 11 E.G. 151.
[10] See the suggested exclusion from the service charge expenditure under para. 2 of part A of the sixth schedule.
[11] Defined in *Terrell v. Murray* (1901) 17 T.L.R. 570 as meaning wear and tear resulting from the reasonable use of the premises by the tenant in the ordinary operation of natural forces.
[12] See clause 2.14 of the agreement for lease.
[13] See clause 9.22.
[14] By placing on the landlord a duty to take care that anyone who might be affected by defects in the premises is safe from personal injury or damage to their property caused by any such defects.
[15] [1996] Ch. 195; [1996] 1 All E.R. 303, CA.
[16] The Landlord and Tenant (Covenants) Act 1995 is intended to give comfort to tenants and relief from the harsh doctrine of privity of contract, by which the

tenant remained liable under the covenants contained in the lease for the duration of the term even though it had assigned the lease in the meantime. Unfortunately, the Act, which took effect on January 1, 1996, does not go as far as some tenants may have wished. For instance, see section 16 of the Act for the circumstances where a landlord can require the outgoing tenant to enter into an authorised guarantee agreement ("AGA"). It should not be forgotten that an AGA can be required even if there is no reference to it in the lease, namely where the lease permits assignment with the landlord's consent and the landlord shows that because of the identity or standing of the assignee it is reasonable for it to require an AGA.

The provisions of the Act apply to tenancies beginning after its commencement, unless they were entered into in pursuance of an agreement made before that date. The Act provides that a tenant who assigns premises demised to him will be released from his liability under the covenants in the tenancy, and, if he assigns part only of the premises demised to him, he will be released to the extent that the covenants fall to be complied with in relation to that part. The corollary for being released from obligations under the covenants is that the tenant ceases to be entitled to the benefits under covenants entered into by the landlord.

There are, however, flies in the ointment. The first is in the Act, namely that where a tenant is released from a covenant on assignment, the landlord may require him to enter into the authorised guarantee agreement within the meaning of the clause, under which the assigning tenant guarantees performance of the covenant by the assignee tenant (but not any later tenant). The second was introduced after discussions between the British Property Federation and the British Retail Consortium, namely that section 19 of the Landlord and Tenant Act 1927 should be modified to enable the parties to a lease to enter into an agreement (whether contained in the instrument creating the tenancy or not and whether made at or after the creation of the tenancy) governing the circumstances in which consent to an assignment may be granted or withheld or stipulating the conditions which the landlord may require to be fulfilled before consent to an assignment is applied for. Circumstances agreed in this way would not be referable to the courts on the grounds of unreasonableness. It remains to be seen how these provisions, if accepted by the tenant, will fetter a tenant in his ability to assign a lease.

The Act also contains a useful provision to protect former tenants who (by virtue of the old law or as guarantors under authorised guarantee agreements) remain liable under covenants to pay rent or service charge. Such tenants will not be liable unless the landlord, within six months (reduced from nine months after discussions between the British Property Federation and the British Retail Consortium) of the rent or service charge having become due, serves a notice on the former tenant warning him of liabilty.

There is also a provision, again pursuant to the discussions mentioned above, that if a tenant (who is subject to the old law) is called upon to pay rent and perform covenants under its privity of contract liability, it should have the option of calling for an overriding lease to be granted to it. As the British

Property Federation pointed out, however, there are a number of detailed issues which arise as a result of this, not the least of which is the terms upon which the overriding lease is to be granted and the right of former tenants and their guarantors to join as tenants in common.

Finally, it is refreshing to note that the Act contains "anti-avoidance" provision in an effort to ensure that parties to a tenancy will be unable to contract-out of the Act.

[17] See *Ashworth Frazer v. Gloucester City Council* [2002] 1 All E.R. 377; [2001] 1 W.L.R. 2180 where the proposed assignee intended to use the premises that would result in a breach of the user covenant contained in the lease.

[18] [2000] 27 E.G. 145.

[19] *O'May v. City of London Real Property Co Ltd* [1983] 1 A.C. 726.

[20] Side agreements between the tenant and undertenant to circumvent this position may not be relied upon unless disclosed to the landlord, pursuant to the case of *Allied Dunbar Assurance plc v. Homebase Ltd* [2001] E.G.C.S. 54, though the result of the appeal is awaited.

[21] *Re Koumoudouros and Marathon Reality Co. Ltd* (1978) 89 D.L.R. (3d) 551.

[22] See comments on distress under clause 9.1.

[23] *Cynon Valley Borough Council v. Secretary of State for Wales and Oi Mee Lam* (1986) 53 P. & C.R. 68

[24] See para. 3.3 of the fifth schedule.

[25] [1984] 1 All E.R. 315.

[26] Under the 1995 Act each successive landlord remains bound by the landlord's covenants comprised in the lease, although there is provision for the landlord to be released under the provisions contained in the Act.

*Chapter 5*

# Landlord's Covenants

## Introduction

**5.01** Not surprisingly, the landlord's covenants are rather fewer than the tenant's and if one was of a mind, and really thought that it was worth the effort, it is possible to invent several pages of landlord's covenants which the tenant would dearly like to have included. The usual quiet enjoyment covenant and some additional covenants are set out below.

## 6 The Landlord's Covenants

**5.02** The Landlord covenants with the Tenant:

### 6.1 Quiet enjoyment

To permit the Tenant peaceably and quietly to hold and enjoy the Premises without any interruption or disturbance from or by the Landlord or any person claiming under or in trust for the Landlord [or by title paramount]

This covenant quite often contains a provision that it is dependent upon the tenant paying the rent reserved by the lease and performing and observing the covenants on its part and the conditions contained in the lease, but these words have no practical effect, and do not render payment of the rent and performance of the covenants conditions precedent to the operation of the covenant (*Edge v. Boileau*[1]).

This covenant applies where the normal enjoyment of the premises is substantially interfered with either in respect of eviction, dispossession or the tenant's use of the premises. However, the covenant will only protect the tenant from interruptions by the landlord and persons claiming under or in trust for it, therefore covering successors in title or persons having authority from the landlord to do the acts complained of,[2] but not covering the acts of a superior landlord or a predecessor in title of the landlord.

The tenant should accordingly extend the covenant to include a reference to title paramount.

### 6.2 Services

> **To observe and perform [its] obligations contained in the sixth schedule**    **5.03**

There should be a landlord's covenant to carry out the services and this covenant should not be qualified by a condition that the landlord's covenant is subject to the tenant having paid the service charge in respect thereof. The service charge may be in dispute or there may be an inadvertent omission to pay on the part of the tenant. These circumstances should not justify the landlord in withholding the services. See also the comments on paragraph 6 of the sixth schedule in respect of the landlord's performance of the services.

The following additional landlord's covenants should also be considered:

### 6.3 Superior lease

Where the lease is an underlease, the tenant should consider inserting the following landlord's covenants:    **5.04**

> **To pay the rents reserved by the [superior lease] dated _____ and made between _____ and to observe and perform the covenants agreements and conditions on the part of the tenant contained therein and to enforce the covenants on the part of the landlord in the said lease**

It is difficult to see how a landlord could object to this clause, which seems fair and reasonable. It is possible that the landlord may try to insert a provision that the tenant should meet the cost of the enforcement of the superior landlord's covenants, but this should be resisted.

> **Not to agree to the variation of any of the terms of the [superior lease] without first obtaining the Tenant's written consent [such consent not to be unreasonably withheld or delayed]**

It is less likely that the landlord will agree to this clause, but it is worthwhile including if possible.

> **To use its best endeavours to obtain the consent of the [superior landlord] whenever the Tenant makes application for any consent required under this Lease and where the**

**consent of both the Landlord and the [superior landlord] is required by virtue of this Lease or the [superior lease]**

Hopefully, the landlord will not take objection to this clause.

Where there is a superior lease it is vital that the tenant has sight of it prior to committing itself to the underlease. There may, for instance, be a covenant in the underlease that the tenant will observe and perform the covenants and other provisions contained in the superior lease; though the tenant's solicitor should try to resist this and to have included in the underlease all relevant provisions. The tenant should also check the superior lease to ensure that there are no break clauses contained in it.

### 6.4 Non-competition

**5.05** It may not be in the best interests of the landlord or the tenant for there to be several units within a shopping centre being entitled to sell the same goods or services. Good estate management should result in the landlord maintaining an even balance of trades, but the following clause is nevertheless prudent:

> **Not to permit or suffer any [adjoining or neighbouring premises in the ownership or control of the Landlord] [other premises in the Centre] to be used for the business from time to time being carried on in the Premises**

### 6.5 Similar leases

**5.06** The tenant, if taking premises in a shopping centre under a lease containing intricate service charge provisions, may wish to ensure that all leases of units in the centre mirror its own lease. It may be that the tenant's lease contains covenants on its part that are for the benefit of other units within the centre and the tenant will expect similar reciprocal provisions to be contained in all other leases. The following additional covenant is therefore suggested:

> **To ensure that all other leases within the Centre contain similar covenants on the part of the Landlord and the Tenant and similar service charge provisions to those contained in this Lease and to enforce the covenants on the part of the tenants contained in such other leases**

### 6.6 Environmental matters

**5.07** See comments under clause 1.14 of the agreement for lease. The tenant should consider including the following additional landlord's covenant, particularly where an environmental survey or searches and enquiries have revealed that the premises or other parts of the centre have been constructed on land containing toxic waste, etc. The types of land uses that are considered to be contaminate are extremely wide and include seemingly innocuous uses such as the repair of electrical and electronic components and equipment, and the manufacture of pet foods.

> **Forthwith at its own expense to carry out and complete any remedial works that may be necessary or required at any time during the Term by any regulatory or other authority in respect of the [Premises] [Centre] pursuant to or in connection with the [Premises] [Centre] having been constructed on land containing toxic waste or any other contaminated or deleterious materials or substances and will at its own expense as soon as possible after the completion of the said remedial works carry out and complete any rebuilding or reinstatement of the [Premises] [Centre] made necessary by the carrying out of the said remedial works**

### 6.7 Common parts

See comments under clause 2.4. If it is desired to include a specific landlord's covenant in respect of the common parts it could be set out here, namely: **5.08**

> **To ensure that there are at all times during the Term sufficient Common Parts [including car parks] and other joint facilities available for use in connection with the user of the Premises to enable the Tenant's and any undertenant's or other lawful occupier's trade and business to be carried on thereat**

The reference to car parks is optional and would depend upon the location of the shopping centre and also whether the definition of the common parts included car parks or if they were separately referred to.

### 6.8 Car park

Where the shopping centre or retail park includes a shopper's car park it may be advisable to include the following covenant: **5.09**

> **Throughout the Term to maintain the car park within the Centre as a shopper's car park serving the Centre (such car**

park having a sufficient number of spaces to comply with the requirements of the local planning authority [and having no fewer than [ ] spaces]) [and any car parking charges for the Centre shall be fair and reasonable taking due account of the charges made generally for car parking in the vicinity of the Centre] [and the Landlord will not impose charges for car parking in the car park without the consent of the majority of the tenants at the Centre]

The tenant may decide to include reference to a specific number of car parking spaces, as the requirements of the local planning authority may result in far fewer spaces being provided by the landlord than the tenant feels adequate. The landlord will, of course, derive more income from the construction of additional units rather than to use valuable space for car parking.

The suggested wording in respect of car parking charges may be appropriate if charges are proposed to be made, or if the tenant is of the opinion that the imposition of charges would be likely to deter potential customers.

**6.9 Kiosks/stalls**

**5.10** There has been a proliferation of kiosks and/or stalls in the malls of shopping centres and retail parks, quite often obscuring the windows of retail units and using services paid for by the tenants of the retail units, *e.g.* litter collection. In order to utilise as much space as possible, a landlord may allow kiosks to open in return for a monthly "composite" rent. It is unfair for a landlord to pocket the whole of the rent and leave the tenants of the shop units to pay for services reasonably attributable to the kiosk–holders. The tenant may consider the following covenant appropriate:

Not to permit the erection or retention of any kiosks and/or stalls on the pavement area in front of the Premises and to ensure that any kiosk/stall-holders pay a fair and reasonable contribution towards the cost of services used by them

**6.10 Signboards**

Quite often, signboards will be constructed by the landlord at the entrance of shopping centres, particular retail parks, detailing the identity of the tenants. This can be a useful advertising tool for tenants and the following landlord's covenant can be considered for inclusion:

**To erect and maintain a signboard[s] at the entrance to the Centre indicating the identity of the tenants trading at the Centre and will ensure that the Tenant's identity is maintained on such signboard[s] without a charge being made to the Tenant.**

The reference to a charge being made is to combat the possibility of the landlord requiring a fee for including the tenant's name. This may be remote, but it has been tried, as the author can confirm.

---

[1] (1885) 16 Q.B. 117.
[2] *Harrison, Ainslie & Co. v. Lord Muncaster* [1891] 2 Q.B. 680.

*Chapter 6*

# Insurance

## Introduction

**6.01** It is obviously essential that the premises and the building or complex (if applicable) are insured to their full reinstatement value from time to time during the lease. The lease will, indeed, quite often contain extensive insurance provisions with this in mind and ensure that all costs in respect of insurance are paid for by the tenant and not the landlord.

From the tenant's point of view, there are various factors that require careful consideration including the risks covered, reinstatement, suspension of rent and determination in the event of frustration, or the landlord's failure to reinstate.

## 7   Insurance

### 7.1   Warranty re-convictions

**6.02**      **The Tenant warrants that prior to the execution of this Lease [it] has disclosed to the Landlord in writing any conviction judgment or finding of any court or tribunal relating to the Tenant (or any director or other officer or major shareholder of the Tenant) of such a nature as to be likely to affect the decision of any insurer or underwriter to grant or to continue insurance of any of the Insured Risks**

The landlord may wish to include this in order to protect its position resulting from insurance contracts being *uberrimae fidei*, with the resultant obligation to disclose to the insurers material facts within its actual or presumed knowledge. This clause could be used to rebut the suggestion by the landlord's insurers that the landlord had actual or presumed knowledge of such facts. It would also give the landlord a right of action against the tenant for any breach. Unfortunately, tenants (particularly directors of tenant companies) will wish to resist this provision on the basis that people are generally reluctant to reveal any such sensitive information about themselves.

### 7.2 Landlord to insure

> **The Landlord covenants with the Tenant to insure the Premises and the Retained Parts [subject to the Tenant paying the Insurance Rent] unless such insurance shall be vitiated by any act of the Tenant or by anyone at the Premises expressly or by implication with the Tenant's authority [and under the Tenant's control]**    **6.03**

While it would be preferable for the insurance to be in the joint names of the landlord and the tenant in order to give the tenant more control over the insurance and to avoid the problem of subrogation referred to below, landlords tend to resist this, presumably on the basis that they wish to retain absolute control and not rely on the tenant in any way as regards the insurance cover.

It is essential to ensure that where the premises form part of a larger building or a shopping centre the building (or the shopping centre) should also be insured as the tenant would wish the whole of the building to be reinstated in the event of damage or destruction and not just the premises. The tenant could, however, specifically except plate glass if it wishes, particularly if the tenant is proposing to seek a waiver in respect of the premises as referred to under paragraph 12.2 of the fifth schedule. The optional words referring to persons under the tenant's control should be included (see clause 5.4) unless, of course, the tenant is able to remove reference to such persons altogether. Although possibly more relevant in connection with reinstatement,[1] the tenant should attempt to place some limitation on the persons who could void the policy. If possible, any reference to undertenants, licensees and casual callers (*e.g.* customers) should be deleted, and there should most certainly not be a reference to the avoidance of the policy by acts or omission of other tenants in a multi-occupied building or shopping centre. There should also be deleted the reference to the landlord not being required to insure where the tenant has failed to pay the insurance rent, although any landlord in its right mind would do so in any event. The clause could be amended to read as follows:

> **The Landlord covenants with the Tenant to insure the Centre (other than plate glass in the windows and doors of the Premises and other units within the Centre and other**

than tenants' fixtures and fittings therein) and all parts thereof except during such periods as the insurance shall be rendered ineffectual or avoided by any act of the Tenant

**7.3 Details of the insurance**

**6.04**  Insurance shall be effected:
7.3.1 in such [substantial and reputable] insurance office or with such underwriters and through such agency as the Landlord may from time to time decide
7.3.2 for the following sums:
7.3.2.1 such sum as the Landlord shall from time to time be advised [by the Surveyor] as being the full cost of rebuilding and reinstatement including architects' surveyors' and other professional fees payable upon any applications for planning permission or other permits or consents that may be required in relation to the rebuilding or reinstatement of the Centre the cost of debris removal demolition site clearance any works that may be required by statute and incidental expenses and
7.3.2.2 the loss of Rent and Service Charge payable under this Lease from time to time (having regard to any review of rent which may become due under this Lease) for [three] years or such longer period as the Landlord may from time to time [reasonably] [consider to be sufficient *or* deem to be necessary] for the purposes of the planning and carrying out the rebuilding or reinstatement
7.3.3 against damage or destruction by the Insured Risks to the extent that such insurance may ordinarily be arranged for properties such as the Centre with an insurer of repute and subject to such excesses exclusions or limitations as the insurer may require

It may be advisable to provide that the insurer should have principal offices in the United Kingdom, but this is no guarantee that the insurer will not succumb to liquidation or contest claims, and one wonders whether this would find favour with our European partners. In addition it is worth noting that "insurance office" would probably not include insurance effected through Lloyds underwriters. This is relevant when considering the provisions of section 83 of the Fires Prevention (Metropolis) Act 1774, by which either party has the right to require insurance monies to be laid out in reinstatement (if a request is made to the insurance company before the monies are paid to the insured) as it seems that the Act does not apply to insurance through Lloyds.[2]

The insurance should cover the full cost of rebuilding and reinstatement from time to time, although it is accepted that a covenant to insure for the "full cost of reinstatement" will be construed as meaning the cost of reinstatement at the time when reinstatement actually takes place, as opposed to the date when the premium is paid, or any other date. The landlord should not be allowed to hide behind the surveyor's advice as to the level of cover. Expressions such as "to insure adequately" and "to insure to the full value of the property" should be amended as the former covenant could be complied with if the cover equates to that recommended by the insurance company,[3] and the latter could be interpreted as meaning the full market value of the property and, as such, could be less than the cost of reinstatement.

It is important to ensure that supplemental fees are included as well as the cost of debris removal, demolition, etc.

Loss of rent should be insured but there should be some upper limitation on the number of years' cover. It is generally thought that if premises cannot be reinstated within three years then something is grossly wrong. If the landlord insists on having the discretion to insure loss of rent for longer than three years, an upper limit of five years could be inserted as a compromise.

**6.05** Some clauses, in referring to loss of rent insurance, mention also the landlord's (reasonable) estimation of the rent following a rent review under the lease. In such an event, the tenant may wish to insert a qualification to the effect that this should not be taken to be an acceptance by the tenant that the rent on review would be at the level insured against by the landlord, though one would not expect the rental valuation to be so fettered in the absence of clear evidence that the tenant had specifically agreed that the landlord's estimate was to be the rent payable on a forthcoming rent review.

The tenant should endeavour to ensure that all reasonable and normal risks are covered by the landlord's insurance. Sometimes the insured risks are stated to be:

> **fire and such other risks as the Landlord may from time to time deem it desirable to insure against**

This is clearly inadequate as there is an interrelationship between the insurance clause, the tenant's repairing covenant and the proviso for suspension of rent. Rent is usually only suspended where the premises are unfit for occupation and use as a result of damage or destruction by an insured risk. Similarly, the exception to the tenant's repairing liability relates principally to damage or destruction by an insured risk. The only alternative is for the tenant to insure the missing risks itself, but this may not be cost effective, particularly if the landlord is a large property company and therefore more able to obtain cheaper cover. Therefore the landlord should be encouraged to insure against all normal risks.

The risks detailed as the insured risks in clause 2.8 are not all-encompassing and could vary depending upon various aspects, including the locality of the premises, *e.g.* subsidence or heave may be advisable in an area of clay subsoil. The tenant's surveyor should be consulted to advise on the risks to be covered should any doubt exist.

The reference in clause 7.3.3 to "such excesses . . ., etc." gives slight cause for concern as it is tilted rather heavily in favour of the insurer. It would be sensible for the tenant to qualify this provision as detailed below.

Clause 7.3 could be amended to read as follows:

**7.3  Details of the insurance**

**6.06**

**Insurance shall be effected:**
**7.3.1    in such substantial and reputable insurance office or with such underwriters and through such agency as the Landlord may from time to time reasonably decide in each case with principal offices in the United Kingdom**
**7.3.2    for the following sums:**
**7.3.2.1  such sum as shall be the full cost of rebuilding and reinstatement including architects' surveyors' and other professional fees payable upon any applications for planning permission or other permits or consents that may be required in relation to the rebuilding or reinstatement of the Centre the cost of debris removal demolition site clearance any works that may be required by statute and proper and reasonable incidental expenses and**
**7.3.2.2  the loss of Rent and Service Charge payable under this Lease from time to time (having reasonable regard to any review of rent which may become due under this Lease) for three years [or such longer period not exceeding five years as the Landlord may from time to time reasonably consider to be sufficient for the purposes of obtaining any necessary planning permission or other permits or consents and for carrying out the rebuilding or reinstatement works]**
**7.3.3    against damage or destruction by the Insured Risks to the extent that such insurance may ordinarily be arranged for properties such as the Centre with an insurer of repute and**

subject to such excesses exclusions or limitations as the insurer may reasonably require and as are normal in the insurance market

### 7.4 Payment of Insurance Rent

The Tenant shall pay the Insurance Rent on the date of this Lease for the period from and including the Rent Commencement Date to the day before the next policy renewal date and subsequently the Tenant shall pay the Insurance Rent on demand (if so demanded) in advance [but not more than [_____ months] in advance] of the policy renewal date  **6.07**

If a rent-free period has been granted to the tenant in respect of the yearly rent, it is likely that the insurance rent will become payable prior to the Rent Commencement Date.

It is obviously advisable that the tenant should not pay the insurance rent too far in advance of the policy renewal date, as there is no reason why the landlord should benefit from the tenant's money. The reference to "months" should accordingly be replaced by a reference to a maximum of four, but preferably two, weeks.

### 7.5 Suspension of rent

7.5.1 If and whenever during the Term:  **6.08**
7.5.1.1 the Premises or the Retained Parts or any part of either of them are damaged or destroyed by any of the [Insured Risks *or* Insured Risks except one against which insurance may not ordinarily be arranged with an insurer of repute for properties such as the Premises unless the Landlord has in fact insured against that risk] so that the Premises or any part of them are unfit for occupation or use and
7.5.1.2 payment of the insurance money is not refused in whole or in part by reason of any act or default of the Tenant or anyone at the Premises expressly or by implication with the Tenant's authority [and under the Tenant's control]
the provisions of clause 7.5.2 shall have effect
7.5.2 When the circumstances contemplated in clause 7.5.1 arise the Rent [and Service Charge] or a fair proportion of the Rent [and Service Charge] according to the nature and the extent of the damage sustained shall cease to be payable until the Premises or the Retained Parts or the damaged

**parts of either of them shall have been rebuilt or reinstated so that the Premises or the affected part are made fit for occupation or use [or until the expiration of [three] years from the damage or destruction whichever period is the shorter] [((the amount of such proportion and the period during which the Rent [and Service Charge] shall cease to be payable to be determined by the Surveyor acting as an expert and not as an arbitrator)** *or* **(any dispute as to such proportion or the period during which the Rent [and Service Charge] shall cease to be payable to be determined in accordance with the Arbitration Act 1996 by an arbitrator to be appointed by agreement between the parties or in default by the President for the time being of the Royal Institution of Chartered Surveyors upon the application of either party)]**

This provision should always be amended to include reference not only to the premises but also to the building of which the premises form part in the event that the premises do not stand alone. In the case of premises forming part of a shopping centre,[4] a similar expansion is recommended. The fact is that damage or destruction of other parts of the building or of the shopping centre (if applicable) may render the premises unusable despite the fact that the premises have not been damaged or destroyed. A reference, as in the precedent, to the retained parts goes some way towards covering the point, but the damage or destruction of neighbouring units in a shopping centre could also render the premises unusable. The tenant should also consider deleting reference to the insured risks completely, as the damage or destruction rendering the premises unusable may not in fact stem from an insured risk. Unfortunately, this would be certain to meet with opposition from the landlord. This is why the amendment to clause 7.5.1.1 below suggests including the words "or otherwise" after "the Insured Risks", but this is unlikely to be accepted. If the landlord is prepared to agree the suggested amendment of the inclusion of the words "or otherwise", there will be no need for the tenant to amend the clause further to provide for damage or destruction by terrorism, where terrorism is not (either at the outset or subsequently) one of the insured risks. If, however, the landlord refuses to accept the suggested amendment, or wishes to have a reference to the specific circumstance or risk in addition to the insured risks that concerns the tenant, it would be as well for the tenant to amend the clause as shown to include a reference to terrorism. An alternative to inserting "or otherwise" is to make reference, as in the suggested amendments, to other risks which the landlord ought to have insured against.

There is a very good argument that not only the rent should be suspended but also the service charge and the insurance rent, particularly where the premises form part of a shopping centre. In such a case, it seems unfair that the tenant should continue to pay these ancillary sums when the premises are unusable. If only "on account" service charge payments are reserved as rent pursuant to the comments under clause 4.2, despite the definition of "rents" in clause 2.16, it may be as well to refer specifically to the Rent Insurance Rent and Service Charge in this clause. A reference to the suspension of "the rent reserved" will not suspend additional rents payable in respect of insurance and service charges.[5]

Any limitation on the period of the suspension of rent should be resisted even if there is included in the lease a clause allowing surrender where the premises are not reinstated within a given period of time.[6] A limitation of three years from the date of the destruction or damage may seem a long time and usually it will be sufficient to allow the landlord to obtain all necessary consents needed to reinstate. There may be instances, however, where, for some unforseen reason, three years is insufficient, with the result that the tenant once again becomes liable to pay rents (and service charges) for premises it is unable to use.

The tenant should also consider amending 7.5.2 to extend the suspension by an additional three months to enable the tenant to fit out the premises, and there is no harm in including a provision that a due proportion of rents paid in advance should be refunded to the tenant as otherwise there is the possibility that the insurers may object to paying the refund on the grounds that the lease contains no obligation for the landord to repay the same.

**6.09** The tenant should also consider protecting any rent free period that may have been granted at the commencement of the lease and which period may not have expired by the date when the damage or destruction occurred.

Clause 7.5 could be amended to read as follows:

**7.5.1** **If and whenever during the Term:**
**7.5.1.1** **the Centre or any part of the Centre or its essential accesses or services are damaged or destroyed by any of the Insured Risks [or otherwise] [or by terrorism whether or not at any time one of the Insured Risks or by any other risk against which the Landlord (acting reasonably) ought to have insured] so as to render the Premises or any part of them unfit for occupation or use or inaccessible or if a substantial part of the Centre is damaged or destroyed so as to make continual use of the Premises impracticable then**
**7.5.1.2** **to the extent that payment of the insurance money is not refused by reason of any act or default of the Tenant or**

anyone at the Premises expressly or by implication with the Tenant's authority while under the Tenant's control and in the employment of the Tenant

the provisions of clause 7.5.2 shall have effect

7.5.2 When the circumstances contemplated in clause 7.5.1 arise the [Rent Insurance Rent and Service Charge] [rents] or a fair proportion of them according to the nature and the extent of the damage sustained shall cease to be payable from the date of such damage or destruction until the date which falls three months after the date when the Premises (with essential accesses and services) and all other relevant parts of the Centre are again rendered fit for occupation and use pursuant to the necessary rebuilding or reinstatement works having been completed and a due proportion of the [Rent Insurance Rent and Service Charge] [rents] paid in advance shall forthwith after the date of such damage or destruction be refunded to the Tenant and any dispute as to such proportion or the period during which the [Rent Insurance Rent and Service Charge] [rents] shall cease to be payable shall be determined in accordance with the Arbitration Act 1996 by an arbitrator to be appointed by agreement between the parties or in default of agreement by the President for the time being of the Royal Institution of Chartered Surveyors upon the application of either party AND in the event that the Rent is suspended by virtue of the foregoing provisions during the operation of the rent free period granted to the Tenant [under] [the provisions of the agreement to grant] [this Lease] the period of the suspension of the Rent shall be extended for a period after the completion of such rebuilding or reinstatement works as aforesaid equal to the balance of the rent free period which the Tenant was unable to enjoy because of the damage or destruction.

7.6 Reinstatement and termination if prevented

6.10 7.6.1 If and whenever during the Term:

7.6.1.1 the Premises the Retained Parts or any part of either of them are damaged or destroyed by any of the [Insured Risks *or* Insured Risks except one against which insurance may not ordinarily be arranged with an insurer of repute for properties such as the Premises unless the Landlord has in fact insured against that risk] and

7.6.1.2 the payment of the insurance money is not refused in whole or in part by reason of any act or default of the Tenant or anyone at the Premises expressly or by implication with the Tenant's authority [and under the Tenant's control]
the Landlord shall use [its] best endeavours to obtain all planning permissions or other permits and consents that may be required under the Planning Acts or other statutes (if any) to enable the Landlord to rebuild and reinstate ("Permissions")

It is insufficient for a landlord to covenant only to reinstate the premises and the retained parts, particularly in the case of a multi-let building or development, where the damage or destruction of other parts could impact on the premises, either physically or financially, *e.g.* where the tenant is unable to use the premises, or where other substantial parts of the development are unusable. The covenant should therefore extend to all other parts of the development, so that the landlord's obligation to rebuild or reinstate applies to all parts even if the premises escape damage.

The insured risks referred to in 7.6.1.1 will hopefully have been specified in clause 2.8 or in the policy details supplied to the tenant from time to time pursuant to clause 7.9.1

Wherever possible, an obligation should be obtained from the landlord to use its best endeavours to obtain all necessary permissions, which should be obtained as soon as possible.

The clause could be amended as follows:

7.6.1 If and whenever during the Term:
7.6.1.1 the Centre or any part thereof or its essential accesses or services are damaged or destroyed by any of the Insured Risks [or otherwise] [or by terrorism (whether or not at any time one of the Insured Risks or by any other risk against which the Landlord (acting reasonably) ought to have insured)][7] then
7.6.1.2 to the extent that the payment of the insurance money is not refused by reason of any act or default of the Tenant or anyone at the Premises expressly or by implication with the Tenant's authority while under the Tenant's control and in the employment of the Tenant
the Landlord shall use its best endeavours to obtain as soon as possible all planning permissions and other permits and consents that may be required under the Planning Acts or other statutes (if any) to enable the Landlord to rebuild and reinstate ('Permissions')

**7.6.2** Subject to the provisions of clauses 7.6.3 and 7.6.4 the Landlord shall as soon as the Permissions have been obtained or immediately where no Permissions are required apply all money received in respect of such insurance (except sums in respect of loss of Rent) in rebuilding or reinstating the Premises or the Retained Parts so damaged or destroyed [making up any difference between the cost of rebuilding and reinstating and the money received out of the Landlord's own money]

It is important to include the words in square brackets in order to ensure that the damaged or destroyed premises are reinstated. This may be particularly important where there is a limitation on the suspension of rent provision, *i.e.* rent resumes after three years, and the landlord claims to have performed its covenants by using the insurance money received. It has been held that there is no implied obligation on the landlord to do more than lay out insurance monies received in making good damage.[8] If the landlord has covenanted "to reinstate", the problem would probably be avoided, and similarly where the covenant is to insure "for the full cost of reinstatement" (without any qualification as included in clause 7.3.2.1), in which case any resultant shortfall would presumably result in a breach of the covenant.[9]

Where relatively substantial reconstruction works are necessary to reinstate, there is every reason for the tenant to expect the benefit of collateral warranties from the contractor, structural engineer and other persons. The tenant may also amend the reinstatement provisions as detailed below in order to try to ensure that the reinstatement works are carried out properly and that the reinstated premises are no less advantageous to the tenant.

The latter part of the clause should be amended as follows:

> ... in rebuilding or reinstating those parts of the Centre including essential accesses and services so damaged or destroyed and the Landlord shall make up any deficiency between the cost of rebuilding and reinstating and the insurance money received by the Landlord out of the Landlord's own money (including making up the non-availability of insurance money where the damage or destruction has been caused by terrorism and no insurance money or insufficient insurance money is made available) [and the Landlord shall carry out such rebuilding and reinstatement works in a good and workmanlike manner in

accordance with good building practice and using good and suitable materials in accordance with the Permissions and shall ensure that the Premises as rebuilt and reinstated shall be similar to the Premises in design function and size [with no less a frontage] location and prominence with ancillary facilities [and Common Parts] no less convenient and commodious as those which existed immediately before the occurrence of the damage or destruction and the Landlord shall use all reasonable endeavours to obtain for the Tenant deeds of collateral warranty from the contractor architect structural engineer mechanical and electrical services engineer and other professional persons in respect of any such rebuilding or reinstatement works insofar as the same apply to the Premises such collateral warranties to be in a form commercially available at the time of the rebuilding or reinstatement]

7.6.3 For the purposes of this clause the expression "Supervening Events" means:

7.6.3.1 the Landlord has failed despite using [its] best endeavours to obtain the Permissions

7.6.3.2 any of the Permissions have been granted subject to a lawful condition with which [it would be impossible for *or* in all the circumstances it would be unreasonable to expect] the Landlord to comply

7.6.3.3 some defect or deficiency in the site upon which the rebuilding or reinstatement is to take place [would render the same impossible *or* would mean that the same could only be undertaken at a cost that would be unreasonable in all the circumstances]

7.6.3.4 the Landlord is unable to obtain access to the site for the purposes of rebuilding or reinstating

7.6.3.5 the rebuilding or reinstating is prevented by war act of God government action [strike lock-out] or

7.6.3.6 any other circumstances beyond the control of the Landlord

7.6.4 The Landlord shall not be liable to rebuild or reinstate the Premises or the Retained Parts if and for so long as such rebuilding or reinstating is prevented by Supervening Events

6.11

7.6.5 If upon the expiry of a period of [three] years commencing on the date of the damage or destruction the Premises and the Retained Parts have not been rebuilt or reinstated so that the Premises are fit for the Tenant's occupation and use either party may by notice served at any time within [six] months of the expiry of such period invoke the provisions of clause 7.6.6

7.6.6 Upon service of a notice in accordance with clause 7.6.5:

7.6.6.1 the Term will absolutely cease but without prejudice to any rights or remedies that may have accrued to either party against the other including (without prejudice to the generality of the above) any right that the Tenant might have against the Landlord for a breach of the Landlord's covenants set out in clauses 7.6.1 and 7.6.2

7.6.6.2 all money received in respect of the insurance effected by the Landlord pursuant to this clause shall belong to the Landlord

The problem is that all of the events set out in clause 7.6.3 seem reasonable, but the fact is that any suspension of the landlord's obligation to reinstate could lead to uncertainty, which is not in the best interests of either party. It is accordingly advisable for the lease to contain a right to terminate the lease if reinstatement has not taken place within a reasonable period. The tenant may wish to dispense with clauses 7.6.3, 7.6.4, 7.6.5 and 7.6.6 and add the following proviso to clauses 7.6.2:

> If for any reason the Premises and all other relevant parts of the Centre sufficient for the Tenant [or any undertenant] to carry on its [or their] normal trade and business including the means of access to the Premises and all essential services therein and thereto shall not be rebuilt or reinstated as they were immediately prior to the date of the relevant damage or destruction (whether the damage or destruction was caused by any of the Insured Risks [or otherwise] [or by terrorism (whether or not at any time one of the Insured Risks)]) by the second anniversary of the date of the damage or destruction the Tenant may thereafter determine the Term by giving not less than one month's notice to the Landlord and upon expiry of such notice the Term will forthwith cease but without prejudice to [the claim of either party for any earlier breach of covenant by the other] *or* [any rights or remedies that may have accrued to either party against the other including (without prejudice to the generality of the above) any right that the Tenant might have against the Landlord for a breach of the Landlord's covenants set out in clauses 7.6.1 and 7.6.2]

This may be resisted by the landlord who will wish to have the unilateral right to terminate. The tenant may be wary of this in case it is used by the landlord to remove the tenant (in a buoyant market) but any dilatoriness on the part of the landlord in reinstating where none of the supervening events applies could be seized upon by the tenant. If a formula similar to the above is chosen, the tenant must ensure that the rent (or rents) does not resume, pursuant to any limitation on the suspension of rent provision, before the tenant has the right to terminate. It may be considered that a three-year period in clause 7.6.5 is too long and that two years is an adequate period for reinstatement to take place, but the landlord will probably hold out for the longer period. As regards the period of notice to be given in clause 7.6.5, the tenant's notice need be only a few days, but (if the security of tenure provisions in the Landlord and Tenant Act 1954 apply to the lease) the landlord will remain subject to its provisions and will have to serve a notice of at least six months. If the Act does apply, the landlord must establish one of the grounds permitted by the Act if the tenant opposes the notice on the basis that it fully intends to resume occupation of the premises when they are reinstated.

If the suggested proviso to clause 7.6.2 is accepted by the landlord, it is likely that the landlord will also want to have the right to terminate the lease in the circumstances envisaged. This will probably be acceptable to the tenant but, as the landlord should not benefit from its own default, it may be as well to amend the proviso as follows, as well as covering the position so that neither party can determine the term once the reinstatement works have been completed:

> ... **by the second anniversary of the date of the damage or destruction then either the Landlord or Tenant may thereafter determine the Term by giving not less than [one] [six] months' notice to the other party and upon expiry of such notice....**

continue as above and then add the following provisos:

> **PROVIDED THAT the Landlord shall not be entitled to determine the Term where the reason for the failure to rebuild or reinstate is the fault or omission of the Landlord AND PROVIDED FURTHER THAT no such notice shall be served following completion of the relevant rebuilding or reinstatement works and any dispute or difference with regard to the completion of the works shall be determined in accordance with the Arbitration Act 1996 by an arbitrator to be appointed by agreement between the parties or in**

default of such agreement by the President for the time being of the Royal Institution of Chartered Surveyors on the application of either party

**6.12** The division of the insurance money in the event of termination can give rise to uncertainty if not provided for in the lease. Authorities seem confused on this topic. In *Beacon Carpets Ltd v. Kirby*,[10] the court decided that the proceeds of insurance should be divided between the landlord and tenant in accordance with their respective interests in the property. This would seem to accord with the dissenting judgment of Lord Denning M.R. in *Re King, Robinson v. Gray*,[11] where the majority of the Court of Appeal decided that a tenant who had insured in the joint names of the landlord and tenant should be entitled to the whole of the proceeds. This cannot be logical, and there is some support for landlords who feel justified in requiring the proceeds to be paid to them on the basis that a lease is for a limited duration but the freehold (where applicable) is for life. Nevertheless, there is no harm in a tenant trying for a compromise and the following provision (adapted for adding to the above amendment to clause 7.6.2) could be considered:

> **AND upon cesser of the Term by notice hereunder the insurance money shall in respect of the damage or destruction of the Premises under the policy maintained under this clause [7] be divided between the Landlord and the Tenant according to the value at the date of the damage or destruction of their respective interests in the Premises (to be determined in default of agreement between the parties by an arbitrator to be appointed by agreement between the parties or in default of such agreement by the President for the time being of the Royal Institution of Chartered Surveyors on the application of either party)**

### 7.7 Tenant's insurance covenants

**6.13** It is important that the lease contains general covenants on the part of the tenant relating to insurance sufficient to ensure that the insurance is not vitiated because of foolish acts on the part of the tenant.

**The Tenant covenants with the Landlord:**
**7.7.1 to comply with all the requirements and recommendations of the insurers**

The problem with the requirements and recommendations of insurers is that some insurers can impose quite unreasonable requirements and recommendations. There is a very good argument for deleting the reference to the tenant complying with insurers' recommendations, on the basis that if the recommendation is sufficiently important to the insurers they will make it a requirement. It is important to try to give the tenant the opportunity of objecting to unreasonable requirements and recommendations, hence the suggested amendment, although it may be that the landlord will make the reasonably valid statement that the actual requirements of the insurers must be complied with as otherwise the landlord will be forever switching insurance companies. It is fair to say, however, that this argument could be countered by the statement that the landlord should not expect the tenant to comply with unreasonable requirements and recommendations, even if it means the landlord changing insurers.

**7.7.1   to comply with the [reasonable] requirements [and [reasonable] recommendations] of the insurers**

An alternative is to provide that the tenant should be permitted to make representations to the insurers in respect of any requirements it may consider to be unreasonable, in which case the clause should be amended accordingly. This is better than nothing, but the insurers could simply refuse to budge.

**7.7.2   not to do or omit anything that could cause any policy of insurance on or in relation to the Premises to become void or voidable wholly or in part nor (unless the Tenant shall have previously notified the Landlord and have agreed to pay the increased premium) anything by which additional insurance premiums may become payable**

This does not seem unreasonable.

**7.7.3   to keep the Premises supplied with such fire-fighting equipment as the insurers and the fire authority may require [or as the Landlord may reasonably require] and to maintain such equipment to their satisfaction and in efficient working order and at least once in every [six] months to cause any sprinkler system and other fire-fighting equipment to be inspected by a competent person**

The same argument as under clause 7.7.1 above applies with regard to fire-fighting equipment. It is clearly essential that the fire authority's requirements are complied with in this regard, be they reasonable or not, but there is no harm in insisting upon any insurers' requirements being reasonable and, in any event, the reference to the landlord's requirements, reasonable or otherwise, should be deleted.

**7.7.4** not to store or bring onto the Premises any article substance or liquid of a specifically combustible inflammable or explosive nature and to comply with the requirements and recommendations of the fire authority [and the [reasonable] requirements of the Landlord] as to fire precautions relating to the Premises

Some tenants sell inflammable, or what may be considered to be otherwise dangerous, substances in the normal course of their business. A specific exclusion should be made in respect of such items which may require the insurer's consent. The tenant should not be surprised if the landlord insists on detailing in this clause the dangerous substances that the tenant offers for sale, *e.g.* lighter fuel. The landlord may also want to provide that any such dangerous substances are stored in suitable fireproof containers, etc. The other amendments to this covenant are self-explanatory.

**7.7.4** not to store or bring onto the Premises any article substance or liquid of a specially combustible inflammable or explosive nature other than such articles as are offered for sale or otherwise used by the Tenant or any undertenant or other lawful occupier in its or their normal trade and business and to comply with the requirements of the fire authority as to fire precautions relating to the Premises

**7.7.5** not to obstruct the access to any fire equipment or the means of escape from the Premises nor to lock any fire door while the Premises are occupied

This is reasonable, and difficult for a tenant to resist.

**7.7.6** to give notice to the Landlord immediately upon the happening of any event which might affect any insurance policy on or relating to the Premises or upon the happening of any event against which the Landlord may have insured under this Lease

This covenant should be resisted by the tenant, although the landlord may try to retain it to show to the insurers that it has done all reasonably expected of it to ascertain the existence of material facts. If the tenant fails to have the covenant deleted, the clause could be amended by the tenant to read:

**7.7.6** to give notice to the landlord as soon as practicable after becoming aware of the happening of any event at the Premises which might adversely affect the Landlord's insurance policy on or relating to the Premises or of the happening of any event at the Premises against which the Landlord may have insured under this Lease in each case in respect of which the requisite particulars have previously been supplied to the Tenant

7.7.7 immediately to inform the Landlord in writing of any conviction judgment or finding of any court or tribunal relating to the Tenant (or any director other officer or major shareholder of the Tenant) of such a nature as to be likely to affect the decision of any insurer or underwriter to grant or to continue any such insurance

The requirement to notify the landlord in respect of convictions, etc., should be deleted for the reason stated above.[12]

7.7.8 if at any time the Tenant shall be entitled to the benefit of any insurance on the Premises (which is not effected or maintained in pursuance of any obligation contained in this Lease) to apply all money received by virtue of such insurance in making good the loss or damage in respect of which such money shall have been received    6.14

The landlord's concern is to avoid the situation by which its insurers may refuse to pay the whole of the proceeds of insurance where the tenant has also taken out insurance cover for the premises, pursuant to a common provision found in insurance policies.[13]

If the following clause is included (which is stated in the precedent possibly to be inappropriate where the premises form part of a larger building or centre), the following comments will apply:

[7.7.9 if and whenever during the Term the Premises or any part of them are damaged or destroyed by an Insured Risk and the insurance money under the policy of insurance effected by the Landlord pursuant to [its] obligations contained in this Lease is by reason of any act or default of the Tenant or anyone at the Premises expressly or by implication with the Tenant's authority [and under the Tenant's control] wholly or partially irrecoverable immediately in every such case (at the option of the Landlord) either:

7.7.9.1 to rebuild and reinstate at its own expense the Premises or the part damaged or destroyed to the reasonable satisfaction and under the supervision of the Surveyor the Tenant being allowed towards the expenses of so doing upon such rebuilding and reinstatement being completed the amount (if any) actually received in respect of such damage or destruction under any such insurance policy or

7.7.9.2 to pay to the Landlord on demand with Interest the amount of such insurance money so irrecoverable in which event the provisions of clauses 7.5 and 7.6 shall apply]

It is not unreasonable for a lease to contain a provision that the tenant will pay for the reinstatement of premises where insurance has been vitiated, subject to a limitation being placed on the persons who can trigger this provision and possibly subject to the tenant being allowed to receive the payable insurance money as the reinstatement progresses, where the tenant is obliged to reinstate, as opposed to being paid upon rebuilding and reinstatement as proposed by clause 7.7.9.1. Having said that, the tenant could be faced with high capital expenditure as a result of this provision, and even worse where the covenant relates to the reinstatement of the whole centre. The tenant would therefore be advised to try to delete this covenant, or at least ensure that it is restricted to the premises alone. Clause 7.7.9 should, in any event, contain the following amendment:

> ... **anyone at the Premises expressly or by implication with the Tenant's authority while under the Tenant's control and in the employment of the Tenant wholly or partially irrecoverable** ...

and the following amendment to 7.7.9.2 should be considered:

7.7.9.2 **to pay to the Landlord on demand with Interest (where the Landlord has rebuilt and reinstated the Premises out of its own money) the amount of such insurance money so irrecoverable in which event the provisions of clauses 7.5 and 7.6 shall apply**

7.8 Increase or decrease of the Centre

6.15  If at any time during the Term the Centre shall be increased or decreased on a permanent basis the Insurance Rent Percentage shall be varied with effect from the first premium or additional premium payable in respect of a period after such a change by agreement between the parties or in default of agreement within [three] months of the first proposal for variation made by the Landlord in such a manner as shall be determined to be fair and reasonable in the light of the event in question by the Surveyor acting as an expert and not as an arbitrator

This does not seem unreasonable, but see the comments under Insurance Rent Percentage in clause 1.15.

[7.9 **Landlord's further insurance covenants**

**The Landlord covenants with the Tenant in relation to the policy of insurance effected by the Landlord pursuant to [its] obligations contained in this Lease:**

7.9.1 **to produce to the Tenant on demand [a copy of the policy and of the last premium renewal receipt or reasonable evidence of the terms of the policy and the fact that the last premium has been paid]**

7.9.2 **to procure that the interest of the Tenant is noted or indorsed on the policy**

7.9.3 **to notify the Tenant of any [material] change in the risks covered by the policy from time to time [and**

7.9.4 **to produce to the Tenant on demand written confirmation from the insurers that they have agreed to waive all rights of subrogation against the Tenant]]**

It is essential that covenants of this nature should be included except where insurance is to be in the joint names of the landlord and tenant.

There should be produced to the tenant not only a copy of the policy and/or a summary of the insured risks but also evidence of the payment of the last premium. It is suggested that where the premises form part of a number of properties insured by the landlord under a block policy, it would be unreasonable to expect the landlord to produce the policy and this is accepted. The point is, however, that as the lease contains a covenant by the tenant not to invalidate the insurance policy, affecting also the exception in respect of the tenant's repairing covenant and the suspension of rent provision, it is vital that the tenant is kept aware of the landlord's insurance policy so that the tenant can ascertain what action or inaction is likely to invalidate it. The suggestion has also been made that the tenant should endeavour to have included in the policy a non-invalidation clause to the effect that no act or omission by the tenant or others should invalidate the policy or render the insurance money irrecoverable. The insurers may, however, require an additional premium for this, and the tenant would be wise to make enquiries in this regard before insisting on a covenant of this nature. The suggested clause 7.9.5 takes this into account, but there may, of course, be no insurer prepared to offer such a clause without an additional premium.

The landlord should either obtain from the insurers a waiver of subrogation rights as regards the tenant, any undertenant and their mortgagees, and possibly also any other lawful occupiers, or if that is not possible or practicable then the landlord should endeavour to note their interests on the policy. This is in order to try to avoid the effects of subrogation, namely where the insurer pays out money to the landlord under an insurance policy he will be subrogated to any rights the landlord may have against the tenant for breaches of covenant which may have given rise to the damage or destruction. The position is now somewhat alleviated by the case of *Rowlands (Mark) Ltd v. Berni Inns Ltd*,[14] where it was held that the intention of the parties to the lease was that the landlord's claim would be against the insurers under the insurance policy and that the landlord would not have a claim against the tenant for breach of covenant, to the effect that there was no claim to which the insurers could be subrogated. Nevertheless, this case turned on a question of construction without any general statement of principle being expounded, and it would therefore seem sensible that a tenant should try to ensure that subrogation rights are avoided wherever possible. A clear waiver of subrogation rights issued by the insurers is obviously preferred, but it is generally accepted that the noting of interests will have the same effect, although there is no guarantee of this. The noting of the tenant's interest on the insurance policy should also entitle the tenant to be given notice by the insurers of any intention to lapse the policy.

**6.16** Clause 7.9.3 is definitely worth including, as it is in the tenant's best interests to know precisely what risks are covered.

The following amendments should be considered:

### 7.9 Landlord's insurance covenants

**6.17** **The Landlord covenants with the Tenant in relation to the policy of insurance effected by the Landlord pursuant to its obligations contained in this Lease:**

**7.9.1** **to produce to the Tenant on demand a copy of the policy and of the last premium renewal receipt *or* reasonable evidence of the terms of the policy and the fact that the last premium has been paid**

**7.9.2** **to procure either that the interest of the Tenant and any undertenant and any other lawful occupier and its or their mortgagees are noted or indorsed on the policy or that the insurers issue a waiver of subrogation rights as regards the Tenant any undertenant and any other lawful occupier and its or their mortgagees**

**7.9.3** to notify the Tenant of any change in the risks covered by the policy from time to time

**7.9.4** to produce to the Tenant on demand written confirmation from the insurers that they have agreed to waive all rights of subrogation against the Tenant any undertenant and any other lawful occupier and its or their mortgagees

**7.9.5** to use reasonable endeavours to ensure that the policy shall contain (without an additional premium being payable therefor) a provision to the effect that the policy cannot be made void or voidable by the Tenant or any undertenant or any other lawful occupier or its or their respective employees or agents so that no act or omission of the Tenant or any undertenant or any other lawful occupier or its or their respective employees or agents or anyone at or near the Premises with the express or implied permission of any of them could cause the policy to become void or voidable or render irrecoverable the whole or part of the insurance money

**7.9.6** not to do or permit to do anything that could cause the policy to become void or voidable whether wholly or in part

---

[1] See clause 7.6.1.
[2] *Portavon Cinema Co. Ltd v. Price and Century Insurance Co. Ltd* [1939] 4 All E.R. 601.
[3] *Mumford Hotels Ltd v. Wheler* [1964] Ch. 117.
[4] References in the text to a shopping centre obviously includes also a retail park.
[5] See *P & O Property Holdings Ltd v. International Computers Ltd* [1999] 18 E.G. 158.
[6] See clause 7.6.
[7] See clause 7.5.
[8] See *Adami v. Lincoln Grange Management Ltd* [1998] 17 E.G. 148.
[9] See *Mumford Hotels Ltd v. Wheler*, n. 3 above.
[10] [1985] Q.B. 755.
[11] [1963] Ch. 459.
[12] See clause 7.1.
[13] See *Halifax Building Society v. Keighley* [1931] 2 K.B. 248.
[14] [1986] Q.B. 211.

*Chapter 7*

# Guarantor's Covenants

## Introduction

**7.01** It is very difficult to muster a cogent argument against the landlord's request for guarantors either on the grant of a lease or on an assignment of the lease where a corporate tenant or corporate assignee has either recently been established or is a concern of limited substance. Where the tenant is an individual or individuals, a guarantor covenant should be resisted. Where the original tenant is not required to provide a guarantor but the alienation provisions permit the landlord to require a guarantor on an assignment if it is reasonable to do so, some landlords and tenants prefer the form of the guarantor's covenants not to be set out in the lease but to rely upon what is reasonable at the time of the assignment, presumably to ensure that the state of the art is employed. This could be dangerous from the tenant's point of view and it is far better to settle the form of the guarantor's covenants at the outset.

The position in respect of guarantors has been affected by the Landlord and Tenant (Covenants) Act 1995. Under that Act, any attempt to provide that a guarantor's liability to observe and perform the tenant covenants contained in a lease should outlast its principal will be void.[1] It is, however, advisable and safer to provide that the guarantor's liability should only last while the tenant is subject to the tenant covenants contained in the lease. There has been some debate as to whether a guarantor of a tenant's obligations in a lease can be required to enter into an authorised guarantee agreement. The 1995 Act does not make it clear as to whether this would be permissible, but the better view is that it would be. The tenant should therefore endeavour to rid the lease of such a provision against the landlord's argument, of course, that the outgoing tenant's covenant under an authorised guarantee agreement may be worthless, *e.g.* where a weak subsidiary company has been guaranteed by a parent company.

8 The guarantor's covenants

The Guarantor covenants with the person named in clause 1.1.1 and without the need for any express assignment with all [its] successors in title that:    7.02

8.1 To pay observe and perform

The Tenant shall during the period ("the Liability Period") when the Term shall be vested in the Tenant and until the Lease is assigned by the Tenant to a third party in accordance with the provisions of this Lease (or if such assignment is an excluded assignment within the meaning of section 11(1) of the 1995 Act until the next subsequent assignment which is not an excluded assignment as aforesaid) punctually pay the rents and observe and perform the covenants and other terms of this Lease and if the Tenant shall make any default in payment of the rents or in observing or performing any of the covenants or other terms of this Lease the Guarantor will pay the rents and observe or perform the covenants or terms in respect of which the Tenant shall be in default and make good to the Landlord on demand and indemnify the Landlord against all losses damages costs and expenses arising or incurred by the Landlord as a result of such non-payment non-performance or non-observance notwithstanding:    7.03

8.1.1 any time or indulgence granted by the Landlord to the Tenant or any neglect or forbearance of the Landlord in enforcing the payment of the rents or the observance or performance of the covenants or other terms of this Lease or any refusal by the Landlord to accept rents tendered by or on behalf of the Tenant at a time when the Landlord was entitled (or would after the service of a notice under the Law of Property Act 1925 section 146 have been entitled) to re-enter the Premises

8.1.2 that the terms of this Lease may have been varied by agreement between the parties [provided such variation is not prejudicial to the Guarantor]

8.1.3 that the Tenant shall have surrendered part of the Premises in which event the liability of the Guarantor under this Lease shall continue in respect of the part of the Premises not so surrendered after making any necessary apportionments under the Law of Property Act 1925 section 140 and

## 142  Guarantor's Covenants

**8.1.4  any other act or thing by which but for this provision the Guarantor would have been released [other than a variation of the terms of this Lease agreed between the parties that is prejudicial to the Guarantor]**

Until the case of *P & A Swift Investments v. Combined English Stores Group plc*[2] it was believed that the benefit of a guarantor's covenants could only be enforced by a successor in title to the landlord's reversion, where there had been an express assignment to it. This case now establishes that such covenants will run with the land and that it is only necessary for the lease to provide that the expression "the landlord" includes its successors in title.

Clause 8.1 provides that the guarantor is not released until the tenant is released pursuant to the provisions of the Landlord and Tenant (Covenants) Act 1995. See the comment under clause 3.8 with regard to the landlord providing that the "term" includes a statutory continuation of the tenancy to ensure that there is no limitation on the guarantee's liability. Clause 8.1.1 is so worded to circumvent the problem by which any time given by a creditor to a debtor could have the effect of releasing the guarantor from its obligations. The latter part of this clause is inserted to try to avoid the difficulty that could arise where a landlord declines to accept rent in order not to waive a breach of covenant by the tenant, which it has been suggested could have a similar effect of releasing the guarantor, but this is not certain.

The optional words in brackets in clause 8.1.2 should be included for obvious reasons, and it is suggested that if those words were included then so should the words at the end of clause 8.1.4 so as to avoid a conflict. The point is that any variation, other than where clearly immaterial, in the obligations of the landlord and tenant will be sufficient to release the guarantor, except where the lease contains a suitably worded exclusion provision.[3] It would, of course, be unreasonable to expect a guarantor to remain liable if there has been a material variation prejudicial to the guarantor. Clause 8.1.3 is included as otherwise the guarantor would be released where the tenant surrenders part of the premises.[4]

**8.2  To take Lease following disclaimer**

**7.04**  If at any time during the Liability Period the Tenant (being an individual) shall become bankrupt or (being a company) shall enter into liquidation and the trustee in bankruptcy or liquidator shall disclaim this Lease the Guarantor shall if the Landlord shall by notice within [60] days after such disclaimer so require take from the Landlord a lease of the Premises for the residue of the Contractual Term which would have remained had there been no disclaimer at the Rent then being paid under this Lease and subject to the same covenants and terms as in this Lease (except that the Guarantor shall not be required to procure that any other person is made a party to that lease as guarantor) such new lease to take effect from the date of such disclaimer and in such case the Guarantor shall pay the costs of such new lease and execute and deliver to the Landlord a counterpart of it

Prior to the case of *Hindcastle Ltd v. Barbara Attenborough Associates Ltd*,[5] on the disclaimer of a lease a guarantor of an insolvent tenant, or indeed a guarantor of a previous tenant who would have been liable under guarantee covenants given to the landlord had it not become insolvent, would automatically be released from its guarantee covenants given to the landlord.[6] The *Hindcastle* case has overruled *Stacey v. Hill* to the effect that on a disclaimer the insolvent's liabilities under a lease will cease but the rights or liabilities of other persons will not and these will include the liabilities of a guarantor under guarantee covenants given to the landlord.

It should, of course, be noted that the *Hindcastle* case was in respect of a pre-1995 Act lease and therefore also involves the preservation of rights of action against former tenants because of the continuation of liabilities referred to above. The liability of these persons under a "new" lease may have been affected by the 1995 Act, but the liability of a previous tenant may be that of guarantor under an authorised guarantee agreement and, as such, this liability will continue because of the preservation of rights on the disclaimer of a lease.

The tenant should ensure that the landlord is not given too long to make up its mind and the period of 60 days suggested by the precedent seems fair to both sides. The tenant should also ensure that this covenant contains a provision that the lease being granted to the guarantor does not itself provide for a new guarantor to be joined.

A minor point, but the words

**to commence on**

may be preferred to

**to take effect from**

in line 13 of clause 8.2.

### 8.3 To make payments following disclaimer

**7.05** If this Lease shall be disclaimed and for any reason the Landlord does not require the Guarantor to accept a new lease of the Premises in accordance with clause 8.2 the Guarantor shall pay to the Landlord on demand an amount equal to [the difference between any money received by the Landlord for the use or occupation of the Premises and] the rents [in both cases] for the period commencing with the date of such disclaimer and ending on whichever is the earlier of the following dates:

**8.3.1** the date [six] months after such disclaimer and
**8.3.2** the date (if any) on which the Premises are relet

This provision is frequently included in guarantors' covenants, probably to cover the position where the landlord has no objection to taking back the premises with a view to a future letting, but in the meantime to secure some form of rental income. The tenant should ensure that a reasonable cut-off date is inserted and the tenant could try to reduce the suggested six months period to three months.

The tenant should also include the following additional clause:

**8.3.3 the date of expiration of the Contractual Term**

remembering of course, to change "earlier" in line nine of clause 8.3 to "earliest" and to add "and" at the end of clause 8.3.2 and to delete "and" at the end of clause 8.3.1.

Some precedents also provide for the tenant to assign the unexpired residue of the term to the guarantor where the guarantor has been required to make any payment under the guarantor's covenants. It is for the tenant to decide whether it would wish such a provision to be included, possibly after discussion with its guarantor, and if so, the landlord's consent would also be required.

---

[1] See ss. 24(2) and 25(1) of the Landlord and Tenant (Covenants) Act 1995.
[2] [1988] 3 W.L.R. 313.
[3] See *Holme v. Brunskill* (1877) 3 Q.B.D. 495; *Howard de Walden Estates Ltd v. Pasta Place Ltd* [1995] 22 E.G. 143 and *West Hornden Industrial Park v. Phoenix Timber* [1995] N.P.C. 42.
[4] *Holme v. Brunskill* (above) on the basis that the guarantor's rights of subrogation would be adversely affected.
[5] [1996] 2 W.L.R. 262; [1996] 1 All E.R. 737.
[6] *Stacey v. Hill* [1901] 1 K.B. 660.

*Chapter 8*

# Provisos

## Introduction

The provisos set out in a lease cover a range of miscellaneous matters which can have an important bearing on the lease. **8.01**

## 9 Provisos

### 9.1 Re-entry

If and whenever during the Term: **8.02**

**9.1.1** the rents (or any of them or any part of them) under this Lease are outstanding for [14 days] after becoming due whether formally demanded or not

**9.1.2** there is a breach by the Tenant [or the Guarantor] of any covenant or other term of this Lease or any document [expressed to be] supplemental to this Lease or

**9.1.3** an individual Tenant becomes bankrupt or

**9.1.4** a company Tenant [or the Guarantor]:

**9.1.4.1** enters into liquidation whether compulsory or voluntary (but not if the liquidation is for amalgamation or reconstruction of a solvent company) or

**9.1.4.2** has a receiver appointed or

**9.1.5** the Tenant enters into an arrangement for the benefit of [its] creditors or

**9.1.6** the Tenant has any distress or execution levied on [its] goods

the Landlord may re-enter the Premises (or any part of them in the name of the whole) at any time (and even if any previous right of re-entry has been waived) and then the Term will absolutely cease but without prejudice to any rights or remedies which may have accrued to the Landlord against the Tenant or the Guarantor [or to the Tenant

**against the Landlord] in respect of any breach of covenant or other term of this Lease (including the breach in respect of which the re-entry is made)**

All leases will, or should, contain a forfeiture provision which is usually in the form of a proviso reserving to the landlord a right of re-entry in the event of non-payment of rent, breach of covenant or circumstances resulting in, or likely to give rise to, the probability of the tenant being unable to perform its obligations under the lease, *e.g.* bankruptcy or liquidation. Given the generous relief against forfeiture provisions contained in section 146 of the Law of Property Act 1925, a tenant should have little to fear from a forfeiture clause unless it is seriously in financial difficulties or has committed a serious breach of covenant which cannot be rectified.

Some re-entry provisions extend the events that could lead to a landlord's right of re-entry and there are arguments that, if possible, these should be resisted, though the landlord would doubtless disagree, *e.g.* appointment of an interim receiver (in the case of an individual tenant) and the making of an administration order (in the case of a corporate tenant). Some amendments to the standard provision are advisable, however, and may be summarised as follows:

(1) The reference to "rents" in clause 9.1.1 should be amended to be a reference to the "Rent", *i.e.* the principal rent, to accord with the definition contained in clause 2.16. It would be inadvisable, as far as the tenant is concerned, for the forfeiture provisions to be brought into effect where any of the additional rents, *e.g.* the insurance rent or the service charge, have not been paid by the tenant, as there may be a legitimate reason why the tenant has not paid these. By including the additional rents in the forfeiture provisions, the landlord is able to exert pressure on the tenant to pay disputed sums, which the tenant may consider unreasonable.

(2) The period of grace before the forfeiture provision bites in respect of outstanding rents should be no less than 14 days and ideally 28, though the usual compromise is 21 days.

(3) Frequently reference is made (as in the precedent) to forfeiture being available on the breach of a covenant by the guarantor or on the bankruptcy of the guarantor. This should be resisted. In the latter case, if there is a provision for the tenant to provide a substitute guarantor on the bankruptcy or liquidation of the original guarantor,[1] the landlord should not be too disadvantaged and it would seem reasonable to resist the stringent forfeiture provision. One would hope that a landlord would not commence forfeiture

proceedings where a guarantor becomes bankrupt, enters into liquidation, etc., where the tenant remains financially sound, but stranger things have happened! It is therefore far safer to delete such references to the guarantor.

(4) The tenant should try to insert reference to the tenant being construed to be:

**the tenant for the time being**

or better still:

**while this Lease shall be vested in the Tenant**

This is to obviate the remote possibility of an argument as to whether the bankruptcy or liquidation of the original tenant (after an assignment) who will presumably still be within the definition of "the Tenant" could affect the re-entry provisions contained in the lease. This is quite academic and, in any event, relief against forfeiture would almost definitely be granted, but many old tried and tested precedents provided for this eventuality and there is no harm in a belt and braces approach.

(5) It may be advisable to amend clause 9.1.2 as follows:

**. . . supplemental to the Lease and which is not remedied within a reasonable period after the Tenant has been given notice thereof by the Landlord or**

although this may possibly be opposed by the landlord.

(6) Many tenants object to forfeiture provisions applying where distress or execution has been levied on its goods at the premises, as even in the best run organisations this sometimes occurs and it is not always an indication that the tenant is in financial difficulty.[2] It is therefore advisable to delete clause 9.1.6, or if that fails, at least ensure that it is amended to refer to the distress or execution being levied

**at the Premises**

and where the reason for the distress or execution is not satisfied within [14] days.

(7) Consider adding the following two provisos:

**PROVIDED HOWEVER that in the event that this Lease is mortgaged at the time of the proposed re-entry and the Landlord has been given notice of the existence of the mortgage then prior to such re-entry or proceedings therefor the**

Landlord will serve a notice of such proceedings and proposed re-entry on the mortgagee at the mortgagee's last known address

AND PROVIDED FURTHER that if the Tenant (being an individual) becomes bankrupt or (being a company) enters into liquidation (whether compulsory or voluntary save for the purposes of amalgamation or reconstruction of a solvent company) or has a receiver appointed the Landlord shall not exercise the right of re-entry by virtue of such bankruptcy liquidation or receivership unless neither the Tenant nor its mortgagee shall pay the Rent hereinbefore reserved on the days and in the manner provided or there shall be any breach or non-performance or non-observance of any of the other covenants or agreements on the part of the Tenant herein contained

### 9.2 Party walls

**8.03** The internal non-load bearing walls that divide the Premises from the adjoining units in the Centre and from the Retained Parts shall be deemed to be party walls within the meaning of the Law of Property Act 1925 section 38 and shall be maintained at the equally shared expense of the Tenant and the other respective estate owners

As the footnote to the precedent states, the object of this provision is that the tenant and the adjoining estate owner (who could be either another tenant or even the landlord) will share the responsibility for the internal divisional walls. If the landlord prefers to covenant to maintain the outer half of all internal non-load bearing walls dividing the premises from other parts of the building and recovering the cost via the service charge, the tenant should ensure that any sums collected by the landlord from other tenants under the terms of their leases to maintain their half of the divisional wall should be deducted from the service charge.

### 9.3 Covenants relating to adjoining Premises

**8.04** Nothing contained in or implied by this Lease shall give the Tenant the benefit of or the right to enforce or to prevent the release or modification of any covenant agreement or condition entered into by any tenant of the Landlord in respect of any property not comprised in this Lease

Tenants have very limited rights to enforce covenants against each other. The general rule is that one tenant cannot enforce covenants contained in another tenant's lease, but there are a number of exceptions, being mainly as follows:

(1) where a tenant has taken an assignment from the landlord of the benefit of a covenant entered into by a tenant of other premises;
(2) where various tenants or their predecessors in title have entered into a mutual deed of covenant (in which case each can enforce the covenants against the others);
(3) where the estate has been laid out under a common scheme for building (known as a building scheme) and the leases have been taken pursuant to that scheme;
(4) where there is a letting scheme, which is similar to a building scheme, but there need be no physical laying out of the estate.

Most leases of commercial centres do not fall within the above categories but if the lease in question does, then it may be advisable to delete the words "to enforce or" from line two of the proviso. In fact, it may be as well to include the following proviso:

> **provided the Premises are not adversely affected thereby**

### 9.4 Disputes with adjoining occupiers

> **If any dispute arises between the Tenant and the tenants or occupiers of other parts of the Centre or the Adjoining Property as to any easement right or privilege in connection with the use of the Premises and any other part of the Centre or the Adjoining Property or as to the boundary structures separating the Premises from any other property it shall be decided [by the Landlord or in such manner as the Landlord shall direct *or* by the Surveyor acting as an expert and not as an arbitrator]**

**8.05**

The problem with this provision is that it restricts the tenant in any action it may wish to take against other tenants, and could result in a dispute being settled against its best interests. Also, it will only bind the other party to the dispute if a similar provision is contained in that tenant's lease. It may therefore be advisable to delete this proviso, but it is not disastrous if it remains. The optional reference to "the Surveyor" acting as an expert is preferable to "the Landlord", unless, of course, the landlord will agree that the reference should be to an independent surveyor.

### 9.5 Effect of waiver

**8.06** Each of the Tenant's covenants shall remain in full force both at law and in equity notwithstanding that the Landlord shall have waived or released temporarily any such covenant or waived or released temporarily or permanently revocably or irrevocably a similar covenant or similar covenants affecting any other part of the Centre or the Adjoining Property

This provision is an attempt to circumvent the rather harsh law of waiver, by which a landlord will lose its right to forfeit the lease where a non-continuing breach has occurred if the landlord does some act to suggest that the landlord is nevertheless satisfied to continue the tenancy, *e.g.* by accepting rent from the tenant.[3]

Some leases contain rather more elaborate provisos such as: "no demand for or acceptance of rent by the landlord or its agents with knowledge of a breach of any of the covenants on the part of the tenant contained in these presents shall be or be deemed to be a waiver wholly or partially of any such breach but such breach shall be deemed to be a continuing breach of covenant". It has been suggested that such provisos are not effective in protecting a landlord from the severity of the law and cannot be set up as a defence to the claim that by accepting rent the breach of covenant has been waived.[4]

The first part of the provision may not therefore be wholly effective in any event and the question is whether the tenant is prepared to accept it in return for a concession from the landlord elsewhere in the lease. The second part of the provision is not unreasonable.

### 9.6 Rights easements, etc.

**8.07** The [operation of the Law of Property Act 1925 section 62 shall be excluded from this Lease and the only rights granted to the Tenant are those expressly set out in this Lease [and such further ancillary rights that arise under the general law or by necessary implication] and the Tenant shall not by virtue of this Lease be deemed to have acquired or be entitled to and the] Tenant shall not during the Term acquire or become entitled by any means whatever to any easement from or over or affecting any other land or premises now or at any time after the date of this Lease belonging to the Landlord and not comprised in this Lease

Section 62 of the Law of Property Act 1925 provides that a lease is deemed to include, in the absence of any contrary intention, all easements, rights and advantages appertaining or reputed to appertain to the premises at the time of the lease. This could have severe repercussions for the landlord in that it could include easements over the adjoining retained land of the landlord, adversely affecting the landlord's ability to use or develop that land. It is also dangerous for a tenant to rely on the provisions of section 62 as the section does not, for example, apply to services and, additionally, as the section takes effect from the date of the demise, it may not be easy to adduce evidence 15 years after the grant that the right complained of was used by the occupants when the lease was granted. It is therefore sensible to set out fully in the lease, for the purpose of clarification, the rights to be granted in order to try to avoid subsequent disputes.

The words

> **and such further ancillary rights that arise under the general law or by necessary implication**

should be included and could be expanded to include ancillary rights that arise

> **by necessity**

## 9.7 Accidents

> **The Landlord shall not be responsible to the Tenant or to anyone at the Premises or the Centre expressly or by implication with the Tenant's authority for any accident happening or injury suffered or for any damage to or loss of any chattel sustained in the Premises or the Centre**

**8.08**

There is a question mark attached to the effectiveness of this provision on the basis that a party cannot exclude its liability for death or personal injuries caused by its negligence. It may be extremely difficult for the landlord to resist a claim by a person at the premises who suffers injury as a result of the landlord's default and who was not a party to the lease. Nevertheless, if the provision is to remain, the following proviso should be added:

> **except where such injury damage or loss is caused as a result of negligence on the part of the Landlord or anyone acting on behalf of the Landlord or as a result of a breach of any of the Landlord's covenants herein contained**

## 9.8 Perpetuity period

> **The perpetuity period applicable to this Lease shall be [80] years from the commencement of the Contractual Term and**

**8.09**

> whenever in this Lease either party is granted a future interest in property there shall be deemed to be included in respect of every such grant a provision requiring that future interest to vest within the stated period and for it to be void for remoteness if it shall not have so vested

Despite the importance of the rule against perpetuities, it is surprising that most leases granted today make no mention of it. Without becoming too detailed, the rule can result in the grant of future interests being void where they do not vest within 21 years from the date of the grant of the lease.[5] For instance, the right reserved under paragraph 1 of the third schedule to this lease refers to "Pipes which *may during* the Term be . . . under . . . the Premises". Without a specific perpetuity period of at least the length of the term (if the term exceeds 21 years) plus a few additional years to cover holding over under the 1954 Act, there would be no right to use pipes placed under the premises during the twenty-third year of the term. The same point applies, of course, to rights granted to the tenant.

The specified period of 80 years is the period referred to in the Perpetuities and Accumulations Act 1964, but there is no reason why the period cannot be less, *e.g.* 30 years for a 25-year term.

### 9.9 Exclusion of use warranty

**8.10** > Nothing in this Lease or in any consent granted by the Landlord under this Lease shall imply or warrant that the Premises may lawfully be used under the Planning Acts for the purpose authorised in this Lease (or any purpose subsequently authorised)

It is for the tenant to ensure that there is a lawful planning permission in existence consenting to the use for which the tenant proposes to put the premises. There is in fact no implied covenant or warranty on the part of the landlord in this regard. It should also be noted that there is no covenant or warranty implied that the premises are legally fit for the purpose for which the tenant intends using them and it is for the tenant to satisfy itself on this point. In the case of an underlease the undertenant should always require sight of the superior lease or leases to satisfy itself that there are no restrictions likely to affect the undertenant's proposed use of the premises.[6]

The tenant may consider adding the following words at the end of this proviso:

> provided that the Landlord shall not do or permit to do anything that could result in the Permitted User becoming an

unlawful lawful or unauthorised use under the Planning Acts.

**9.10 Entire understanding**

This Lease embodies the entire understanding of the parties relating to the Premises and to all the matters dealt with by any of the provisions of this Lease    8.11

This provision has merit from both parties' points of view. It is perhaps a reminder to the parties' advisers to encourage the parties to have one final read through the engrossments before execution.

**9.11 Representations**

The Tenant acknowledges that this Lease has not been entered into in reliance wholly or partly on any statement or representation made by or on behalf of the Landlord except any such statement or representation that is expressly set out in this Lease [or was made in writing by the Landlord's solicitors to the Tenant's solicitors in reply to an enquiry made in writing by the Tenant's solicitors in connection with the grant of this Lease]    8.12

This is self-explanatory, but see the comments on misrepresentation under clause 11 of the agreement for lease. The words in square brackets are not often included in the actual lease and are more usually in the agreement for lease. The same comments apply as under clause 11 of the agreement for lease in respect of replies to the tenant's solicitors' written enquiries.

**9.12 Licences, etc., under hand**

Whilst the Landlord is a limited company or other corporation all licences consents approvals and notices required to be given by the Landlord shall be sufficiently given if given under the hand of a director the secretary or other duly authorised officer of the Landlord [or the Surveyor on behalf of the Landlord]    8.13

Without this provision, the effectiveness of licences and consents granted by the landlord during the term and not executed by the company could be in doubt. It may, however, be that even without this provision, a landlord who had granted a licence to a tenant signed by an authorised director could expect to be estopped from denying its effectiveness.

**9.13 Tenant's property**

**8.14** If after the Tenant has vacated the Premises on the expiry of the Term any property of the Tenant remains in or on the Premises and the Tenant fails to remove it within [seven] days after being requested in writing by the Landlord to do so or if after using [its] best endeavours the Landlord is unable to make such a request to the Tenant within [fourteen] days from the first attempt so made by the Landlord:

9.13.1 the Landlord may as the agent of the Tenant sell such property and the Tenant will indemnify the Landlord against any liability incurred by [it] to any third party whose property shall have been sold by the Landlord in the mistaken belief held in good faith (which shall be presumed unless the contrary be proved) that such property belonged to the Tenant

9.13.2 if the Landlord having made reasonable efforts is unable to locate the Tenant the Landlord shall be entitled to retain such proceeds of sale absolutely unless the Tenant shall claim them within [six] months of the date upon which the Tenant vacated the Premises and

9.13.3 the Tenant shall indemnify the Landlord against any damage occasioned to the Premises and any actions claims proceedings costs expenses and demands made against the Landlord caused by or related to the presence of the property in or on the Premises

This provision has become rather popular of late and it is difficult to argue against its inclusion. Quite clearly, if a tenant vacates premises and decides to leave all manner of items behind, thereby inhibiting the landlord from reletting the premises, the tenant can hardly complain if the landlord sells the discarded property. Furthermore, a landlord cannot be expected to spend years chasing after a tenant in order to avail the tenant of the proceeds of sale. The retention of such money by the landlord after a reasonable period of time is not unfair. It is more a case of striking a fair balance between the landlord and the tenant. The periods of 7 and 14 days should certainly be amended to 14 and 28 days respectively, and the tenant should at least amend clause 9.13.3 by the removal of the words "any damage occasioned to the Premises and" from lines one and two.

**9.14 Compensation on vacating**

**8.15** Any statutory right of the Tenant to claim compensation from the Landlord on vacating the Premises shall be excluded to the extent that the law allows

Basically, the landlord can deny the tenant statutory compensation[7] if there has been a change of ownership during the last five years of the term prior to its expiration and the assignee is not a successor to the business of the assignor. This is quite unreasonable and should be resisted as it could affect the marketability of the lease in the last five years of the term, which the tenant may find unacceptable despite the fact that its inclusion could result in a small reduction in rent on review if the tenant is successful in arguing the point.

### 9.15  Service of notices

> **The provisions of the Law of Property Act 1925 section 196 as amended by the Recorded Delivery Service Act 1962 shall apply to the giving and service of all notices and documents under or in connection with this Lease except that section 196 shall be deemed to be amended as follows:** **8.16**
>
> 9.15.1  **the final words of section 196(4) . . . "and that service . . . be delivered" shall be deleted and there shall be substituted ". . . and that service shall be deemed to be made on the [third] Working Day after the registered letter has been posted". "Working Day" means any day from Monday to Friday (inclusive) other than Christmas Day Good Friday and any statutory bank or public holiday**
>
> 9.15.2  **any notice or document shall also be sufficiently served on a party if served on solicitors who have acted for that party in relation to this Lease or the Premises at any time within the year preceding the service of the notice or document**
>
> 9.15.3  **any notice or document shall also be sufficiently served if sent by telex [telephonic facsimile transmission or any other means of electronic transmission] to the party to be served (or its solicitors where 9.15.2 applies) and that service shall be deemed to be made on the day of transmission if transmitted before 4 p.m. on a Working Day but otherwise on the next following Working Day (as defined above)**
> **and in this clause "party" includes the Guarantor**

These provisions are designed to introduce certainty to the service of notices and documents and, unless a particular tenant takes exception to any aspect, they do not seem unreasonable. Many large corporate tenants, however, prefer notices to be served at their registered office and not at individual units. This is to avoid the possibility of an important notice not being considered important by a local shop manager. In such circumstances, therefore, it may be prudent to include the following additional proviso:

> **PROVIDED THAT while this Lease is vested in _____ (Tenant's name) any notice or document to be served on the Tenant shall be served at its registered office and not at the Premises**

The tenant may object to the amendments suggested to be made to s 196 and wish to amend or delete them. Clause 9.15.2 may in particular be objected to, and so may clause 9.15.3 for that matter.

It should be noted that in the case of *Claire's Accessories UK Ltd v. Kensington High Street Associates LLC*[8] the court held that a proviso that notices should be served at a company's registered office was mandatory. Although not included in the precedent, the following provisos are also frequently included:

### 9.16 Developing neighbouring property

**8.17** Landlords frequently include a proviso stating that nothing contained in the lease shall prevent them from altering, adding to, refurbishing and generally executing works to neighbouring property.

Any deletion of this provision will normally be resisted vehemently by a landlord, particularly in a shopping centre, as it will not wish to have any infringement that may interfere with its development of neighbouring property. The proviso set out below may be a fair compromise to be added to such a provision:

> **PROVIDED THAT in so doing the Landlord shall cause as little inconvenience or disturbance to the Tenant or any undertenant or other lawful occupier of the Premises as is reasonably practicable in the circumstances and shall not prohibit or unreasonably interfere with or prevent the use of the Premises for the Permitted User**

In addition it may be as well for the tenant to stipulate in such a provision that any development of neighbouring or adjoining premises should not include the building of which the premises form part, unless, of course, adequate safeguards are included to ensure that the premises do not suffer as a result.

### 9.17 Frustration of reinstatement

**8.18** Landlords sometimes include a proviso that the landlord should have the right to terminate the lease in the event of reinstatement being frustrated or delayed as a result of circumstances beyond the landlord's control. This should ideally be dealt with under the insurance provisions,[9] but should it appear in the provisos, the tenant should ensure that it is a bilateral right and that in any event the landlord should not be permitted to terminate the lease until it has taken all reasonable measures to procure the rebuilding or reinstatement of the centre or the part so destroyed or damaged (as appropriate).

### 9.18 Value Added Tax

There will most likely be a proviso contained in the lease to the effect that any sums specified in the lease are exclusive of VAT and that any obligation of the tenant in the lease to make any payment to the landlord shall include an obligation to pay, in addition, any VAT that may be chargeable. There is a great temptation to delete such a provision, but this would not find favour with the landlord and is therefore not worthwhile. The present unsatisfactory state of the law relating to VAT could mean that VAT paid by the tenant may not be recoverable, and therefore the tenant should consider amending such a provision to provide that it will only pay VAT on such sums where it is first presented with a valid VAT invoice in the tenant's name or at least that a VAT invoice in the tenant's name will be given to the tenant shortly after payment.

**8.19**

### 9.19 Rights of light

There may be a proviso to the effect that the tenant cannot complain if its light is subsequently affected by any building works being carried out by the landlord to neighbouring property. The very least that the tenant should tolerate is a proviso that the light to the premises should not be "materially" affected by any such works.

**8.20**

### 9.20 Limitations on liability

It may be worthwhile to include the following additional proviso:

**8.21**

> **On an assignment of this Lease in pursuance of the Landlord's licence authorising the assignment the Landlord shall forthwith release the assignor from its future liability under this Lease**

Although the Landlord and Tenant (Covenants) Act 1995 has now been added to the statute book, it may still be preferable for the tenant (*i.e.* the assignor) to obtain a specific release of its future liability under the lease than to rely on the Act, in order to avoid the guarantee obligations contained in the Act.

### 9.21 Provisions relating to entry

**8.22** Almost all modern commercial leases contain provisions for the landlord and other persons to enter the premises for various reasons. Such entry could be extremely disruptive to the tenant and the following proviso may be advisable:

> **Anyone entering the Premises under any of the provisions contained in this Lease shall only do so if the purpose of such entry cannot reasonably be achieved otherwise than by effecting entry on to the Premises and any person or persons entering the Premises pursuant to the provisions of this Lease shall cause the minimum of disturbance to the business being carried on in the Premises and shall forthwith make good all loss or damage caused by such entry and shall not in any event prevent the Tenant or any undertenant or other lawful occupier from carrying on its or their business at the Premises (provided that if the Tenant or any undertenant or other lawful occupier shall be prevented from carrying on business at the Premises the rents payable hereunder shall cease to be payable until the Tenant or such undertenant or other lawful occupier shall be able to recommence its or their business) and in the carrying out of any works to adjoining or neighbouring premises or any other property by or with the authority of the Landlord there shall not be erected any scaffolding or any other structures within the Premises or in front of or to the rear or sides (if applicable) of the Premises in such a position so as to obstruct the windows of the Premises or so as to prevent or interfere with access to the Premises by customers or other persons entering the Premises or in connection with the servicing of the same**

### 9.22 Environment

**8.23** In addition to the suggested landlord's covenant set out in clause 6, the tenant should also consider inserting the undermentioned proviso to deal with the suspension of rents if the premises become unusable as a result of the land on which they (or other parts of the development) have been constructed containing toxic materials:

> **If the Premises or any part thereof or the means of access thereto or any essential services therein or thereto become unfit for occupation or use as a result of the Centre or any**

part thereof having been constructed on land containing toxic waste or any other contaminated or deleterious materials or substances the rents shall be suspended from the date when the Premises and/or the means of access thereto and/or the essential services therein or thereto become unfit for occupation or use until the date when the Premises and/or the means of access thereto and/or the essential services therein or thereto (as the case may be) are once again rendered fit for occupation and use and a due proportion of such rents paid in advance shall forthwith be refunded to the Tenant PROVIDED THAT if the Premises and/or the means of access thereto and/or the essential services therein or thereto (as the case may be) shall not have been so rendered fit for occupation and use within two years from the date when they became unfit for occupation and use the Tenant may at any time thereafter give written notice to the Landlord to determine the Term wherepon the Term will forthwith cease but without prejudice to the claim of either party for any earlier breach of covenant by the other AND PROVIDED FURTHER THAT no such notice shall be served by the Tenant following the date when the Premises and/or the means of access thereto and/or the essential services therein or thereto (as the case may be) are rendered fit for occupation and use

## 9.23 Break Clause

The tenant may have negotiated, as part of the heads of terms, an option to determine the lease on perhaps the fifth or tenth anniversary (or both) of the commencement of the lease term. The "break" clause, as drafted by the landlord's solicitors, may read as follows:

**8.24**

> **If the Tenant wishes to determine this Lease [on [the . . . day of . . . *or* the expiry of the . . . year of the Term. [*or* Contractual Term (*as the case may be*)] ] ] and shall give to the Landlord not less than . . . months' notice in writing and shall up to the time of such determination pay the rents reserved by and perform and observe the covenants contained in this Lease and shall on the date of such determination give vacant possession of the Premises then upon the expiry of such notice the Term [*or* Contractual Term] shall immediately cease and determine but without prejudice to the respective rights of either party in respect of any antecedent claim or breach of covenant**

The problems stemming from the drafting and interpretation of break clauses could easily warrant a chapter, or indeed a whole book, but, as that is not possible, the following points may perhaps be helpful:

(1) It is probably better, if possible, to stipulate an actual break date rather than to refer to "the fifth anniversary of the commencement of the term", or similar provisions. Certainty is vital in respect of break clauses and the tenant can perhaps consider itself fortunate in the case of *Mannai Investment Co Ltd v. Eagle Star Life Assurance Co. Ltd.*[10]

(2) The tenant must avoid the inclusion of any pre-conditions. They can, and will, trip up even the most assiduous tenant, as the courts will strictly enforce them. The reference to the "rents" would include (in this lease) the yearly rent, the insurance rent and the service charge. The tenant could be in dispute with regard to the insurance rent and the service charge, and even if the rent pre-condition relates only to the yearly rent, a technical problem could result in its non-payment. Similarly, the tenant will almost invariably be in breach of at least one of the tenant's covenants, *e.g.* in *Osbourne Assets Ltd v. Britannia Life Ltd*,[11] where the tenant's break notice failed as it had redecorated using two rather than three coats of paint, as stipulated in the lease. The tenant should not rely on the landlord's suggested "watering down" of the provision to there being no "material" breaches of covenant. What may not be material to one landlord may be extremely material to another, despite the attempt by the court in *Commercial Union Life Assurance Co Ltd v. Label Ink Ltd* (July24, 2000, unreported) to lay down some useful guidelines. Even a reference to the tenant giving up vacant possession can be dangerous, *e.g.* if the tenant leaves behind fixtures and fittings. It is therefore strongly recommended that the tenant should accept no pre-conditions in any shape, manner or form.

(3) A frequently overlooked principle is that rent is not apportionable once it has accrued due and, therefore, if a break date falls between two rent payment dates the tenant will not, in the absence of specific wording, be entitled to a refund of rent from the break date to the expiration of the rent payment period in question.

(4) The landlord and tenant must consider whether the break clause is to form part of the hypothetical lease on rent reviews under the lease and, indeed, at which date the break clause is to be deemed to be operable.

The break clause may therefore be amended to read as follows:

> **If the Tenant wishes to determine this Lease on [the . . . day of . . . ] and shall give to the Landlord not less than . . .**

months' notice in writing then upon the expiry of such notice the Term (*or* Contractual Term] shall immediately cease and determine but without prejudice to the respective rights of either party in respect of any antecedent claim or breach of covenant [and the Landlord shall on such determination repay to the Tenant any part of the [rents] paid in advance by the Tenant in respect of the period from the date of such determination to [the day before the next payment date of such [rents]]

Depending on the identity of the "rents", it would be preferable for the tenant to be more specific as regards dates, *e.g.* "to the day before the next quarter day" in respect of the yearly rent.

### 9.24 Agreement for Lease

Sometimes the lease may contain a provision that the lease is granted pursuant to an agreement for lease, *e.g.*:

> This Lease is granted pursuant to an Agreement for Lease dated [ ]

There is no objection to this.[12]

### 9.25 New tenancy

Some leases contain a proviso indicating whether or not the lease is a new lease for the purposes of the Landlord and Tenant (Covenants) Act 1995, *e.g.*

> This Lease is a new tenancy for the purposes of the 1995 Act section 1

### 9.26 Contracts (Rights of Third Parties) Act 1999

Section 1 of the Contracts (Rights of Third Parties) Act 1999 enables a third party to enforce a term of a contract (which will include a lease and documents entered into pursuant to a lease) even though it was not a party to the contract if the contract so provides, or where the contract purports to confer a benefit on him. This will be the position unless the parties decide specifically to exclude the Act from the contract in question. It comes as no great surprise that most landlords prefer to exclude the provisions of the Act from leases, licences and other similar documentation, usually by including a provision along the following lines:

Unless it is expressly stated that the Contracts (Rights of Third Parties) Act 1999 is to apply nothing in this Lease will create rights in favour of anyone other than the parties to this Lease

### 9.27 Certificate of value

A certificate of value may be appropriate where the tenant is paying a capital sum to the landlord for the grant of the lease, but quite rare in the author's view for commercial leases at a full rack rent.

---

[1] See clause 5.23 of the precedent.
[2] The Lord Chancellor's Department has published a consultation paper on the law of distress for rent, which suggests various options ranging from complete abolition to compromise proposals. The view has also been expressed that, without modification, the present law relating to distress may not withstand challenge under the Human Rights Act 1998.
[3] Although in *Legal and General Assurance Society Ltd v. General Metal Agencies Ltd* (1969) 113 S.J. 876 it was held that a mechanical acceptance of rent by a computer was not a waiver.
[4] *Davenport v. R.* (1877) 3 App. Cas. 115.
[5] See the Perpetuities and Accumulations Act 1964.
[6] In *Hill v. Harris* [1965] 2 Q.B. 601, an undertenant was prevented from using premises for its proposed use as a result of a restriction contained in the headlease. It was held that despite the landlord knowing of the undertenant's proposed use, the landlord was not liable in damages as no express warranty had been given.
[7] The statutory compensation currently payable is equal to the rateable value of the premises, or twice the rateable value where either the current tenant has occupied the premises for the purposes of its business for the whole of the 14-year period immediately prior to the termination date originally specified in the lease, or if the current tenant is a successor to a business which has been carried on at the premises for that period.
[8] February 23, 2001, unreported.
[9] See comments under clause 7.6.
[10] [1997] E.G.L.R. 57, in which the tenant's break notice expired on the last day of the third year of the term, whereas the lease provided that it should expire on the third anniversary of the term. The notice was saved by the House of Lords under the principle of the "reasonable recipient" by which any obvious error should be appreciated by a reasonable recipient of a break notice. This is, however, far too tenuous a principle for a tenant to rely upon in respect of notices and absolute care is vital.
[11] 1997, unreported.
[12] See also Chapter 9. The suggested certificate could be inserted under this heading.

*Chapter 9*

# Execution of Deeds

At the end of the body of the lease prior to the schedules there will be what is known as the testimonium and, while there is in law no necessity for a testimonium, one is almost invariably included. **9.01**

The old form of the testimonium was usually as follows:

> **IN WITNESS whereof the parties hereto have caused their common seals (for corporations) to be hereunto affixed the day and year first before written**

or

> **IN WITNESS whereof the parties hereto have hereunto placed their hands and seals (for individuals) the day and year first before written**

Section 1 of the Law of Property (Miscellaneous Provisions) Act 1989 coupled with section 36A of the Companies Act 1985 have introduced changes to the execution of deeds by providing that a document shall not be a deed unless it is clear on its face that it is intended to be a deed. Furthermore, deeds made by individuals need no longer be sealed, although they may seal them if they wish to do so, and deeds made by a company need only be signed by a director and the company secretary (or by two directors) and, provided that the deed is expressed to be executed by the company, it has the same effect as if it was executed under the company's seal. Unfortunately, problems still remain with regard to delivery and it seems that in the case of an individual, delivery will still be necessary as the old law still applies, with the result that a document will be treated as delivered when it is clear that it was intended by one of the parties that he was to be bound by the terms of the document. In the case of a company, delivery is still necessary and a document is presumed to have been delivered on its execution unless the contrary is proved.

The testimonium should therefore read as follows:

**IN WITNESS whereof this Deed has been executed by the parties hereto and is intended to be and is hereby delivered on the day first before written**

This may be an appropriate place to mention section 240 of the Finance Act 1994. The effect of this section is that no lease is to be treated as duly stamped unless it contains a certificate that there is no agreement to which it gives effect, or it is stamped with a stamp denoting that there is an agreement to which it gives effect which is not chargeable to duty or the duty has been paid on the agreement to which it gives effect.

The section was implemented as a result of the Inland Revenue receiving legal advice that both the agreement and the lease should be stamped. For the purpose of stamp duty penalties for late stamping, an agreement is treated as made at the same time as the lease, provided that it relates to substantially the same property and term of the lease. Therefore, if the agreement and lease are presented for stamping together within 30 days after execution of the lease, there will be no penalty.

The upshot of the above section is that where a lease is not granted pursuant to an agreement for lease, the following certificate should be added, preferably immediately before the testimonium:

**The Landlord and the Tenant hereby certify that there is no Agreement for Lease to which this Lease gives effect**

*Chapter 10*

# The Premises

## Introduction

It is absolutely vital for the tenant to ensure that the premises are correctly described in the lease and that the rights granted are sufficient for the tenant to carry on its business and the exceptions and reservations do not adversely affect the premises or the business.

10.01

**FIRST SCHEDULE**

**The Premises**

The Premises means the unit referred to in clause 1.3 shown [for the purposes of identification only] edged [red] on the Plan including:

10.02

1   the floor and ceiling finishes (but not any other part) of the floor slabs and ceiling slabs that bound the Premises
2   the inner half severed medially of the internal non-load bearing walls that divide the Premises from the adjoining unit[s] in the Centre or from the Retained Parts
3   the whole of the shop front
4   the doors and windows and door and window frames at the Premises
5   all additions and improvements to the Premises
6   all the Landlord's fixtures and fittings and fixtures of every kind which shall from time to time be in or upon the Premises (whether originally fixed or fastened to or upon the Premises or otherwise) except any such fixtures installed by the Tenant that can be removed from the Premises without defacing the Premises
7   all Pipes that are in or on and that exclusively serve the Premises and

8          any equipment or apparatus (for air extraction or otherwise) that is in or on and that exclusively serves the Premises but excluding the air space above the Premises the foundations all external or structural or loadbearing walls columns beams and supports and any of the pipes that do not exclusively serve the Premises

As mentioned, it is essential that the premises are accurately described in the lease and the tenant should liaise closely with its surveyor for this purpose. The precedent suggests the inclusion of a plan and, while it is suggested that where the premises are clearly defined there is no need for a plan, there is little doubt that a plan stated to be for identification purposes (and thereby preventing the plan from prevailing over the verbal description) is advisable.

What is included in the definition of the premises depends very much on the nature of the premises and the building. This lease is, of course, a lease of part of the building and therefore the structure has been excluded. If the lease is of premises forming the whole of a building, *e.g.* as in some retail parks, the structure and other parts of the building may be included, in which case the definition of the premises will have been worded accordingly. The tenant will certainly wish to ensure that its own fixtures and fittings are excluded from the definition of the premises, which could otherwise have adverse consequences so far as the tenant is concerned when construing the tenant's covenants and valuing "the Premises" for rent review purposes. The tenant may try to rid the definition of paragraph 5 completely to avoid any confusion on rent review or arguments as to the ownership of any such additions or improvements, failing which a possible "belt and braces" amendment to paragraph 5 could be:

5          **(without prejudice to the disregard contained in paragraph 1.4.3 of the fourth schedule) all additions and improvements to the Premises**

One other point worth mentioning is that when dealing with a lease of the whole of a building, the landlord and the tenant will have to consider whether the airspace above the building is to be included or excluded from the demise, as without specific reference it seems that a lease of a building will include the airspace above it, at least to such height as may be necessary for the use and enjoyment of the land and any structure upon it.[1] The precedent purports to exclude the airspace above the premises, which may not suit the tenant if it wishes to place air-conditioning equipment, telecommunications equipment, aerials, etc., on the roof. Consideration must be given to this when amending the lease.

## SECOND SCHEDULE

### Rights granted

The tenant must make absolutely certain that there are full and sufficient rights available to it so that the premises can be enjoyed for the whole of the term for any purpose currently permitted by the lease or to which the premises may be put with the landlord's consent.  **10.03**

The general law in fact implies various rights and easements, but it is bad practice and quite dangerous to rely on this, and all necessary rights should therefore be specifically spelled out.

### 1  Common Parts

> **The right for the Tenant and all persons expressly or by implication authorised by the Tenant (in common with the Landlord and all other persons having a like right) to use the Common Parts for all proper purposes in connection with the use and enjoyment of the Premises provided that the Landlord shall not be obliged to keep the malls and other pedestrian ways open [to the general public] earlier than [one hour] before the Shop Opening Hours or later than [one hour] after the Shop Opening Hours**  **10.04**

It will be for the landlord and the tenant to negotiate shop opening hours at the commencement of the term and which from the tenant's point of view should be sufficient for the tenant to carry on its normal trade and business. One aspect the tenant should consider is access to the common parts for making deliveries of goods. Some tenants "service" during the night, or very early in the morning, and would expect appropriate areas of the common parts to be open for this purpose subject, of course, to any planning restrictions in this regard. See also the suggested landlord's covenant at clause 6.7 where the common parts are not identified on a plan. It may also be advisable to include the words . . . **and other joint facilities** . . . after . . . **Common Parts** . . . in line 4.

It is also worth noting the case of *B & Q plc v. Liverpool & Lancashire Properties Ltd*[2] in which it was held that a landlord could not reduce a service area to an extent less than that which the tenant had originally negotiated and had considered important for its operation.

## 2 Pipes

**10.05** **The right to free passage and running (subject to temporary interruption for repair alteration or replacement) of water sewage gas electricity telephone and other services or supplies to and from the Premises in and through the Pipes that now serve the Premises presently laid in on under or over other parts of the Centre and (if any) the Adjoining Property (in common with the Landlord and other persons having a like right)**

The tenant should ensure that the grant of a right to use the service media should extend not only to the service media in existence at the date of the lease but also to those which may be provided during the course of the lease, subject, of course, to the perpetuity provisions. In addition, there should, if possible, be a right to enter upon adjoining premises to make connections and for the purpose of repair. This right should accordingly be amended as follows:

**The right to free passage and running (subject to temporary interruption for repair alteration or replacement) of water sewage gas electricity telephone and all other services or supplies to and from the Premises in and through the Pipes that now (or at any time during the Term) serve the Premises presently (or at any time during the Term) laid in on under or over other parts of the Centre and (if any) the Adjoining Property (in common with the Landlord and other persons having a like right) together with the right to enter the other parts of the Centre and (if any) the Adjoining Property to make connections to the Pipes and to inspect and repair such connections**

## 3 Support

**10.06** **The right of support and protection for the benefit of the Premises as is now enjoyed from all other parts of the Centre**

It is suggested that this right strengthens the landlord's covenant for quiet enjoyment, and the only question is as to whether to extend it to include "shelter", but this is probably unnecessary, although the landlord has seen fit to include it in the rights reserved under paragraph 5!

In addition to the above rights, and those which the tenant would be advised to require as a result of the nature of the premises and the centre to cover such matters as access, stairs and passages, lifts, sanitary facilities and car parking, the tenant should also consider amending the lease to include the following rights:

4   Entry

**10.07**   **The right for the Tenant and all persons expressly or by implication authorised by the Tenant to enter upon other parts of the Centre and (if any) the Adjoining Property to carry out works to the Premises where such works would otherwise not be possible or may be possible but rendered more expensive than they would otherwise be if this right was available**

The problem of access over a neighbour's land has been greatly alleviated by the passage of the Access to Neighbouring Land Act 1992, which sets out a procedure whereby a person may obtain a court order permitting access to a neighbour's property in order to carry out works to protect, repair or maintain their property in circumstances where the neighbour refuses consent to such access. It would appear that tenants are bound by the provisions of the Act and could therefore be affected adversely by it, but it remains to be seen as to whether a tenant in such a position could maintain an action against its landlord for breach of the landlord's covenant for quiet enjoyment where there is no reservation of such a right of access in the tenant's lease.

5   Fire escape

**10.08**   The tenant should certainly consider whether a right should be included in the lease over adjoining or neighbouring premises in the event of fire or other emergency.

6   Other rights

**10.09**   The tenant may also wish to include specific additional rights, *e.g.* to place telecommunications equipment on the roof of the building of which the premises form part; to place a refuse receptacle in the common parts; to erect signage in the common parts, etc.

THIRD SCHEDULE

Rights reserved

**10.10**   These may be extremely disruptive and, as such, may need to be given careful consideration by the tenant.

## 1 Use of Pipes

**10.11** The right to the free and uninterrupted passage and running of water sewage gas electricity telephone and other services or supplies from and to other parts of the Centre or any Adjoining Property in and through the Pipes which now are or may during the Term be in under or over the Premises

This is a standard reservation and the tenant may wish to ascertain at the outset just exactly which are the pipes at the commencement of the term that will be the subject of this right.

## 2 Construction of Pipes

**10.12** The right to construct and to maintain in on under or over the Premises at any time during the Term any Pipes for the benefit of any other part of the Centre or any Adjoining Property

This is not a standard right and could be highly disruptive. The tenant should consider its deletion, particularly where the premises form part of a shopping centre and the other units have already been constructed or are about to be so. The tenant should at least consider a proviso to the effect that the works should cause the minimum of disturbance to the business being carried on at the premises and that any damage should be made good with all due expedition.

## 3 Access

**10.13** 3.1 The right at [any time during the Term *or* reasonable times and upon reasonable notice except in cases of emergency] to enter (or in cases of emergency to break and enter) the Premises:

3.1.1 to inspect the condition and the state of repair of the Premises

3.1.2 to inspect cleanse connect to repair remove replace with others alter or execute any works whatever to or in connection with the Pipes easements or services referred to in paragraphs 1 and 2 of this schedule

3.1.3 to view the state and condition of and repair and maintain the Centre where such viewing or work would not otherwise be reasonably practicable

3.1.4 to carry out work or do anything whatever comprised within the Landlord's obligations in this Lease

| | | |
|---|---|---|
| 3.1.5 | to take schedules or inventories of fixtures and other items to be yielded up on the expiry of the Term and | |
| 3.1.6 | to exercise any of the rights granted to the Landlord by this Lease | |
| 3.2 | The right with the Surveyor and any person acting as the third party determining the Rent in default of agreement between the parties under the provisions for rent review contained in this Lease at [any time *or* convenient hours and on reasonable prior notice] to enter and to inspect [and measure] the Premises for all purposes connected with any pending or intended step under the 1954 Act or the implementation of the above provisions | |

Any right of access given to the landlord is likely to be disruptive to the tenant's business unless exercised outside normal business hours and in accordance with an arrangement previously settled by the landlord with the tenant. Unfortunately, certain landlords tend to abuse rights of access and as a first step the tenant should ensure that the right is subject to reasonable notice and may only be exercised at reasonable times, except, of course, in cases of emergency. The suggested proviso under clause 9.21 is designed to give the tenant some comfort in respect of certain of these rights of access, which could otherwise be disruptive. Paragraph 3.1.3 could be extremely disruptive and, if the configuration of the centre is such that it is a vital right for the landlord to include, the tenant should consider replacing "reasonably practicable" with the word "possible".

Paragraph 3.1.5 could be annoying if the landlord is of an interfering disposition, and could be preceded by the words:

**(in the last six months of the Term)**

The optional words in respect of convenient hours and reasonable prior notice in paragraph 3.2 are, of course, preferred.

## 4   Scaffolding

| | |
|---|---|
| The right to erect scaffolding for [any purpose connected with or related to the Centre *or* the purpose of repairing or cleaning the Centre] notwithstanding that such scaffolding may temporarily restrict the access to or use and enjoyment of the Premises | **10.14** |

This right is included in order to overcome the problem resulting from *Owen v. Gadd*,[3] where the Court of Appeal held that the construction of scaffolding poles in front of a shop, where there was no reservation of such a right, infringed the landlord's covenant for quiet enjoyment. It is fair to say that scaffolding placed in front of premises is extremely detractive, and the following amendments to this paragraph may be advisable:

> **The right to erect scaffolding for the purpose of repairing or cleaning the Centre provided that there shall not be erected any scaffolding or other structures in front of or to the rear or sides (if applicable) of the Premises in such a position so as [materially] to obscure the windows of the Premises or so as to prevent or [unreasonably] interfere with access to the Premises by customers or other persons entering the Premises or in connection with the servicing thereof**

The suggested proviso under clause 9.21 does, of course, also deal with the question of scaffolding and if there is included in the lease a paragraph along the lines of paragraph 4 above, then the above amendment can be inserted instead of the similar parts of the wording of the proviso under clause 9.21.

### 5 Support, etc.

**10.15** **The rights of light air support protection shelter and all other easements and rights now or after the date of this Lease belonging to or enjoyed by other parts of the Centre**

The following proviso should be added at the end of this paragraph:

> **provided that such rights and easements shall not [adversely] or [materially] affect the Premises or the business being carried on therein**

### 6 Light, etc.

**10.16** **Full right and liberty at any time after the date of this Lease to alter or to erect new structures within or adjoining the Centre (such expression here excluding the Premises) in such manner as the Landlord shall think fit notwithstanding the fact that the same may obstruct affect or interfere with the amenity of or access to the Premises or the passage of light and air to the Premises**

It may be as well to include the words in parentheses to remove any suggestion that the landlord may have the right to alter the premises. The other point to consider is that any interference with the light and air to the premises could adversely affect the tenant's business and the tenant should consider the latter part of this paragraph being amended as follows:

> **provided that the same shall not [materially] obstruct affect or interfere with the amenity of or access to the Premises or the passage of light and air to the Premises**

There may, of course, be various other specific or general rights reserved to the landlord and the tenant must decide whether or not they are reasonable, *e.g.*:

> **The right to affix to [and thereafter to maintain] on the Premises lighting equipment necessary for the purpose of lighting the Common Parts**

and possibly:

> **The right to vary alter or control the Common Parts and access to the whole or any part of the Centre**

In the examples given above, the first right may be tolerable, but the second right could adversely affect the tenant's business and, therefore, if the tenant was forced to accept it, the right should at least be qualified by a proviso that the right should not adversely affect the tenant's business.

---

[1] *Bernstein of Leigh (Baron) v. Skyviews and General Ltd* [1978] Q.B. 479.
[2] [2000] E.G.C.S. 101.
[3] [1956] 2 Q.B. 99.

*Chapter 11*

# Rent Review Provisions

## Introduction

**11.01** In an ideal world without inflation and market factors, rent would be set at the commencement of the lease and remain static throughout the term. This is not the position in reality and the landlord will be endeavouring to ensure that provisions are contained in the lease sufficient to increase the rent periodically (or at least not to decrease it), whereas the tenant will wish to be certain that the rent payable on review is fairly and reasonably settled.

Advisers should have regard to the recommendations in respect of rent review provisions contained in the Code of Practice for Commercial Leases in England and Wales.

**FOURTH SCHEDULE**

**Rent and rent review**

1 Definitions

**11.02** 1.1 **The terms defined in this paragraph shall for all purposes of this schedule have the meanings specified**
1.2 **"Review Period" means the period between any Review Date and the day prior to the next Review Date (inclusive) or between the last Review Date and the expiry of the Term (inclusive)**

Certainty in a lease is a characteristic that should be welcomed by the parties if not by litigators. One area which should be certain is the actual dates on which the rent reviews should take place. In the precedent there is no problem as clause 1.7 envisages that the actual review dates will be specified. Some leases, however, provide that rent reviews will take place on a specified date and thereafter at the expiration of every fifth year of the term or even at the expiration of every fifth year of the term without specifying an initial rent review date. The latter can lead to uncertainty as to the precise rent review date and both of the foregoing give rise to the problem as to whether they imply that there should be a rent review on the first day of the continuation tenancy created by the Landlord and Tenant Act 1954. The better view is that there is such an implication if the definition of "the Term" includes any period of holding over or extension or continuance of the term of years granted by the lease whether by statute or otherwise. It is also possible that a rent review would still be implied even without this definition, although perhaps in such an event there would be a strong counter-argument. Some rent review provisions in fact quite blatantly provide for a last-day rent review, which at least makes the position clear.

The landlord will argue that the requirement of an end of term rent review is merely to ensure that the rent is uplifted to a market level while a renewal under the 1954 Act is being negotiated, which would not necessarily be the position pursuant to an interim rent application under section 24 of the Act. Suggestions of procrastination by the tenant are also put forward by landlords in defence of this provision, but the tenant will argue that the landlord is quite often to blame, particularly in trying to impose unreasonable new lease provisions on the tenant in contravention of the guidelines laid down in the *O'May* case.[1] There is, of course, an argument that in a depressed or falling market tenants may have no objection to an end of term rent review, but the tenant may still prefer to avoid this imposition.

1.3 **"the Assumptions" means the following assumptions at the relevant Review Date:**

1.3.1 **that no work has been carried out on the Premises by the Tenant [its] undertenants or their predecessors in title during the Term which has diminished the rental value of the Premises [other than work carried out in compliance with clause 5.7.1]**

It is essential that regard is had to work which the tenant has been forced to carry out in accordance with statutory provisions, where such work may have diminished the rental value of the premises. The tenant should argue that there is no reason why it should suffer as a result of this. The square brackets should therefore remain or be replaced with words to similar effect, *e.g.*:

> **except to the extent that it has been carried out pursuant to any statutory requirements or the requirements of any local authority or other public body**

**1.3.2** **that if the Premises have been destroyed or damaged they have been fully restored**

This assumption appears in almost all institutionally acceptable leases nowadays, and the landlord will argue for its inclusion on the basis that it would be unfair for the rent to be ascertained for the premises in their damaged condition as the damage is likely to be repaired within a few years, or hopefully considerably less, whereas the revised rent is to last for [five] years. Furthermore, the landlord will state that the tenant will be enjoying a suspension of rent until the premises are reinstated. Against this, however, the tenant could argue that the suspension of rent may be of limited duration (so that the revised increased rent could become payable before the premises are reinstated), that the damage may not have been caused by an insured risk (in which case the suspension of rent provisions would probably not apply) or that the premises may not be reinstated because of the default of the landlord. The first of these provisions will hopefully have been covered by the tenant either by insisting on an unlimited suspension of rent or providing for a break option, or even effecting its own insurance. The other two are possibilities which could be covered by the tenant by suitable amendments if it so wishes, although they are likely to be met by opposition from the landlord. The suggested amendments are:

**1.3.2** **that if the Premises have been destroyed or damaged by any of the Insured Risks they have been fully restored except where such restoration has not taken place as a result of default by the Landlord**

**1.3.3** **that the covenants contained in this Lease on the part of the [Landlord and the] Tenant have been fully performed and observed**

**11.03** It is quite fair for this assumption to be included so far as the tenant's covenants are concerned, but unfair as regards the landlord's covenants, despite the landlord arguing that it should not be disadvantaged because of a breach which may be complied with shortly after the review date. The counter-argument is that the landlord should have remedied the breach prior to the review date, knowing that a review was pending. The worst that the tenant should accept is as follows:

**1.3.3** **that the covenants contained in this Lease on the part of the Landlord (other than in respect of material breaches) and the Tenant have been fully performed and observed**

**1.3.4** **that the Premises are available to let by a willing landlord to a willing tenant in the open market by one lease without a**

**premium being paid by either party and with vacant possession**

The assumptions contained in this paragraph are reasonable and essential from the tenant's point of view, but the following comments may be of interest by way of explanation and it may be useful to include the amendments detailed at the end of the comments.

The rent should be reviewed as at the relevant review date and, while this is referred to in paragraph 2.3, often there is a reference to the relevant review date in this assumption.

It is considered advisable to make reference to a willing landlord and a willing tenant to ensure that on the review date there would be a market for the premises, but it is likely that even without such an assumption a willing landlord and a willing tenant would be inferred. While section 34 of the Landlord and Tenant Act 1954 makes reference to a willing lessor it does not make reference to a willing lessee, but nevertheless, it was held in *Dennis and Robinson Ltd v. Kiossos Establishment*[2] that a willing lessee would be assumed.

It is useful to include "let as a whole" on the basis that the valuer may decide to disregard the possibility of underletting part, but there is some difficulty in agreeing this conclusion if the lease provisions enable the tenant to create underleases of part. In such circumstances it is suggested that the valuer may well disregard the assumption and look to the actual lease terms unless, of course, there is a provision that the valuer is to disregard the possibility of an underlease of part. There is also an argument that while "let as a whole" suggests only one lease, the phrase may be consistent with the grant of two or more hypothetical leases, each demising part of the premises and between them demising the whole. The suggestion is, therefore, that a reference to "one lease" or "a lease" of the whole may be preferable, though this will not prevent the valuer disregarding the possibility of an underlease of part as referred to earlier.

It is preferable to direct the valuer to assume that neither party is paying a premium to the other party as such premiums could affect valuation to the advantage or disadvantage of one or other of the parties. This may, for instance, be relevant at a time when landlords are paying incentives to tenants to take leases.

There should be a reference to the premises being let with "vacant possession", although this could have implications for the landlord. The provision assumes that the tenant has moved out of the premises or has never in fact occupied them. The case of *99 Bishopsgate Ltd v. Prudential Assurance Co. Ltd*[3] is authority for the fact that with such a provision it could be contended that the tenant should be allowed a rent-free period in order to fit out the premises for its business. The adverse position so far as the landlord is concerned is exacerbated by the fact that the tenant would be assumed to have removed all of its fixtures and fittings as well.[4]

The assumption could be amended to read as follows:

**1.3.4** **that the Premises are available to let at the relevant Review Date by a willing landlord to a willing tenant in the open market by one lease of the whole without a fine or premium being paid by either party and with vacant possession**

**1.3.5** **that the Premises are ready for and fitted out and equipped for immediate occupation and use for the purpose or purposes required by the willing tenant referred to in paragraph 1.3.4 and that all the services required for such occupation and use are connected to the Premises**

This assumption may take several forms including "fitted out and available for immediate occupation and use" or "fit for immediate occupation and use", the general effect being to make a declaration that there should be no allowance made against the rental value of the premises to reflect a period of time during which the tenant would expect to carry out its fitting out works.

**11.04** The problem is whether these words negate the disregard of the tenant's improvements and assume (even without reference to "fitted out") that the premises have already been fitted out to the willing tenant's requirements, resulting in the tenant having to pay rent for its own fixtures and fittings. Arbitrators, and indeed some commentators, seem to be taking different views on the general effect of this assumption and there has recently been a spate of cases attempting to deal with it. In *Pontsarn Investments Ltd v. Kansallis-Osake-Pankki*,[5] the expression was "vacant but fit for immediate occupation and use" and the landlord argued for an uplift in rent on the basis that the assumption meant that the premises were fitted out for immediate occupation and use. The judge preferred the tenant's interpretation that the meaning of the assumption was that the premises were defect free and ready for the tenant to commence fitting-out works. It has been suggested that even with the words "fitted out" included in the assumption, the position may not be disastrous for the tenant if the lease contains the standard disregard of tenant's improvements and the tenant has actually paid for the works in question. In such an event it is suggested that part of the rent attributable to the works should be deducted from the rental value of the premises as assessed. In *London & Leeds Estates Ltd v. Paribas Ltd*,[6] the lease contained an assumption that the demised premises were fit for immediate occupation and use, and that all fitting out and other tenant's works required by the willing tenant had already been completed. The Court of Appeal held that the purpose of this sort of clause was to preclude the actual tenant from arguing for a discount on the ground that the hypothetical tenant would have required further or different works from those carried out by the actual tenant whose improvements were to be disregarded.

The position is far from satisfactory, however, and the tenant should delete this paragraph. If, however, the landlord refuses to budge, it may be possible to persuade it that the following assumption could be substituted, which is based on an assumption in the Law Society/RICS model form of rent review clause (1985 edition):

> **that no discount or deduction is to be made in the yearly rent representing any rent-free period which on a new letting with vacant possession might be granted to an incoming tenant for a reasonable period [not exceeding [three] months] to reflect the length of time it would take for the incoming tenant to carry out its initial fitting-out works**[7]

The tenant may decide to stipulate an actual period during which the fitting-out works would be expected to take place, rather than for it to be open-ended. If the landlord objects to the above assumption and insists on a provision to the effect that the rent free period has already been enjoyed by the incoming tenant, the following wording could be added to paragraph 2.3 as an alternative to the above assumption, but with paragraph 1.3.5 in any event being deleted:

> **and after the expiry of a rent-free period which on a new letting with vacant possession it may then be the practice in open market lettings for a willing landlord to grant to an incoming tenant for a reasonable period [not exceeding [three] months] to reflect the length of time it would take for the incoming tenant to carry out its initial fitting-out works**

1.3.6     **that the lease referred to in paragraph 1.3.4 contains the same terms as this Lease except the amount of the Initial Rent and any rent-free period allowed to the Tenant for fitting out the Premises for [its] occupation and use at the commencement of the Term but including the provisions for rent review on the Review Dates and at similar intervals after the last Review Date and except as set out in paragraph 1.3.7**

Having regard to the cases emanating from the decision in *National Westminster Bank v. Young (Arthur) McCelland Moores & Co.*,[8] the tenant should make absolutely certain that this assumption does not, by neglect or otherwise, provide that the hypothetical lease is to have no rent review provisions contained in it, as this would lead to an uplift in rent. The landlord will wish to ensure that any rent-free period granted at the commencement of the term of the actual lease is not reflected in the hypothetical lease, because of the assumption that the hypothetical lease is on the same terms as the lease, for fear of an argument by the tenant that the rent should be discounted accordingly. The tenant may wish to delete the last part of this assumption and rely on the amendment proposed to be inserted in paragraph 1.3.7, but if not, paragraph 1.3.6 could be amended to read as follows:

**1.3.6** **that the lease referred to in paragraph 1.3.4 contains the same terms as this Lease except the amount of the Initial Rent and except any rent-free period allowed to the Tenant for fitting out the Premises for its occupation and use at the commencement of the Term but including the provisions for rent review on the Review Dates and at similar intervals after the last Review Date where on the relevant Review Date the term of the lease referred to in paragraph 1.3.7 exceeds the Contractual Term remaining unexpired at the relevant Review Date**

**1.3.7** **that the term of the lease referred to in paragraph 1.3.4 is equal in length to [the Contractual Term *or* the Contractual Term remaining unexpired at the relevant Review Date *or* the Contractual Term remaining unexpired at the relevant Review Date or a period of [15] years whichever is the greater] and that such term begins on the relevant Review Date and that the rent shall commence to be payable from that date and that the years during which the tenant covenants to decorate the Premises are at similar intervals after the beginning of the term of such lease as those specified in this Lease**

Until recently it was considered that the shorter the term of the hypothetical lease the lower would be the rent. There is now the suggestion that a longer term could give rise to a lower rent as a result of the onerous liabilities of a tenant under a long lease. There appear to be no certain conclusions, however, and as the position may well change from building to building it may be as well for the tenant to seek its surveyor's advice on this point so that all material factors in respect of the subject premises can be taken into account. Possibly the best solution is to agree to a minimum term of either 10 or 15 years.

The other point to note as regards this assumption is that the contractual term will be spelt out, which will at least avoid an argument as to the

## Rent Review Provisions 181

duration of the term where phrases are used such as "for the residue of the term hereby granted". If no term is stated, the term of the hypothetical lease will be equivalent to the residue of the term granted by the lease as at the review date.[9]

Where there is a minimum stated term it is advisable to state specifically that the term should be subject to a rent review every five years to avoid any argument on the last review (when the term of the hypothetical lease will be 10 or 15 years) that the term will be void of rent reviews as the actual lease itself will have no further rent review after that date.

**11.05**

This paragraph could be amended as follows:

**1.3.7** **that the term of the lease referred to in paragraph 1.3.4 is equal in length to the Contractual Term remaining unexpired at the relevant Review Date or a period [10] [15] years (with a rent review every five years) whichever is the greater and that such term begins on the relevant Review Date and that the rent shall commence to be payable from that date and that the years during which the tenant covenants to redecorate the Premises are at similar intervals after the beginning of the term of such lease as those specified in this Lease**

**[1.3.8** **that the Lease referred to in paragraph 1.3.4 will be renewed at the expiry of its term under the provisions of the 1954 Act]**

The tenant should delete this paragraph, although even without this assumption the valuer would be entitled to take into account the possibility of the tenancy being renewed under the Landlord and Tenant Act 1954.[10] If the tenant is of the opinion that it is unlikely to obtain a renewal, it may try to insert an assumption that the tenancy will not be renewed, but this is likely to be resisted by the landlord and it is suggested that the best solution is to let the matter rest on the general law, *i.e.* delete this assumption.

**1.3.9** **that every prospective willing landlord and willing tenant is able to recover VAT in full**

**11.06**

Various VAT assumptions have been finding their way into leases of late, including the above.[11] It was thought that if an exempt or partially exempt tenant could not recover VAT imposed on rent, then this would be reflected in the amount of rent it would be prepared to pay. The threat of a "two-tier" market has not yet materialised, but this is not to say that it will not in the future. The tenant should be wary of artificial assumptions of this nature, however, and therefore, from the tenant's point of view, it is better for this assumption to be deleted.

The following three points should also be noted:

(1) The tenant should delete any reference to an assumption of having been given the benefit of any rent-free period (other than in respect of a reasonable period of time for the purpose of fitting out as referred to above) or other financial inducement (or similar wording or provisions) which it may be the practice to give incoming tenants at the time of the rent review. As mentioned under paragraph 1.3.4, the case of *99 Bishopsgate Ltd v. Prudential Assurance Co. Ltd* had the effect of tenants being able to claim on rent reviews that they should be entitled to certain concessions being offered to incoming tenants in the open market, *e.g.* rent-free periods to enable fitting-out works to be completed. A benefit of this nature on each rent review under the lease seemed unfair to landlords, who contrived by wording in rent review clauses to counteract this situation. Typical wording may be the assumption referred to above. Unfortunately, it may be that at the review date, rents are depressed and tenants in the open market are being allowed several years' rent-free period or other inducements by landlords in order to keep rents up to an acceptable level, called "the headline rent". The side effect of such an assumption, depending on the wording used, appeared to be that the tenant was left with a headline rent for the whole of the review period, as the tenant would be assumed to have had the concession referred to in order to hoist the rent to the headline level. Not surprisingly, landlords did not take too long to latch on to this windfall. The Court of Appeal has, however, come to the aid of these unfortunate tenants, but the spectre of "headline rent" has not been entirely exorcised. Tenants should therefore remain extremely wary of any wording that could possibly extend further a normal rent-free period for fitting-out works to take place.

The Court of Appeal heard four principal "headline rent" cases together, being: *Co-operative Wholesale Society Ltd v. National Westminster Bank plc*; *Broadgate Square plc v. Lehman Brothers Ltd*; *Scottish Amicable Life Assurance Society v. Middleton Potts & Co.* and *Prudential Nominees Ltd v. Greenham Trading Ltd.*[12] It is fair to say that the Court's reasoning, though applauded by tenants with enthusiastic relief, was more in keeping with expediency than logical deductive discourse. Although the Court managed to construe the offending words in the *Co-operative*, *Scottish Amicable* and *Prudential* cases in favour of the tenants, *i.e.* as not producing "headline rents", the wording in the *Broadgate* case was just too clear to circumvent. The open market rent in the *Broadgate* case was defined as that "which would reasonably be expected to become payable in respect of the premises after the expiry of a rent-free period of such length as would be negotiated in the open market between a willing landlord and a willing tenant". The Court was faced with no alternative but to accept that this wording produced a "headline rent" and that the first instance decision could not be reversed.

We are therefore left with the position that the courts will approach the construction of rent review clauses having regard to reality and that, wherever possible, they will construe a lease to give effect to the main purpose of a rent review and not to uplift the rent unfairly. That said, the courts will be left with no option but to give clear wording the meaning that such clear wording produces, and for this reason tenants should still exercise extreme care and refuse to accept wording that could even remotely look as though it could give rise to a "headline rent" situation.

(2) Some business premises have residential flats above them, which are not infrequently occupied by Rent Act tenants. A valuation with assumed vacant possession could result in a higher rent being attributable to the flats than is actually the position. For this reason a proviso along the lines detailed below may offer the tenant some protection:

> **provided however that the [market value] of the [residential flat] shall be deemed to be the greater of the rent actually being received by the Tenant therefor or the rent permitted under the Rent Act for the time being in force**

(3) If the landlord has agreed that the tenant will not pay more rent on rent review for the premises than by reference to a specific gross internal area, the following assumption may be inserted by the tenant pursuant to the clause suggested in clause 2 of the agreement for lease:

> **that the gross internal area of the Premises shall be [ ] square [feet/metres] and that the willing tenant shall not be assumed to be willing to pay more rent for the Premises as a result of the actual gross internal area of the Premises exceeding [ ] square [feet/metres]**

1.4 "the Disregarded Matters" means:
1.4.1 any effect on rent of the fact that the Tenant [its] undertenants or their respective predecessors in title have been in occupation of the Premises

**11.07** The disregard of occupation should also extend to undertenants, other lawful occupiers and predecessors in title and be in respect of the premises or any part thereof. The disregard is required to avoid any assumption that a tenant in occupation of the premises may pay a rent higher than the market rent in order not to have to move, and is accepted to be different from an assumption of vacant possession.[13] Where the tenant occupies adjoining premises the tenant should consider the disregard being extended to deal with the occupation of other properties in the locality to avoid any element of "marriage" value, *i.e.* that the tenant may be prepared to pay a higher rent to avoid having to move in order to expand.

The disregard should be amended to read as follows:

**1.4.1** any effect on rent of the fact that the Tenant its undertenants or their respective predecessors in title or other lawful occupiers have been in occupation of the Premises or any part thereof

**1.4.2** any goodwill attached to the Premises by reason of the carrying on at the Premises of the business of the Tenant [its] undertenants or their predecessors in title in their respective businesses

Goodwill should be disregarded, despite some commentators' advice that it is possibly against strict logic, in order not to penalise the tenant for its efficiency in running its business. Once again, this disregard should extend to undertenants, or other lawful occupiers and to be in respect of the premises or any part thereof. It may also be as well to include the word "respective" before "predecessors in title" to accord with paragraph 1.4.1 and to assist clarification There is also the suggestion that the disregard should extend back to before the commencement of the current lease term in certain circumstances, *e.g.* where a new tenant has taken over a business under a new lease that has been carried on for many years at the premises.

**1.4.3** any increase in rental value of the Premises attributable to the existence at the relevant Review Date of any improvement to the Premises carried out with consent where required otherwise than in pursuance of an obligation [except an obligation contained in clause 5.7.1] to the Landlord or [its] predecessors in title either:

**1.4.3.1** by the Tenant [its] undertenants or their respective predecessors in title [or by any lawful occupiers] during the Term or during any period of occupation prior to the Term arising out of an agreement to grant or

**1.4.3.2** **by any tenant or undertenant of the Premises [or by any lawful occupiers] before the commencement of the Term so long as the Landlord or [its] predecessors in title have not since the improvement was carried out had vacant possession of the relevant part of the Premises**

It would be possible to continue at length on this subject and comments will therefore be kept to a strict minimum. The amendments detailed below are self-explanatory to a degree but the following points should be noted:

**11.08**

(1) There are four main ways of expressing the disregard, these being:
   (a) disregarding the improvement itself (it is suggested that this may be over-generous to the tenant);
   (b) disregarding the effect on rent of the improvement (this seems to be the fairest method of expressing the disregard, but there is the problem that there is no judicial authority as to what it means);
   (c) disregarding any increase in rent (this follows the Model Clause prepared by the Law Society/RICS and indeed the precedent and seems to hold no patent pitfalls for the tenant); or
   (d) to make a fair allowance to the tenant in respect of improvements (this may avoid the tenant arguing for a rent-free period at each review but concern has been expressed as to the imprecise nature of this valuation).

(2) Without a disregard of improvements, the rent on review will be calculated by reference to the premises as they stand as at the review date[14] and for this reason it is vital to include the disregard as otherwise the tenant will be paying for its own improvements.

(3) It is suggested that an improvement is something which alters or adds to an existing building and which includes something that amounts to a landlord's fixture.[15] The alteration is to be something more than mere repair, but is at least to be judged from the tenant's point of view.

(4) **Any increase in rental value**
A point worth noting is that it is possible for an improvement to decrease the rental value of the premises.

(5) **Carried out with consent where required**
It is difficult for the tenant to resist this provision as the landlord will wish to include an element of certainty as to what improvements are to be disregarded. It should also be remembered that the requirement for consent is likely to be strictly construed.[16] The tenant,

however, may wish to avoid this clause in order to include "improvements" for which consent has not for some reason been obtained, or may not be necessary (though the precedent caters for this), or which has become lost.

(6) **Otherwise than in pursuance of an obligation to the Landlord**
This possibly has its origin in an attempt by the landlord to ensure that the tenant does not gain from works which it is obliged to carry out, *e.g.* in repairing the premises, and there is a similar provision contained in section 34 of the Landlord and Tenant Act 1954. A typical obligation in a lease is that contained in clause 5.7.1, but fortunately paragraph 1.4.3 makes specific reference to that clause. The majority of rent review provisions, however, do not contain such an exception and, if not, the tenant should amend the disregard either to refer to the clause containing the statutory obligation or by including general wording as suggested in the amended paragraph 1.4.3. As mentioned under clause 5.7.1, a particular concern is the impact of the Disability Discrimination Act 1995. This requires works to be carried out, usually by the tenant, and as they will be carried out pursuant to statute, the tenant will need to be certain that they are disregarded on rent review, despite being effected pursuant to an obligation to the landlord, *i.e.* to comply with statute.

The difficulty with this phrase is where it is suggested that a covenant given to the landlord in a licence for alterations to effect the improvement works requested by the tenant could be construed to be such an obligation to the landlord with the result that the works are not disregarded. Courts are tending to lean against such a construction,[17] but there is no harm in including the amendment detailed below.

(7) **By the Tenant its undertenants or their respective predecessors in title or by any lawful occupiers**
It is important to ensure that improvements carried out by all persons in occupation of the premises from time to time shall be disregarded. Another consideration is that paragraph 1.4.3 refers to improvements "carried out" by the tenant, etc. It may be that, in certain circumstances, the tenant pays for the improvements but they are carried out by a third party. It would be sensible to expand this provision to read "by or at the expense of."[18]

(8) **During the Term or during any period of occupation prior to the Term arising out of an agreement to grant**
This is self-explanatory and it is essential to avoid the construction that the improvements should be limited to those carried out by the tenant during the term granted by the lease, as well as avoiding the

possible exclusion of improvements carried out under a previous lease. The inclusion of the words

**or at the expense of**

may, in addition to the point referred to above, assist the tenant to argue that improvements paid for by the tenant through the service charge provisions but carried out by the landlord should nevertheless be disregarded. It is a tenuous argument, but one worth promoting. Alternatively, the tenant should consider specifically disregarding works carried out to the premises with money provided via the service charge.

The disregard could be amended to read as follows: **11.09**

**1.4.3** **any increase in rental value of the Premises or any part thereof attributable to the existence at the relevant Review Date of any alteration or improvement (and for the avoidance of doubt the expressions "alteration" and "improvement" shall include fitting-out works and similar alterations) to the Premises or any part thereof carried out or being carried out otherwise than in pursuance of an obligation under this Lease to the Landlord or its predecessors in title (except where such obligation is imposed by statute[19] or is a requirement or direction of a local authority or other public body or where the obligation is a covenant to carry out the alterations or improvements contained in any licence or consent authorising the same or regulating the manner or time in which such works are to be carried out) either:**

**1.4.3.1** **by or at the expense of the Tenant its undertenants or their respective predecessors in title or by or at the expense of any lawful occupiers during the Term or during any period of occupation prior to the Term arising out of an agreement to grant the Term or otherwise [*or* during the term granted by any previous Lease of the Premises][20] or**

**1.4.3.2** **by or at the expense of any tenant or undertenant of the Premises or by or at the expense of any lawful occupiers before the commencement of the Term so long as the Landlord or its predecessors in title have not since the alteration or improvement was carried out had vacant possession of the relevant part of the Premises**

Some tenants prefer specifically to disregard the tenant's fixtures and fittings, but it is likely that with a vacant possession assumption it will be presumed that the tenant will have removed them.[21]

The tenant should also try to ensure that any special concessions given to the tenant on rent review, *e.g.* a provision that the actual tenant need only pay a set percentage of the open market rent are not lost because the willing tenant may pay more because of the concession.[22]

Where there is a break clause included in the lease, the parties must decide whether or not it is to be included in the hypothetical lease and therefore taken into account on rent review and, if so, when during the term of the hypothetical lease the break clause is to be exercised. For example, a tenant's break right could be considered valuable and therefore enhance the rent on review.[23]

**1.5 "the President" means the President for the time being of the Royal Institution of Chartered Surveyors the duly appointed deputy of the President or any person authorised by the President to make appointments on his behalf**

This requires no comment; suffice to say that the reference to the deputy is to avoid an argument as to the validity of an appointment by a deputy where there is no authority to do so in the lease.

**11.10** **1.6 "the Arbitrator" means a person appointed by agreement between the parties or in the absence of agreement within [fourteen] days of one party giving notice to the other of [its] nomination or nominations nominated by the President on the application of either party made not earlier than [six] months before the relevant Review Date or at any time afterwards**

The first consideration is to decide whether the valuer is to be an expert or an arbitrator. Opinion is generally divided as to who is preferable from the tenant's point of view, and circumstances do vary from case to case. The tenant should seek its surveyor's opinion on this aspect at the outset. At a very simplistic level, an expert will be cheaper and quicker with an element of finality and, whilst he can be sued in negligence, his decision cannot be appealed against—although if he gives reasons for his decision which are subsequently shown to be incorrect, then it is possible that the court will be able to set aside his decision[24]—whereas an arbitrator has far greater powers under the Arbitration Act 1996, including powers to force the attendance of witnesses, discovery of documents and orders as to costs. The expert will fix the rent from his own knowledge and is not obliged to invite the parties to make submissions or produce evidence. It is suggested that even if there is a provision in the rent review clause that he should do so, he may legitimately disregard them if he so wishes. He is therefore a person who arrives at his opinion from his own judgment, hence his exposure to proceedings by either party. Some tenants prefer arbitration where the premises are unusual or where it is considered that, in view of their size and value, full and open argument should be available, whereas an expert may be preferred where the premises are of standard design and character and where numerous comparables are available in the locality.

The tenant should ensure that if there is a dispute with regard to the identity of the valuer, either party will be able to apply to the President (or some other presiding person) to have an independent valuer appointed and that the appointment can be made by no later than the relevant review date in order to settle the review which may be in the tenant's interests either where an assignment is in prospect or interest is being charged on the reviewed rent.

There is sometimes included a provision that the valuer should have experience of lettings of properties similar to the premises in the locality. However, there is a suggestion that this could cause uncertainty as a result of the difficulty in defining "locality" and "experience", but it could be argued that "experience" is definable and the tenant may at least wish to include the following additional words at the end of this paragraph:

> **the Arbitrator having at least ten years' experience in the valuation of [retail] [office] premises**

## 2    Ascertaining the Rent

2.1      **The Rent shall be:**                                                                                          **11.11**
2.1.1    **until the first Review Date the Initial Rent and**
2.1.2    **during each successive Review Period a rent equal to the greater of:**
2.1.2.1  **the Rent payable immediately prior to the relevant Review Date or if payment of Rent has been suspended pursuant to the proviso to that effect contained in this Lease the Rent which would have been payable had there been no such suspension or**
2.1.2.2  **such Rent as may be ascertained in accordance with this schedule**

As drafted, the paragraph provides for an upwards-only rent review and it may be that the tenant is able to negotiate an upwards or downwards review, even in the face of strong opposition from the landlord.[25] This may be particularly so in a recession and the tenant should at least try to negotiate this.[26] There is no objection to the latter part of 2.1.2.1.

**2.2** **Such revised Rent for any Review Period may be agreed in writing at any time between the parties or (in the absence of agreement) will be determined [not earlier than the relevant Review Date] by the Arbitrator**

The notes to the precedent refer to the point that there is nothing in this provision to commence the process of rent review, *e.g.* the service of a rent review notice. It was omitted in the interests of avoiding any arguments as to whether time was of the essence. There is no harm in having a notice provision included, but there should be avoided at all cost a "trigger notice" procedure by which the tenant could be lumbered with paying an exorbitant rent (as detailed in the landlord's notice) if the tenant does not respond with a counter-notice in time or make application to the independent valuer. Even if there is no reference to time being of the essence, the latter can be implied by contra-indications in the rent review clause or by the interrelationship of the rent review clause and other clauses in the lease.[27] In *Starmark Enterprises Ltd v. CPL Distribution Ltd*[28] a "deeming provision", by which the tenant was deemed to have agreed to pay the increased rent specified in the landlord's rent notice if the tenant failed to serve a counter-notice within one month of receipt of the rent notice, was held by the court to be a sufficient contra-indication to displace the presumption that time was not of the essence.

By far the safest procedure is for either party to be able to instigate the rent review, perhaps not earlier than 12 months prior to the relevant review date and not later than the next following review date, with either party in any event having the right to apply for the appointment of the expert or arbitrator if the rent review is not underway by the relevant review date. This should be the position even if the landlord has the sole right to commence the rent review, as the tenant may wish to have the review settled quickly pending a proposed assignment or underletting of the lease. If the lease makes no reference to the point then either party may apply for the appointment of the expert or arbitrator but if the landlord (as opposed to either party) is the only party who may apply but refuses to do so for some reason, the question is whether the tenant can enlist the assistance of the court by asking for a mandatory injunction to force the landlord to apply for the appointment. There have, in fact, been four recent cases on the point[29] and the court has assisted the tenant only where the review is not upwards only. It is therefore essential for the tenant to be alert to this provision when amending the lease.

The independent valuer is most often the President of the Royal

Institution of Chartered Surveyors who has at his command a full and efficient machinery to ensure that an appropriate appointment is made. The tenant should consider whether there should be included an obligation on the landlord's part to notify the tenant of an application being made to the independent valuer.

**2.3 The revised Rent to be determined by the Arbitrator shall be such as he shall decide to be the rent at which the Premises might reasonably be expected to be let in the open market at the relevant Review Date making the Assumptions but disregarding the Disregarded Matters**

This generally follows section 34 of the Landlord and Tenant Act 1954, and is the preferred formula despite the fact that there is no authority as to the meaning of "reasonably". Words such as "highest", "full" and "best" rent should be avoided, for while "highest" and "full" may not in fact add very much to the valuation of the rent, a reference to "best" rent would most certainly bring into the equation a rent paid by a special bidder.

Care should be taken to avoid the standard precedent that the valuer should disregard the "disregarded matters", as this could be construed to be a double negative.

The paragraph should be amended to read:

**2.3 The revised Rent to be determined by the Arbitrator shall be such as he shall decide to be the rent at which the Premises might reasonably be expected to be let in the open market at the relevant Review Date making the assumptions but disregarding the matters detailed in paragraph 1.4 of this schedule and defined as "the Disregarded Matters"**

**2.4 The arbitration shall be conducted in accordance with the Arbitration Act 1996 except that if the Arbitrator nominated pursuant to paragraph 1.6 shall die or decline to act the President may on the application of either party discharge the Arbitrator and appoint another in his place**

This requires no amendment.

**2.5 Whenever the Rent shall have been ascertained in accordance with this schedule memoranda to that effect shall be signed by or on behalf of the parties and annexed to this Lease and its counterpart and the parties shall bear their own costs in this respect**

**11.12**

This requires no amendment but the following points should be noted:

(1) It is in both parties' interests that the rent review is evidenced by a memorandom, putting beyond doubt any subsequent argument as to what rent has been agreed.

(2) There is no reason whatsoever why the new rent should be evidenced by a deed under seal provided the lease contains provisions for the rent to be reviewed from time to time. This merely adds to expense.

(3) Under no circumstances should the tenant be required to pay the landlord's costs incurred in connection with rent review memoranda, on the basis that the tenant probably would prefer there to be no review at all, unless a downwards review is permitted.

### 3 Arrangements pending ascertainment of revised Rent

**11.13** **3.1 If the revised Rent payable during any Review Period has not been ascertained by the relevant Review Date Rent shall continue to be payable at the rate previously payable such payments being on account of the Rent for that Review Period**

Possibly because of the mildly contentious nature of rent reviews, it is becoming increasingly rare for the review to be settled prior to the review date and this provision is self-explanatory. The tenant should, however, delete any reference that may be inserted in this provision (or elsewhere in the lease) to the tenant being obliged to make an interim payment as notified by the landlord[30] until the new rent is agreed.

**3.2 If one party shall upon publication of the Arbitrator's award pay all the Arbitrator's fees and expenses such party shall be entitled to recover [(in default of payment within [21] days of a demand to that effect in the case of the Landlord as Rent in arrears or in the case of the Tenant by deduction from Rent)] such proportion of them (if any) as the Arbitrator shall award against the other party**

This is not an unreasonable provision and, while the optional part of the paragraph provides for the payment to the landlord to be recoverable as rent in arrears, it also at least specifies how the tenant is to recover payment, although if the reference to set-off is allowed to remain in clause 5.1.1, a reference to this provision will have to be inserted in 5.1.1 and the notes to the precedent suggest "except that referred to ..." in order to avoid an inconsistency.

## 4 Payment of revised Rent

**4.1** If the revised Rent shall be ascertained on or before the relevant Review Date and that date is not a quarter day the Tenant shall on that Review Date pay to the Landlord the amount by which one quarter's Rent at the rate payable on the immediately preceding quarter day is less than one quarter's Rent at the rate of the revised Rent apportioned on a daily basis for that part of the quarter during which the revised Rent is payable

**4.2** If the revised Rent payable during any Review Period has not been ascertained by the relevant Review Date then immediately after the date when the same has been agreed between the parties or the date upon which the Arbitrator's award shall be received by one party the Tenant shall pay to the Landlord:

**4.2.1** any shortfall between the Rent which would have been paid on the Review Date and on any subsequent quarter days had the revised Rent been ascertained on or before the relevant Review Date and the payments made by the Tenant on account and

**4.2.2** interest at the base lending rate of the bank referred to in or nominated pursuant to clause 1.8 prevailing on the day upon which the shortfall is paid in respect of each instalment of Rent due on or after the Review Date on the amount by which the instalment of revised Rent which would have been paid on the relevant Review Date or such quarter day exceeds the amount paid on account and such interest shall be payable for the period from the date upon which the instalment was due up to the date of payment of the shortfall

**11.14**

Until the revised rent has been ascertained, rent will continue to be payable at the rate prior to the relevant review date. When the revised rent has been ascertained, there should be due from the tenant the difference in rent between the new rent and the rent paid on account on each rent day since and including the relevant review date, together with interest at no higher than the base lending rate of any of the major clearing banks.

Arguments are often made by landlords that the interest should be higher as it would be impossible for a tenant to borrow money at base rate, but a counter-argument could be that the landlord should ensure that it instigates the rent review at the earliest date possible under the lease and thereafter pursues it vigorously to ensure that there is the minimum period of time between the relevant review date and the date of ascertainment of the new rent.

Many older leases contain a provision that once the new rent has been ascertained the "shortfall" should be paid "with interest thereon at the base lending rate of XYZ Bank plc". This form of wording should be avoided, as the landlord could ask for interest on the total of the shortfall for the whole of the period from the relevant review date to the date of payment.

There may also be a provision that the old rent is to continue to be payable up to the quarter day following the date of ascertainment whereupon the shortfall and interest become payable. If the rent is ascertained on June 26, a tenant may not wish to continue to pay interest on the relevant part of the shortfall until September 29 (unless the interest rate is particularly low). It may be in the tenant's best interests to ensure that the date of payment of the shortfall is no later than 28 days after the date of ascertainment and perhaps 14 days is a fair compromise as the tenant will not want too short a period either, for fear of the penal interest rate applying.

A practical point worth noting is that where there is no provision for interest to be payable on the shortfall, the landlord will not be entitled to charge interest from the relevant review date at the rate for late payment contained in the main body of the lease, as that interest rate only becomes payable when money has not been paid after it has become due. What should be noted, however, is that if the shortfall is not paid on the date of ascertainment (or within the period of grace (if any) provided) interest will be payable on the total sum due at that date at the penal rate of interest for late payment contained in the body of the lease.

**11.15** A final point is that it may be fairer to both parties if the interest payable is stated to be at the base lending rate from time to time as opposed to the rate prevailing on the day upon which the shortfall is paid (and both of these options are set out below).

Paragraph 4 could therefore be improved upon by the substitution of the following wording:

> **4.1** **If the revised Rent shall be ascertained on or before the relevant Review Date and that date is not a quarter day the Tenant shall on that Review Date pay to the Landlord the amount by which one quarter's Rent at the rate payable on the immediately preceding quarter day is less than one quarter's Rent at the rate of the revised Rent apportioned on a daily basis from and including that Review Date to the day before the next following quarter day**

4.2 If the revised Rent payable during any Review Period has not been ascertained by the relevant Review Date then within fourteen days after the date ("the date of ascertainment") when the same has been agreed between the parties or upon which the Arbitrator's award shall be received by or otherwise made known to the Tenant the Tenant shall pay to the Landlord:

4.2.1 any shortfall ("the shortfall") between the Rent which would have been payable if the revised Rent had been ascertained by the relevant Review Date and the payments made by the Tenant on account thereof in respect of the period ("the interim period") commencing on the relevant Review Date and ending on the day before the quarter day following the date of ascertainment or ending on the day before the date of ascertainment if the revised Rent is ascertained on a quarter day and

4.2.2 interest at the base lending rate [from time to time] of the bank referred to in or nominated pursuant to clause 1.8 [prevailing on the day upon which the shortfall is paid] in respect of each instalment of Rent due during the interim period on the difference between the amount of Rent that would have been payable under this Lease on each of the quarter days during the interim period had the revised Rent been ascertained by the relevant Review Date and the amount paid on account thereof such interest being payable for the period beginning on the date upon which each instalment of Rent was due and ending on the date of payment of the shortfall

## 5 Arrangements when increase in Rent prevented, etc.

5.1 If at any of the Review Dates there shall be in force a statute which shall prevent restrict or modify the Landlord's right to review the Rent in accordance with this Lease and/or to recover any increase in the Rent the Landlord shall when such restriction or modification is removed relaxed or modified be entitled (but without prejudice to [its] rights (if any) to recover any Rent the payment of which has only been deferred by law) on giving not less than [one] month's nor more than [three] months' notice in writing to the Tenant [at any time within [six] months (time being of the essence) of the restriction or modification being removed relaxed or modified] to invoke the provisions of paragraph 5.2

11.16

5.2 Upon the service of a notice pursuant to paragraph 5.1 the Landlord shall be entitled:

5.2.1 to proceed with any review of the Rent which may have been prevented or further to review the Rent in respect of any review where the Landlord's right was restricted or modified and the date of expiry of such notice shall be deemed for the purposes of this Lease to be a Review Date (provided that without prejudice to the operation of this paragraph nothing in this paragraph shall be construed as varying any subsequent Review Dates)

5.2.2 to recover any increase in Rent with effect from the earliest date permitted by law

It is hoped that counter-inflation legislation will never again trouble the property market, at least in the form imposed between 1972 and 1975. Nevertheless, landlords' advisers are not in the risk business as such, and rent review clauses in leases almost invariably include provisions dealing with the possibility of subsequent rent control. These tend to follow a standard form but if possible the tenant should try to ensure that there is not more than one intermediate rent review between any two rent review dates and should also consider inserting a provision that the rent shall nevertheless be calculated at the intermediate rent review by reference to rental values as at the review date subjected to the rent control. This is not unreasonable as new lettings will presumably continue to be granted during any rent freeze, hopefully providing adequate comparable evidence. Once counter-inflation legislation is repealed, it is likely that rents will increase rapidly, in which case the tenant could be severely prejudiced if its rent is to be reviewed as at a date which could be two or three years after the contractual review date.

It is also essential to include the words in square brackets in paragraph 5.1 in order to ensure that the landlord does not hold back and impose the rent review at a time which is likely to be more favourable to its interests.

The following proviso should be added at the end of 5.2.1

> except that the revised Rent shall nevertheless be calculated by reference to rental values at the Review Date subjected to the rent restriction and provided that there shall be no more than one such additional rent review between any two Review Dates

One final point is that where the independent surveyor is to act as an expert and not as an arbitrator it may be advisable to include the following provisions if omitted from the lease:

(1)   The fees and expenses of the valuer including the cost of his nomination shall be borne equally by the Landlord and the Tenant who shall otherwise bear their own costs
(2)   The valuer shall afford the Landlord and the Tenant an opportunity to make written representations to him [and also an opportunity to make written counter-representations on any representations made to him by the other party] but is not to be in any way limited or fettered by such representations [and counter-representations] and is to be entitled to rely on his own judgment and opinion
(3)   If the valuer shall die delay or become unwilling or incapable of acting or if for any other reason the President for the time being of the Royal Institution of Chartered Surveyors or the person acting on his behalf shall in his absolute discretion think fit he may on the application of either the Landlord or the Tenant by writing discharge the valuer and appoint another in his place
(4)   If either party requests the valuer shall be under an obligation to provide reasons for his rental valuation the cost to be borne by the party requesting such reasoned determination

---

[1] *O'May v. City of London Real Property Co. Ltd* [1983] 2 A.C. 726.
[2] [1987] 1 E.G.L.R. 133.
[3] [1985] 1 EGLR 72; [1985] 273 E.G. 984.
[4] *Young v. Dalgety plc* [1987] 1 E.G.L.R. 116. See also *Ocean Accident Guarantee Corporation v. Next plc and Commercial Union Assurance Co plc v. Next plc* [1995] E.G.C.S. 187, in which it was held that the tenant's trade fixtures would not be expected to increase the yearly rent, even though they were installed by the tenant pursuant to an obligation contained in the lease.
[5] [1992] 22 E.G. 103.
[6] [1993] 30 E.G. 89.
[7] The author has, however, heard the suggestion that this assumption could be construed against the landlord to be an onerous provision which could have a depressive effect on the rent, but this is not to be relied upon.
[8] [1985] 2 All E.R. 817. In which the words "other than the rent hereby reserved" were adjudged to have had the effect of excluding rent reviews from the hypothetical lease for valuation purposes; though the problem has now been alleviated in most instances by a more rational approach being adopted by the courts.
[9] *Norwich Union Life Insurance Society v. Trustee Savings Bank Central Board* [1986] 1 E.G.L.R. 136.

[10] *Secretary of State for the Environment v. Pivot Properties Ltd* [1980] 256 E.G. 1176.
[11] Stemming principally from the extension of VAT to land transactions in 1989, but also pursuant to the Budget speech made on November 26, 1996 in respect of the ineffectiveness of elections to waive exemption from VAT in certain circumstances and the adverse effect of this on the recovery by the landlord of VAT on construction costs.
[12] All reported under [1994] E.G.C.S. 184; [1995] 01 E.G. 111.
[13] *Scottish & Newcastle Breweries plc v. Sir Richard Sutton's Settled Estates* [1985] 2 E.G.L.R. 130.
[14] *Ponsford v. HMS Aerosols Ltd* [1978] 2 All E.R. 837; *Laura Investment Co. Ltd v. Havering London Borough Council* [1992] 24 E.G. 136.
[15] *New Zealand Government Property Corporation v. H M & S Ltd* [1982] Q.B. 1145.
[16] See *Hamish Cathie Travel England Ltd v. Insight International Tours Ltd* [1986] 1 E.G.L.R. 244.
[17] *Godbold v. Martin (The Newsagents)* [1983] 268 E.G. 1202.
[18] See *Durley House Ltd v. Viscount Cadogan* [2000] 1 WLR 246, [2000] 09 E.G. 183, in which it was held that "carried out" could include works that were not physically carried out by the tenant, but the court made it clear that the tenant had to do something more than simply require a third party to carry out the works.
[19] Or make specific reference to the tenant's covenant contained in the lease requiring compliance with statutory obligations if included, *e.g.* "except an obligation contained in clause 5.7.1" (as in the precedent).
[20] This may be appropriate on a renewal.
[21] See *New Zealand Government Property Corporation, v. HM & S Ltd* (above, n. 15).
[22] See *British Railways Board v. Ringbest* [1996] 30 E.G. 94; [1996] 2 E.G.L.R. 82. See also point (3) at the end of para. 1.3.9 in respect of the "pegging" of the area of the premises for the purpose of rent review.
[23] It is likely that a break right that is stated to be personal to the tenant will not be included in the hypothetical lease, in the absence of an express provision: *St Martin's Property Ltd v. Citicorp Investment Bank Properties Ltd* [1998] E.G.C.S. 161, CA.
[24] *Burgess v. Purchase & Sons (Farms)* [1983] Ch. 216.
[25] Also, as mentioned in the introduction, advisers should have regard to the recommendations contained in the Code of Practice for Commercial Leases in England and Wales.
[26] See also *Boots The Chemists Ltd v. Pinkland Ltd* [1992] 28 E.G. 118.
[27] *United Scientific Holdings Ltd v. Burnley Borough Council* [1978] A.C. 904.
[28] [2001] 32 E.G. 89.
[29] *Harben Style Ltd v. Rhodes Trust* [1995] 1 E.G.L.R. 118; *Royal Bank of Scotland plc v. Jennings* [1995] 2 E.G.L.R. 87; *Royal Insurance Property Services Ltd v. Cliffway Ltd* [1996] E.G.C.S. 189; and *Addin Investments Ltd v. Secretary of State for the Environment* [1996] E.G.C.S. 195. But also see the

recent case of *Barclays Bank plc v. Saville Estates Ltd* [2002] 18 E.G. 152 in which it was held that in order to give the lease business efficacy, the tenant was able to serve a notice making time of the essence.

[30] *e.g.* 75 per cent of the difference between the current rent and the landlord's estimate of the market rent.

*Chapter 12*

# The Shop Covenants

## Introduction

**12.01** These covenants are tenants' covenants relating particularly to leases of shop premises, although some of the covenants below are also appropriate for leases of non-retail premises.

**THE FIFTH SCHEDULE**

**The shop covenants**

1   Fitting out

**12.02**      At [its] own expense within _____ weeks from the date of this Lease to install in the Premises in accordance with the specification and drawings annexed as the eighth schedule the shop front and floor surface and all usual tenant's shop fixtures fittings and decorations and electricity and water fittings and apparatus and such fixtures and fittings as may be necessary to enable the Tenant to use occupy and trade from the Premises all such works ("the Tenant's Works") to be executed in a good and workmanlike manner with good quality materials in accordance with the specifications and drawings and with all necessary licences permits authorities permissions and consents [and notwithstanding that the fourth schedule paragraphs 1.4.3 and 4[1] provide (*inter alia*) that any increase in rental value due to the existence of an improvement carried out in pursuance of an obligation to the Landlord will not be disregarded on a review of the Rent any increase in rental value due to the Tenant's Works shall for all purposes of the fourth schedule be deemed to be improvements falling within the definition "the Disregarded Matters"]

This covenant is more normally contained in an agreement for lease but if it is included as one of the tenant's covenants then it is vital that there is a reference that the fitting-out and other works, despite their being carried out pursuant to an obligation to the landlord, will nevertheless be disregarded when ascertaining the revised rent on rent review. If not, then the works will not be disregarded despite having been carried out at the expense of the tenant. A particular example of this would be works carried out pursuant to the Disability Discrimination Act 1995.

The obligation to the landlord to carry out works may not necessarily be contained in the lease[2] but may be comprised in a licence permitting the alterations.[3] As in the *Godbold* case, however, the courts will be reluctant to accept that a licence for alterations can comprise an obligation to the landlord for this particular purpose.[4]

## 2 User

| | | |
|---|---|---|
| 2.1 | To use the Premises for the Permitted User only | **12.03** |
| 2.2 | Not to stand place deposit or expose outside any part of the Premises any goods materials articles or things whatever for display or sale or for any other purpose nor cause any obstruction of the Common Parts | |
| 2.3 | Not to discharge into any of the Pipes serving the Premises or any other property any oil grease or other deleterious matter or any substance which might be or become a source of danger or injury to the drainage system of the Premises the Centre or any Adjoining Property | |
| 2.4 | Not to install or use in or upon the Premises any machinery or apparatus which causes noise or vibration which can be heard or felt in nearby premises or outside the Premises or which may cause damage | |
| 2.5 | Not to play or use any musical instrument loudspeaker tape recorder gramophone radio or other equipment or apparatus that produces sound in the Premises so as to be heard in nearby premises or outside the Premises [if the Landlord shall [in [its] absolute discretion *or* reasonably] consider such sound to be undesirable and shall give written notice to the Tenant to that effect] | |
| 2.6 | Not to display any flashing lights in the Premises that can be seen from outside the Premises [nor to display any other lighting arrangement that can be seen from outside the | |

Premises if the Landlord shall [in its absolute discretion *or* reasonably] consider such lighting to be undesirable and shall give written notice to the Tenant to that effect]

**2.7** **Not to cook or heat any food in the Premises other than for the purpose of making hot drinks**

The problem is one of achieving a happy medium between the landlord's likely desire, particularly in shopping centres, of maintaining a balance of differing uses and thereby restricting the use to which premises can be put, and the tenant's wish to have the right to widen the use where necessary, *e.g.* where the tenant wishes to underlet or assign. If the use is too restrictive the tenant could argue that this should be taken into account on rent review. If too wide, this could favour the landlord on review, resulting in a higher rent than may be justified by the tenant's actual use. Care must therefore be taken in settling the permitted user.

It is better for the covenant to use the premises to be put into the negative to avoid any suggestion that there is a positive obligation to trade, although the covenant may be likely to be construed as being negative in any event,[5] therefore paragraph 2.1 should be amended to read:

**Not to use the Premises otherwise than for the Permitted User**

The remainder of the paragraph will be a matter of negotiation depending upon the tenant's proposed business and the nature of any additional restrictions affecting the user that may be set out in the lease. Certain tenants may object to paragraph 2.6 on the grounds that, with modern shopfronts, a relatively innocuous interior lighting display, visible from the exterior, could breach this covenant. In addition, paragraph 2.7 could perhaps be amended as follows:

**2.7** **Not to cook or heat any food in the Premises other than for staff consumption**

**3** **Alterations**[6]

**12.04** **3.1** Save as permitted by paragraph 3.2 not to make any alteration or addition whatsoever to the Premises or to install or erect any exterior lighting shade or awning or place or install any structure or other thing in front of or elsewhere outside the Premises

**3.2** Not without the consent of the Landlord such consent not to be unreasonably withheld [or delayed] to make any alteration or addition to the shop front of the Premises

3.3  At the end of the Term (if so required by the Landlord) substantially to reinstate the Premises to the same condition as they were in at the date of the grant of this Lease such reinstatement to be carried out under the supervision and to the [reasonable] satisfaction of the Surveyor

3.4  To procure that any alterations or additions to the Premises which shall be permitted by the Landlord under this paragraph shall be carried out only by contractors first approved by the Landlord [such approval not to be unreasonably withheld [or delayed]]

3.5  To make connection with any Pipes serving the Premises only in accordance with plans and specifications approved by the Landlord [such approval not to be unreasonably withheld [or delayed]] subject to consent to make such connection having previously been obtained from the competent statutory authority or undertaker

Alterations' covenants are absolute or qualified; the former where no alterations are permitted and the latter where none are permitted without the previous consent of the landlord. There is in fact no provision implied in a qualified covenant that the landlord's consent will not be unreasonably withheld. Where the covenant is qualified, section 19(2) of the Landlord and Tenant Act 1927 will apply to the extent that the alterations constitute improvements and will imply a provision that the landlord's consent is not to be unreasonably withheld. An "improvement" need not necessarily add to the letting value of the premises,[7] provided that it improves the comfort, convenience and beneficial use of the premises from the point of view of the tenant.[8]

A tenant will wish to have the right to carry out such alterations as would be likely to be necessary or arise during the duration of the term, which may be 25 years. Circumstances change in that time and therefore a well-advised tenant should have the right to carry out, to both the interior and exterior of the premises, structural and non-structural alterations with consent not to be unreasonably withheld. A landlord may, however, try to resist the tenant's right to carry out structural alterations, in which case the tenant should try to pinpoint any structural alterations that it would be likely to want to carry out, *e.g.* the insertion of a hole in the structural slab to accommodate a conveyor installation for the transfer of goods from storage to the retail part of the premises, or, indeed, structural alterations necessary for the purpose of creating a permitted underletting.

The alterations provisions may also contain a covenant by the tenant, in the case of works of a substantial nature, to provide security in the form of a deposit of money or the provision of a bond, as assurance to the landlord that any permitted works will be fully completed. If implemented this will probably result in a dispute as to what are works of a substantial nature and what is adequate security. The tenant would be advised to delete such a covenant.

Another point to consider is the extent to which the tenant would expect to have to reinstate the premises at the end of the term. The tenant may, for example, have installed a mezzanine floor as part of its works and may prefer not to have to dismantle it on vacating, though the landlord may have a valid case to the contrary. The tenant may therefore endeavour to exclude substantial items from its reinstatement obligation, either in the lease or the licence for alterations permitting their construction. The Code of Practice for Commercial Leases may also be a relevant factor. In addition, the tenant may wish to avoid having to obtain the landlord's consent for the erection of aerials etc.

Ideally, the paragraph should be amended to read:

**3.1** **Not without the consent of the Landlord such consent not to be unreasonably withheld or delayed to make any alteration or addition whatsover to the Premises [or to the Retained Parts**

(namely parts of the structure situated within the definition of the premises)

> **situated within the Premises or dividing one floor of the Premises from another]**
> **PROVIDED THAT consent shall not be necessary for**
>
> **(1)  internal non-structural alterations or additions or**
> **(2)  the installation or removal of internal demountable partitioning or**
> **(3)  the erection of aerials satellite dishes and other telecommunications equipment on the roof of the Premises [or other parts thereof]**

**3.2** At the end of the Term (if reasonably required by the Landlord) substantially to reinstate the Premises to the same condition as they were in at the date of the grant of this Lease such reinstatement to be carried out to the reasonable satisfaction of the Surveyor

**3.3** To procure that any alterations or additions to the Premises which shall be permitted by the Landlord under this paragraph shall be carried out only by reputable contractors

3.4    To make connection with any Pipes serving the Premises only in accordance with plans and specifications approved by the Landlord such approval not to be unreasonably withheld or delayed subject to consent to make such connection having previously been obtained from the competent statutory authority or undertaker

4    To take precautions

4.1    To take all necessary precautions against frost damage to the Pipes in on under or over the Premises  12.05
4.2    To take all necessary care and precautions to avoid water damage to any other part of the Centre by reason of bursting or overflowing of any pipe or water apparatus in the Premises

The tenor of these covenants is not unreasonable, but the substitution of the word "reasonable" for "necessary" is an improvement from the tenant's point of view.

5    Hours of trading access and display

5.1    During the Shop Opening Hours  12.06
5.1.1    to keep the Premises open for business and properly cared for and
5.1.2    to trade actively throughout substantially the whole of the Premises except in so far as:
5.1.2.1    the Tenant may be prevented from doing so by reason of destruction or damage to the Premises or the Centre by an Insured Risk or by any other cause not involving default by the Tenant
5.1.2.2    may be necessary for the carrying out with all reasonable speed of any major repairs alterations or additions to the Premises
5.1.2.3    may be necessary to complete a permitted assignment [or underletting] of this Lease or
5.1.2.4    to do so would be contrary to any regulation or requirement of any competent statutory or local authority

See comments under clause 1.12 as to shop opening hours.

Most retailing tenants object to keep open provisions because circumstances could result in the tenant wishing to close the premises either because they have become uneconomic or the tenant has moved to larger premises in the area. Having regard to rents and other outgoings that will continue to be payable in respect of the premises, the tenant is likely to be seeking either an assignee or undertenant, but in the event of a slow market, this could take a considerable period of time. What the tenant does not want is to be forced to re-open the premises or, possibly, to have the lease forfeited, although it may not object to that if the market is depressed. The courts have, however, shown a reluctance to grant an injunction requiring a tenant to trade[9] and we now have the House of Lords judgment in *Co-op Insurance Society Ltd v. Argyll Stores Holdings Ltd.*[10] In this case the House of Lords declared that they would not overturn the settled practice of refusing to grant an order to enforce trading, but it should not be forgotten that the landlord may have a claim for substantial damages stemming from the breach of a keep-open covenant[11] and it may be possible for the landlord to establish quite a substantial loss particularly in the case of a "key" tenant.[12] The landlord may also, of course, bring forfeiture proceedings, though that may not necessarily be in the landlord's best interests. The keep-open covenant should therefore be deleted.

One option available is to agree an amendment by which the tenant must keep the premises open for business during the first [three] *or* [five] years of the term. This gives the landlord some initial comfort and hopefully will not prove to be too burdensome for the tenant—depending, of course, on the length of the lease term and the likely success of the tenant's business! If paragraph 5.1 has to remain, the tenant should consider amending paragraph 5.1.2.1 as follows:

**5.1.2.1 the Tenant may be prevented from doing so by reason of destruction or damage to the Premises or the Centre by any of the Insured Risks (or by terrorism (whether or not at any time one of the Insured Risks)) or by any other cause not involving default by the Tenant**

... and by rewording paragraph 5.1.2.3 to read as follows:

**5.1.2.3 the Tenant may wish to close the Premises where it proposes to seek an assignment or underletting of this Lease in which event it shall market the Premises and use all reasonable endeavours to complete such assignment or underletting with all due expedition or**

**[5.2 Not to open the Premises for business outside Shop Opening Hours]**

This clause should be deleted where the premises are self-contained. If the premises are part of a shopping centre, the tenant should ensure that arrangements for access outside specified hours can at least be made for servicing and stock-taking if necessary. See also comments under clause 1.12 as to shop opening hours.

5.3 To keep all those parts of the interior of the Premises that are visible from a pedestrian mall [or a street] attractively laid out and furnished and with goods well displayed and to keep any display windows or showcases in the Premises clean and adequately and attractively dressed at all times to the [reasonable] satisfaction of the Landlord

5.4 Unless prevented by any regulation or requirement of a competent statutory or local authority or by any interruption in the supply of electricity by the statutory undertaker to keep all display windows and showcases of the Premises well lit during such hours as the Surveyor shall from time to time determine or in the absence of such determination during the Shop Opening Hours and the [30] minutes immediately preceding those hours and the [30] minutes immediately following those hours provided that this obligation shall not apply during the periods specified in paragraphs 5.1.2.1 to 5.1.2.4 but during those periods the Tenant shall take such steps as the surveyor shall [reasonably] require to ensure that [a reasonably *or* an] attractive external appearance to the Premises is maintained

Landlords of shopping centres often try to impose covenants along the lines of paragraphs 5.3 and 5.4 stating that they are in the interests of good estate management. Both of these paragraphs should be deleted. As regards paragraph 5.3, some of the larger retail stores no longer have dressed display windows. If they are to be accepted, the "reasonable" options should definitely be included. Also, paragraph 5.3 could be amended to commence:

**While the Tenant is trading from the Premises to keep ...**

and the words ...

**at all times to the [reasonable] satisfaction of the Landlord ...**

should be deleted. Paragraph 5.4 should certainly be resisted whenever possible. The determination of the surveyor as to the hours during which the display windows and showcases should be lit is really a discretion too far and should be deleted, unless, of course, it is made clear that such hours are to be less than the shop opening hours. The reference to paragraphs

5.1.2.1 to 5.1.2.4 will depend upon what is agreed in respect of paragraph 5.1.

### 6 Signs and advertisements

**12.07**
- **6.1 At all times to display and maintain a suitable sign of a size and kind first approved in writing by the Landlord showing the Tenant's corporate or trading name**
- **6.2 Not to place or display on the exterior of the Premises or on the windows or inside the Premises so as to be visible from outside the Premises any name writing notice sign placard poster sticker or advertisement other than:**
- **6.2.1 normal price tickets attached and relating to goods sold in the display area inside the Premises (but not on the window glass) [and]**
- **6.2.2 the sign referred to in paragraph 6.1 [and]**
- **[6.2.3 trade placards posters or advertisements of a temporary and not excessive nature and necessary or usual for the Permitted User [provided that not more than [25] per cent of the surface area of the shop window of the Premises shall be obscured by such placards posters or advertisements]]**

The landlord will wish to maintain some control over signs and advertisements to ensure, for instance, that the prestige of the shopping centre is maintained. Paragraph 6.1 should be qualified to provide that the landlord's consent will not be unreasonably withheld or delayed. Some substantial tenants insert a proviso exempting them from the effect of this provision on the basis that they would not wish the landlord to object on any grounds, reasonable or otherwise, to their corporate signage. The tenant's own business practice will be pertinent to decide whether the provisions relating to trade placards, posters and advertisements are acceptable, although they may be necessary for a subsequent assignee or underlessee. The percentage figure in paragraph 6.2.3 could, hopefully, be open to negotiation. For instance, some retailers require virtually total coverage of their windows and doors during sale periods.

### 7 Clean and tidy

**12.08**
- **7.1 Not to cause the Common Parts to become untidy or dirty but at all times to keep the Common Parts free from deposits of materials and refuse**
- **7.2 To clean both sides of the shop front [and the doors and windows and door and window frames] of the Premises [at**

least [once] every [week] or as often as is [reasonably] necessary]

It is important to avoid an obligation on the tenant to keep the common parts clean and tidy where the tenant is not in default. The following amendment is therefore suggested:

**7.1** Not to cause the Common Parts to become untidy or dirty or to deposit materials or refuse on any part of them

Clause 7.2 should be amended to read:

**7.2** To clean both sides of the shop front [and the doors and windows and door and window frames] of the Premises as often as is reasonably necessary

**8** **Ceiling and floor loading**

**8.1** Not to bring or permit to remain upon the Premises any safes machinery goods or other articles which shall or may strain or damage the Premises or any part of them

**8.2** Not without the consent of the Landlord to suspend anything from the ceiling of the Premises

**8.3** On any application by the Tenant for the Landlord's consent under paragraph 8.2 the Landlord may consult and obtain the advice of an engineer or other person in relation to the loading proposed by the Tenant and the Tenant shall repay to the Landlord on demand the fees of such engineer or other person

**12.09**

The tenant should endeavour to ascertain the maximum floor loadings of the premises. As regards paragraph 8.2, it is unlikely that the tenant would wish to suspend anything from the ceiling, but there is no harm in seeking to amend the qualification to provide that the landlord's consent will not be unreasonably withheld or delayed. The fees referred to in paragraph 8.3 should be qualified to read:

the reasonable and proper fees

**9** **Loading and unloading**

**9.1** Not to load or unload any goods or materials from any vehicle except where such vehicles are parked in the loading bay coloured [brown] on the Plan and not to cause congestion of that or any adjoining loading bays nor inconvenience to any other user of it or them

**12.10**

9.2 Not to permit any vehicles belonging to the Tenant or any persons calling on the Premises expressly or by implication with the authority of the Tenant to stand on the service roads [or the pavements of them] or (except when and for so long as the same are actually loading or unloading goods and materials) on the loading bays and [to use [its] best endeavours] to ensure that such persons calling on the Premises do not permit any vehicle to stand on any such road pavement or loading bay

9.3 Not to convey any goods or materials to or from the Premises except through the entrances and service areas provided for the purpose and not (without prejudice to the generality of the above) to convey the same via the shopping malls

A shopping centre quite often comprises numerous premises each needing to be serviced on a regular basis. If the landlord does not impose restrictions and regulations to control the use of service facilities and accesses, no doubt there would be a plethora of complaints from all tenants affected, including those who have added to the chaos. It is merely a question of arriving at a solution that is fair to all concerned. The "best endeavours" qualification in paragraph 9.2 should in any event be amended to "reasonable endeavours".

### 10 Security and fire alarms

**12.11**

10.1 To permit the duly authorised employees and agents of the Landlord to enter the Premises upon reasonable notice during the Shop Opening Hours [accompanied by an employee of the Tenant] for the purpose of servicing and maintaining the intruder and fire alarm systems in the Centre [provided that the Landlord shall cause as little disturbance as possible and shall make good any damage to the Premises or to any furniture fittings stock or equipment in the Premises caused by such entry]

10.2 To permit the duly authorised employees and agents of the Landlord to have such access to the Premises as may be required in the event of an intruder alarm call

10.3 To maintain repair and when necessary renew the intruder and fire alarms and ancillary equipment installed in the Premises

10.4 Not to install or maintain in the Premises any equipment or apparatus which:

10.4.1 is intended to be an extension of the intruder alarm or fire alarm systems and to be connected to either such system other than such apparatus or equipment as is compatible with the equipment of such systems and that has been approved by the Landlord [such approval not to be unreasonably withheld [or delayed]] or

10.4.2 which may affect the performance of the intruder alarm or fire alarm systems

10.5 Not to make any connection to such systems without the prior written consent of the Landlord [such consent not to be unreasonably withheld [or delayed]]

10.6 To install and maintain in the Premises a telephone which is connected to the British Telecom system

These provisions appear satisfactory depending upon what has been agreed between the landlord and the tenant during negotiations.

The tenant may, however, wish to delete paragraph 10.6 as there are now other competitors to British Telecom.

**11 Heating cooling and ventilation**

11.1 Not to do anything which interferes with the heating cooling or ventilation of the Common Parts or which imposes an additional load on the heating cooling or ventilation plant and equipment  **12.12**

11.2 During the Shop Opening Hours to operate the ventilation equipment in the Premises which comprises part of the system for the air conditioning of the Common Parts in accordance with the regulations for such purpose made by the Landlord from time to time

This seems satisfactory (subject to the word "adversely" preceding "interferes" in paragraph 11.1) although paragraph 11.2 depends on the particular circumstances of the letting. Any regulations made by the landlord as referred to in paragraph 11.2 should be "reasonable" and an amendment in that regard should be made.

**12 Plate glass**

12.1 To maintain in force throughout the Term insurance against damage to all plate glass in the Premises and to produce to the Landlord on demand the policy relating to such insurance and evidence of payment of the current premium  **12.13**

**12.2** Notwithstanding anything to the contrary contained elsewhere in this Lease wherever any plate glass is broken or damaged to lay out all money received in respect of such insurance as quickly as possible in reinstating with new glass of the same quality and thickness and to make good any deficiency in such money

Insurance of plate glass can be quite expensive and therefore many retailers prefer to carry this risk themselves on the basis, hopefully, that they would not expect to have too many breakages a year. Quite often, the tenant agrees that the covenant can remain but in return is given a letter of waiver stating that the covenant will not apply to the tenant while the lease is vested in it and the tenant is trading at the premises. Unfortunately, such a letter can easily become lost. Furthermore, the landlord's own insurance covenant will often give the landlord the right to insure against such other risks as the landlord may require, and this risk could therefore be covered "through the back door". The tenant may also wish to delete any provision which states that the tenant is to insure plate glass in the joint names of the landlord and tenant, even if the tenant decides to add a proviso to the end of this paragraph that it will not apply to the particular named tenant while the lease is vested in it. An obligation on the tenant to produce the insurance policy to the landlord on demand is also usually resisted and replaced with an obligation to produce evidence of cover and/or details of such insurance. The following proviso is suggested:

> **PROVIDED THAT this provision shall have no effect while this Lease is vested in [_____]**

**13 Regulations**

**12.14** To comply with all regulations made by the Landlord from time to time for the management of the Centre [and notified to the Tenant in writing] [provided that nothing in the regulations shall purport to amend the terms of this Lease and in the event of any inconsistency between the terms of this Lease and the regulations the terms of this Lease shall prevail]

This provision could impose on the tenant unknown restrictions which could adversely affect the tenant's business or give rise to capital expenditure. In *Bristol & West Building Society v. Marks & Spencer plc*,[13] a landlord failed in his attempt to obtain a mandatory injunction as a result of a new "regulation" imposed by him, but the court nevertheless accepted that a landlord can impose additional obligations on a tenant by this method, and if the clause has to be accepted, which the tenant may try to resist, the words in square brackets must remain. In addition, the tenant should amend the first line to provide that the regulations are "reasonable", as well as possibly adding the following proviso at the end of the paragraph:

> **PROVIDED FURTHER THAT any such regulations shall only be made by the Landlord where they are in the best interests of the tenants in the Centre [and there shall be no regulations relating to keeping the Premises open for business or requiring the Tenant to join a traders' or similar association]**

The optional amendment (in square brackets) is merely to cover the situation where the landlord makes a regulation requiring the premises to be "kept open" for trade either during certain hours of the day or generally.

---

[1] The reference to para. 4 in the precedent would appear to be incorrect and was probably intended to be a reference to para. 2.3.

[2] See fourth schedule, para. 1.4.3.

[3] *Godbold v. Martin (The Newsagents)* [1983] 268 E.G. 1202.

[4] For an interesting variation on the landlord's attempt to gain from works carried out by the tenant, see *Historic Houses Hotels Ltd v. Cadogan Estates* [1995] 11 E.G. 140, where the landlord tried to take advantage of wording in several licences for alterations that "upon completion of the permitted works the provisions of the lease should apply to the premises as if the premises in their altered state had originally been comprised in the lease"! Fortunately, the court saw through this argument.

[5] As an "emphatic negative": see *Tea Trade Properties v. CIN Properties* [1990] 22 E.G. 67.

[6] It is more usual for the alterations covenant to be contained in the tenant's covenants, and this has been recognised in the fifth edition 1997 reissue of volume 22(2) of the *Encyclopaedia*.

[7] *Balls Bros Ltd v. Sinclair* [1931] 2 Ch. 325 (the letting value can be reduced from the landlord's standpoint).

[8] *F.W. Woolworth & Co. Ltd v. Lambert* [1937] Ch. 37.

[9] See, for example, *F.W. Woolworth plc v. Charlwood Alliance Properties Ltd* [1987] 1 E.G.L.R. 53, in which the judge refused a mandatory injunction because of previous case law to the contrary. See also *Braddon Towers Ltd v. International Stores Ltd* [1987] 1 E.G.L.R. 209.

[10] [1997] 23 E.G. 141.

[11] In *Costain Property Developments Ltd v. Finlay & Co. Ltd* [1989] 1 E.G.L.R. 237, damages for breach were awarded in the sum of £147,000.

[12] In *Transworld Land Co. Ltd v. J Sainsbury plc* [1990] 2 E.G.L.R. 255, the closure of the "anchor" tenant affected rent review negotiations of neighbouring premises and loss of rent as a result of rent reviews following closure were taken into account in calculating damages.
[13] [1991] 41 E.G. 139.

*Chapter 13*

# Service Charges

## Introduction

The landlord's intention in including service charge provisions is to try to ensure that the rents obtainable from various units within a multi-occupied development are not diminished by the landlord having to pay for various "services" provided to those units, or in respect of areas where the units have joint rights.     **13.01**

The intention here is to try to establish a satisfactory medium between the landlord, who will be endeavouring to include within the service charges everything from weeding the ornamental grass forming part of a shopping precinct to dusting artificial flowers, and the tenant. There are indeed occasions where a tenant can find itself paying almost as much by way of service charges as rent, which is, of course, a most unhappy state of affairs. It is perhaps an obvious statement to make, but the tenant should ascertain from the landlord a detailed estimate of the first year's service charge (and previous years' service charges, if the lease is of an existing building) prior to committing itself to take the lease.

The ideal situation is where premises stand alone and are therefore subject to full repairing covenants without the necessity for a service charge. Any party walls can be dealt with by means of a standard tenant's covenant to contribute towards the cost of repairs as and when the need arises. Unfortunately, now more often than not service charge provisions are found in leases to cover either the situation where premises form part only of a building in joint occupation or where premises form part of a shopping centre or retail park.

Leases contain many different ways of dealing with the provision and payment of services, but the constituent parts are mainly:

(1) the performance of the services;
(2) the payment of the service charge;
(3) the composition of the services.

The provisions contained in the precedent are clear and form the backbone of many lease precedents.

It should be appreciated that if a tenant carries out works to its premises which would ordinarily be carried out by the landlord and paid for via the service charge, the tenant will still be obliged to contribute to the cost of similar works carried out to the remainder of the units by the landlord.[1]

## SIXTH SCHEDULE

### Service charge
### Part A—Definitions

**13.02**  1      "Services" means the services facilities and amenities specified in Part C of this schedule

**13.03**  2      "Annual Expenditure" means:

  2.1    all costs expenses and outgoings whatever [reasonably and properly] incurred by the Landlord during a Financial Year in or incidentally to providing all or any of the Services and

  2.2    all sums [reasonably and properly] incurred by the Landlord during a Financial Year in relation to the matters specified in Part D of this schedule ("the Additional Items") and any VAT payable on such items but:

  2.3    excluding any expenditure in respect of any part of the Centre for which the Tenant or any other tenant shall be wholly responsible and exluding any expenditure that the Landlord shall recover or which shall be met under any policy of insurance maintained by the Landlord pursuant to [its] obligations in this Lease and

  2.4    including (when any expenditure is incurred in relation to the Centre and other premises) the proportion of such expenditure that is reasonably attributable to the Centre to be determined from time to time by the Surveyor (acting as an expert and not as an arbitrator)

The words in square brackets should remain in paragraphs 2.1 and 2.2, but apart from that the definition does not seem unreasonable although the exception in paragraph 2.3 in respect of insurance should make reference to terrorism (where not an insured risk) and may be better expressed separately as:

> excluding the cost of any works of repair or otherwise where such works are the result of damage or destruction by any of the Insured Risks or as a result of terrorism (whether or not at any time one of the Insured Risks) or by any other risk

**against which the Landlord (acting reasonably) ought to have insured**

In addition to the exclusions from the expenditure of the items detailed in paragraph 2.3, the tenant may also consider excluding the following items:

(1) The cost of any refurbishment or enhancement of any part of the centre.
(2) The cost of any works to be carried out to the centre as a result of the centre having been constructed on land containing toxic waste or any other deleterious material or substances.[2]
(3) The cost of any works where money has been or is recoverable from third parties (including insurers) in respect thereof.
(4) The cost of any works necessitated by structural or inherent defects.
(5) Any expenditure incurred by the landlord properly and fairly attributable to any other premises within the centre.
(6) All costs occasioned as part of the initial construction and equipping of the centre and/or the premises as well as the capital cost of substantial plant equipment or fabric installed during the term.
(7) All costs in relation to or connected with the promotion or advertising of the centre.
(8) All costs and expenses relating to the collection of rent or service charges or licence fees.
(9) All costs (including without limitation) solicitors' surveyors' and agents' fees incurred by or on behalf of the landlord in the collection of rents and/or service charges and/or in any proceedings against any lawful or unlawful occupier at the centre.
(10) Any fees or expenses attributable to the review of rents or to the letting of vacant units or in respect of any dispositions or dealings with the landlord's interest in the centre or any part thereof.
(11) The cost of adding to the centre or replacing renewing reconstructing or building any additional units or other buildings within the centre.

A number of these exclusions will be met with opposition from the landlord, in which case it is a question of negotiation as to which exclusions will remain. One exclusion in particular worth mentioning is (4). It is obviously quite impracticable for the tenant to have carried out a structural survey of the whole centre and it is therefore worth pressing for this exclusion, though landlords fight tooth and nail to resist this. A possible fallback is to obtain an obligation from the landlord to pursue its builders and other relevant members of its professional team.[3]

There should also be a provision that the tenant should not be required to pay any part of the annual expenditure attributable to any unlet premises. In this lease, there is an actual service charge percentage set out in clause 1.13, but the majority of leases adopt the perhaps preferred course of stating that the service charge attributable to the tenant should be a fair and proper proportion of the annual expenditure, thereby giving the tenant the chance to contest unfair treatment. In such circumstances, there should be a definition of the "unlet premises" together with a landlord's covenant to pay the service charge attributable to the unlet premises and possibly also, as mentioned above, a proviso in the service charge provisions that the tenant shall not be required to pay any part of the service charge attributable to any unlet premises. The tenant should take care to ensure that the definition of "unlet premises" is not so narrow that many units that are vacant may not fall within the definition (or may result in a dispute) because the landlord has defined them as being premises "available to be let for the same term as and on a lease containing the same provisions as this lease". The tenant should be wary to avoid having a full repairing obligation for its own premises and also paying via the service charge for repairs being carried out to "unlet premises" or for repairs to the structure of other premises at the centre where those premises are let on internal repairing terms only. Also see under clause 1.12 the comments in respect of Sunday trading and consider whether a tenant who does not intend to trade on a Sunday should insert a provision exempting it from having to pay for services incurred as a result of the centre being open on Sundays.

Paragraph 2.4 is included principally to cover the position where the landlord also owns adjoining property, not forming part of the centre and the landlord carries out repairs or incurs expenditure in respect of both properties. The provision does not seem unreasonable.

The tenant should also consider inserting the following provision to cover the situation where the landlord imposes car parking charges but intends that the management and maintenance of the car park should be a service charge expense. The same could apply in respect of kiosks and stalls and promotions and displays within the common parts from which the landlord may derive an income, but in respect of which no service charge will be paid despite the use of services, although the landlord may not be expected to hand over the whole of the income in respect of those, but may make an appropriate contribution:

> **The Landlord shall in the calculation of the expenditure give credit for all income derived from charges for car parking at the Centre [as well as derived from kiosks and stalls and promotions and displays within the Common Parts] to the effect**

|     | that the expenditure shall be reduced by the crediting of such income | |
| --- | --- | --- |
| 3 | 'Computing Date' means [December 31] in every year of the Term or such other date as the Landlord may from time to time nominate and 'Computing Dates' shall be construed accordingly | **13.04** |

It may be advisable to qualify line three by amending it to read:

**time to time reasonably nominate**

in order to avoid the landlord chopping and changing throughout the term.

|     |     |     |
| --- | --- | --- |
| 4 | "Financial Year" means the period: | |
| 4.1 | from the commencement of the Term to and including the first Computing Date and subsequently | **13.05** |
| 4.2 | between two consecutive Computing Dates (excluding the first Computing Date but including the second Computing Date in the period) | |

This seems generally acceptable.

|     |     |     |
| --- | --- | --- |
| 5 | "Service Charge" means the Service Charge Percentage of the Annual Expenditure | |

As mentioned, it may not always be advisable to have a specific percentage. The definition of the centre in the precedent is precise (see clause 1.2), but most service charge provisions allow the landlord to extend or reduce the centre. If the service charge is by reference to a specific percentage and the centre is reduced, the tenant could be penalised; the converse may be the case if the centre is extended. Fortunately, these service charge provisions cater for this potential problem by the inclusion of paragraph 8.2. The landlord may provide for the tenant's percentage to be properly determined by a surveyor who may have the discretion to allocate or assess different proportions of the cost of the services to the premises having regard to the various different services being supplied. This is not unfair where one type of property imposes a substantial burden on certain expensive services. What is unfair, however, is where the person or persons deciding the contribution are inextricably linked to the landlord and whose decision is stated to be final and binding on the parties.[4] In such circumstances there should be included a provision that in the event of dispute the determination should be made by an independent surveyor acting as an expert and appointed by the President of the Royal Institution of Chartered Surveyors on the application of either the landlord or the tenant. **13.06**

The percentage of the total service charges payable by a tenant may therefore either be based on a straight percentage of the total service charges or calculated by reference to weighted floor areas, or indeed arrived at by some other formula. In all cases the tenant must endeavour to ensure that the service charge attributable to the premises is fair and reasonable.

## Part B—Performance of the Services and payment of the Service Charge

**6    Performance of the Services**

**13.07**   Subject to the Tenant paying to the Landlord the Service Charge and complying with the covenants and other terms of this Lease the Landlord shall perform the Services throughout the Term provided that the Landlord shall not be liable to the Tenant in respect of:

6.1   any failure or interruption in any of the Services by reason of necessary repair replacement maintenance of any installations or apparatus or their damage or destruction or by reason of mechanical or other defect or breakdown or frost or other inclement conditions or shortage of fuel materials water or labour or any other cause beyond the Landlord's control [provided and to the extent that:

6.1.1   any such failure or interruption could not [reasonably] have been prevented or shortened by the exercise of proper care attention diligence and skill by the Landlord or those undertaking the Services on behalf of the Landlord and

6.1.2   the Landlord uses and continues to use [[its] best *or* reasonable] endeavours to restore the Services in question] or

6.2   any act omission or negligence of any porter attendant or other person undertaking the Services or any of them on behalf of the Landlord [provided that this clause shall not be construed as relieving the Landlord from liability for breach by the Landlord of any covenants on the part of the Landlord contained in this Lease]

The landlord's performance of the services should not be made subject to the tenant paying the service charge, although the landlord will doubtless be able to justify that the tenant should not be entitled to have something for nothing. It would, of course, be difficult to exclude the tenant from enjoying services supplied to other tenants in the centre. The words would, however, probably prevent the tenant from suing the landlord for non-performance of the services. A reference to complying with the covenants and other terms of the lease should definitely be deleted.

The tenant may be advised to specify a standard to which the landlord is to perform the services as referred to in the amendment to this paragraph below. The words in square brackets in paragraphs 6.1 and 6.2 should be included and if possible a reference to "best" as opposed to "reasonable" endeavours inserted in paragraph 6.1.2.

The tenant should in fact try to delete paragraph 6.2 as there is no reason why the landlord should avoid liability because of the incompetence of the persons to whom it has delegated authority.

The opening paragraph of this provision should be amended to read:

> **The Landlord shall perform the Services throughout the Term in a proper and efficient and economic manner in accordance with the principles of good estate management and without imposing any unfair or unreasonable burden on the Tenant and (where appropriate) using good and suitable materials provided that the Landlord shall not be liable to the Tenant in respect of:**

The tenant may decide to include, either in the schedule or in clause 6, a covenant by the landlord to enforce the obligations in respect of the payment of service charges by the other tenants of the centre.[5]

## 7 Payment of the Service Charge

**7.1** The Landlord shall as soon as convenient after each Computing Date prepare an account showing the Annual Expenditure for the Financial Year ending on that Computing Date and containing a fair summary of the expenditure referred to in it and upon such account being certified by the Accountant it shall be conclusive evidence for the purposes of this Lease of all matters of fact referred to in the account [except in the case of manifest error]     **13.08**

The landlord may not wish to have to produce the accounts by a specified date and there may even be an advantage to the tenant in delaying the payment of a possible balancing charge, if on account payments are less than the service charge. Nevertheless, most substantial tenants prefer the calculation of the service charge to be subject to a time limitation if possible and therefore the commencing part of this paragraph could be amended to read:

**7.1** **The Landlord shall as soon as possible (and in any event no later than [three] months) after each Computing Date ...**

In addition, it is vital that the words in square brackets should remain, possibly with the words "or genuine dispute" added, and there should be provision in the service charge clauses for reference to an independent surveyor for determination in the event of dispute. It is certainly advisable to avoid an unqualified statement that a certificate is final and conclusive. It is considered that a certificate can be final and conclusive on questions of fact, but there is still debate as to whether a certificate purporting to be conclusive as to a question of law can be challenged. The better view is that it cannot be challenged, but the certifier may owe a duty of care.[6] It certainly seems that where the amount is certified by the landlord's accountant, as in the present case, the certificate will be open to challenge despite reference to it being conclusive.[7]

**7.2** **The Tenant shall pay for the period from the Rent Commencement Date to the Computing Date next following the date of this Lease the Initial Provisional Service Charge the first payment being a proportionate sum in respect of the period from and including the Rent Commencement Date to and including the day before the next quarter day to be paid on the date of this Lease the subsequent payments to be made in advance on the relevant quarter days in respect of the relevant quarters**

This is self-explanatory and quite often the date of the first payment of the service charge will be governed by the provisions of the agreement for lease, *e.g.* the service charge may commence to be payable from the access date or the date of practical completion, either of which may precede the rent commencement date.

**7.3** **The Tenant shall pay for the next and each subsequent Financial Year a provisional sum [equal to the Service Charge payable for the previous Financial Year *or* what the Service Charge would have been had the previous Financial Year been a period of 12 months calculated by establishing by apportionment a monthly figure for the previous Financial Year and multiplying this by [12] increased by [10] per cent *or* calculated upon [an] *or* [a] reasonable and proper] estimate by the Surveyor acting as an expert and not**

> as an arbitrator of what the Annual Expenditure is likely to be for that Financial Year] by four equal quarterly payments on the usual quarter days

The footnote to the precedent provides wording where the annual expenditure for the previous financial year has not been ascertained by the first quarter day of the next year, the wording allowing for a provisional sum to be paid being equal to the provisional sum paid for that quarter day in the previous financial year. Most service charge provisions, however, adopt the alternative wording in this paragraph that the provisional payments should be calculated on the basis of a reasonable and proper estimate by the landlord's surveyor. This is possibly the fairest method of dealing with the matter, as long as there is the safeguard that the tenant can challenge the calculation where there has clearly been an error.

**7.4 If the Service Charge for any Financial Year shall:**
**7.4.1 exceed the provisional sum for that Financial Year the excess shall be due to the Landlord on demand or**

The tenant should seek an amendment endeavouring to provide for a period of grace of at least 14 days before the excess referred to in paragraph 7.4.1 becomes due in order to avoid the payment of interest, *e.g.*:

> ... the excess shall be due to the Landlord within 14 days after demand or

**7.4.2 be less than such provisional sum the overpayment shall be credited to the Tenant against the next quarterly payment of the Rent and Service Charge**

There would appear to be a good argument for the overpayment to be refunded to the tenant immediately, possibly also with interest if the overpayment is a substantial sum. Nevertheless, landlords tend to resist such a suggestion, but in any event, the following words should be added at the end of paragraph 7.4.2:

> except in respect of the final year of the Term (howsoever determined) when any such overpayment by the Tenant shall be repaid to the Tenant within 14 days after the issue of the said account and certificate

Needless to say, the tenant should not accept a provision that interest should be payable on any shortfall due to the landlord.

Wherever possible the tenant should try to include the following additional paragraph which is self-explanatory and reasonable:

**7.5** Any sums paid by the Tenant on account of the Service Charge shall until expended be held by the Landlord in a separate account with interest to accrue to the account and not to the Landlord and which said sums and interest shall belong to the Tenant until the relevant expenditure in respect thereof has been incurred[8]

The tenant should also add the following obligation on the part of the landlord in a convenient and suitable part of the service charge provisions:

> **The Landlord will make available to the Tenant the records and vouchers relating to the performance of the Services either by supplying copies to the Tenant or making them available at such location as the Landlord may reasonably appoint for the purpose of inspection during normal business hours**

It should be noted that a tenant is now able to recover from its landlord an overpayment of service charge made by it under a mistake of law and a landlord is able to recover from its tenant an underpayment of service charge under a mistake of law, even though a certificate has been issued.[9]

In order to be certain that the landlord will not be permitted to maintain a sinking fund, the tenant could insert the following additional paragraph:

**7.6** The Landlord will not maintain a sinking or reserve fund to provide for any anticipated expenditure in respect of any of the Services or the Additional Items

**8 Variations**

**8.1** The Landlord may withhold add to extend vary or make any alteration in the rendering of the Services or any of them from time to time [if the Landlord at [its] absolute discretion deems it desirable to do so *or* provided that the same complies with the principles of good estate management and is reasonable in all the circumstances]

The landlord will wish to include this provision to ensure that it can vary the services to take account of changing circumstances. The tenant should be careful to place some limitation on the landlord's ability in this regard and the second option in square brackets is most definitely preferred coupled with the following proviso:

PROVIDED THAT the foregoing shall not result in the Services being so extended varied or altered so as adversely to affect the Tenant's enjoyment and occupation of the Premises

8.2 If at any time during the Term the total property enjoying or capable of enjoying the benefit of any of the Services or the Additional Items is increased or decreased on a permanent basis or the benefit of any of the Services or the Additional Items is extended on a like basis to any adjoining or neighbouring property [or if some other event occurs a result of which is that the Service Charge Percentage is no longer appropriate to the Premises] the Service Charge Percentage shall be varied with effect from the Computing Date following such event by agreement between the parties or in default of agreement within [three] months of the first proposal for variation made by the Landlord in such a manner as shall be determined to be fair and reasonable in the light of the event in question by the Surveyor (acting as an expert and not as an arbitrator) except that nothing contained in this Lease shall imply an obligation on the part of the Landlord to provide the Services or the Additional Items to any adjoining or neighbouring property

This is inserted to enable the landlord to extend the services to neighbouring developments within its ownership or control, or possibly to deal with any decrease in the extent of the centre. Also, as the footnote to the precedent points out, the words in square brackets give greater flexibility to the landlord by allowing a change in the percentage in circumstances other than an increase or decrease in the extent of the centre. It is more appropriate where there is a fixed service charge percentage payable by the tenant, and if it is accepted it would be advisable for the tenant to amend the paragraph to provide for any disagreement to be referred to an independent surveyor in the event of the landlord's surveyors' determination being in dispute.

## Part C—The Services

The services listed in the precedent are not extensive, having regard to heavyweight commercial leases of premises in city shopping centres nowadays, and the tenant must use its discretion as to which of the services are appropriate by reference to the size of the centre and which should be deleted as being unduly burdensome. For instance, some tenants object to the landlord having an absolute discretion to include the cost of promotional activity and may try to exclude it, as in the suggested exclusions detailed under paragraph 2. The landlord may wish to promote a shopping centre, for example, by local (or sometimes national) advertising. There is no harm in this provided the cost of such promotion (which could be exorbitant) is kept within reason and possibly the promotional activity should firstly be subject to consultation with the tenants in the centre or the tenants' association, if one exists. If the tenant is a large national retailer, it may already be spending a sizeable sum on advertising and may object to paying a further amount to an advertising programme over which it has no control.

Another point is that service charge provisions quite often, as in this lease, include reference to the cost of "providing" various services. Quite frequently, tenants will object to this because they expect at least some of these services to have been, or to be, provided at the landlord's expense as part of its construction of the centre. An example may be closed-circuit television or other security arrangements, which could be expensive and which the tenant may consider ought to have been provided at the landlord's expense at the outset rather than a few months into the lease term and thereby passing through the service charge. The tenant should therefore be wary to delete reference to the "provision" of any service it feels should be provided at the landlord's cost, and when amending the lease the tenant should consider the words "provision" and "supplying" very carefully indeed.

Some comfort has recently been afforded to tenants by two cases. In the case of *Fluor Daniel Properties Ltd v. Shortlands Investment Ltd*[10] the court held that the standard to which works, carried out by a landlord and payable by a tenant, should be reasonable and take into account the length of the lease term. In *Scottish Mutual Assurance plc v. Jardine Public Relations Ltd*[11] the court held that a tenant of a three year lease should not have to contribute towards non-urgent roof repairs that were more appropriate to fulfilling the landlord's obligations over a 20-year period.

9 **Maintaining, etc., Retained Parts**

**13.10**   **Maintaining repairing [amending altering rebuilding renewing and reinstating] and where appropriate treating washing down painting and decorating [to such standard as the Landlord may from time to time consider adequate] the Retained Parts**

The landlord's covenant in respect of the maintenance and repair of the retained parts should be comprehensive in order to include damage resulting from structural or inherent defects, and no doubt the landlord will expect to recover the cost of all such works, including the remedying of defects, from the tenants. In practice, it is difficult to resist this, but the tenant should attempt to do so and the tenant may also consider inserting a proviso to the effect that the landlord will use its best or all reasonable endeavours to pursue such claims as it may have against the building contractor or other members of the landlord's professional advisers. A structural survey may also be advisable.

The tenant should consider some limitation on the landlord's right to amend, rebuild or renew the retained parts as these words could incorporate substantial rebuilding works for which the tenant would be likely to have to share the cost. Reference to amending and altering should be deleted altogether and rebuilding and renewing qualified as below.

As to the standard of maintenance and repair, the landlord will normally wish to provide that this will be as the landlord or its surveyor considers adequate, as otherwise the courts will imply that the costs recoverable should be fair and reasonable.[12]

The paragraph could be amended to the following form:

> **Maintaining repairing rebuilding renewing and reinstating (but only rebuilding or renewing in so far as may be necessary for the purposes of repair) and where reasonably appropriate treating washing down painting and decorating (to such standard as may be reasonable) the Retained Parts**

10    Maintaining, etc., apparatus plant machinery, etc.

> **Inspecting servicing maintaining repairing amending overhauling replacing and insuring (save in so far as insured under other provisions of this Lease) all apparatus plant machinery and equipment within the Retained Parts from time to time including (without prejudice to the generality of the above) [lifts lift shafts] stand-by generators and boilers and items relating to mechanical ventilation heating cooling public address and closed-circuit television**

13.11

This does not seem unreasonable and may be extended to cover various other specific items, depending upon the nature of the centre (or indeed limited as the case may be), although the tenant should consider including the following words in line five:

### 11 Maintaining, etc., Pipes

**13.12** Maintaining repairing cleansing emptying draining amending and renewing all Pipes within the Retained Parts and all other Pipes on any Adjoining Property which serve the Centre

This could perhaps be amended to read as follows:

Maintaining repairing cleansing emptying draining amending and renewing (but only amending or renewing where reasonably necessary) all Pipes within the Retained Parts and all other Pipes on any Adjoining Property which serve the Centre subject to the Landlord contributing or ensuring that a contribution is made towards such works where such Pipes also serve the Adjoining Property

### 12 Maintaining, etc., fire alarms, etc.

**13.13** Maintaining and renewing any fire alarms and ancillary apparatus and fire prevention and fire fighting equipment and apparatus in the Retained Parts

It may be advisable to qualify this by inserting the words "(where necessary)" after "renewing".

### 13 Cleaning, etc., Retained Parts

**13.14** Cleaning treating polishing [heating] and lighting the Retained Parts to such standard as the Landlord may from time to time consider adequate

The tenant should consider amending this paragraph to end as follows:

... to such standard as may be reasonably adequate

### 14 Heating, etc.

**13.15** Providing such mechanical ventilation heating and (if deemed desirable by the Landlord) cooling for such parts of the Retained Parts and for such hours and times of year as the Landlord shall in [its] absolute discretion determine

It is important that the views of the tenants should be obtained not only with regard to heating and ventilation but also with regard to the opening hours of the centre in general. Some service charge provisions include the supply of heating (or other services) to individual premises. The tenant should consider such a provision carefully, as it may intend supplying its own heating (or other services) and not be happy to pay a proportion of the cost of such supply (or supplies) to other premises. This should be amended as follows:

> **Providing such mechanical ventilation heating and (if reasonably deemed desirable by the Landlord) cooling for such parts of the Retained Parts and for such hours and times of year as the Landlord shall in its reasonable discretion determine after consultation with the [tenants in the Centre] [Tenants' Association]**[13]

### 15 Malls open

> **Keeping the malls and other public pedestrian ways of the Centre open to the general public during the Shop Opening Hours and the [30] minutes immediately preceding and the [30] minutes immediately following those hours**    13.16

See comments under clause 1.12 above.

### 16 Speakers, etc.

> **Maintaining operating and replacing any signs loudspeakers public address or music broadcast system or closed-circuit television or the like in the Retained Parts as the Landlord shall in [its] absolute discretion determine**    13.17

The landlord should perhaps use its reasonable discretion, but subject to that point this provision is not unreasonable as it does not refer to the "provision" of the items.

### 17 Ornamental features garden, etc.

> **Providing and maintaining (at the Landlord's absolute discretion) any architectural or ornamental features or murals and any plants shrubs trees or garden or grassed area in the Retained Parts and keeping the same planted and free from weeds and the grass cut**    13.18

This should commence:

> Providing and maintaining to a reasonable standard any architectural...

It should also be noted that this head of expenditure quite frequently extends to the provision of seats and benches, drinking fountains, decorative lights, etc., some of which the tenant may expect the landlord to provide at its own expense at the outset. Architectural features can also be interesting—and expensive and should therefore be deleted. The tenant should attempt to delete a "sweeper" at the end of this provision.

### 18 Fixtures fittings, etc.

**13.19** > Supplying providing purchasing hiring maintaining renewing replacing repairing servicing overhauling and keeping in good and serviceable order and condition all fixtures and fittings bins receptacles tools appliances materials equipment and other things which the Landlord may deem desirable or necessary for the maintenance appearance upkeep or cleanliness of the Centre or any part of the Centre

There is no basic objection to this provision depending on the nature of the centre although the latter part could perhaps be amended as follows:

> ...which the Landlord may reasonably deem desirable or necessary...

although the tenant may try to delete the opening three words. The tenant may also prefer to add the following words after "and other things":

> ...within the Retained Parts...

### 19 Windows

**13.20** > Cleaning as frequently as the Landlord shall in [its] absolute discretion consider adequate the exterior and interior of all windows and window frames in the Retained Parts

This is perhaps a minor point, but it may be better for this provision to begin:

> Cleaning as frequently as may be reasonably necessary the exterior and interior...

### 20 Refuse

**13.21** > Collecting and disposing of refuse from the Centre and the provision repair maintenance and renewal of plant and

> equipment for the collection treatment packaging or disposal of the same

This may be necessary in a large centre but could add considerably to costs by a landlord being over-enthusiastic. The following proviso at the end of the paragraph may be advisable:

> ... provided that the Landlord shall endeavour to ensure that costs in this regard are kept to a fair and reasonable level

Individual tenants may, of course, also have their own arrangements for the collection and disposal of refuse.

## 21   Traffic

**Controlling traffic on the service roads**  13.22

Whether this will be necessary depends on the size of the centre.

## 22   Other services

**Any other services relating to the Centre or any part of the Centre provided by the Landlord from time to time and not expressly mentioned [which shall at any time during the Term be:**  13.23

**22.1**  **capable of being enjoyed by the occupier of the Premises**
**22.2**  **[reasonably] calculated to be for the benefit of the Tenant and other tenants of the Centre or be [reasonably] necessary for the maintenance upkeep or cleanliness of the Centre and**
**22.3**  **in keeping with the principles of good estate management]**

Almost all service charge provisions contain something of this nature and, in fact, the form of this provision is far more generous to tenants than most other forms. The usual provision is a general sweeping-up clause to include expenditure on any other items that the landlord may in its absolute discretion think proper for the more efficient management, use and promotion of the centre. There must obviously be a provision of some sort to include services which do not necessarily occur to the landlord at the time of drafting but which could be necessary during the term of the lease, and the question is whether some limitation can be placed on the landlord's right to extend the services to include the imaginable and unimaginable. This will be for the tenant to negotiate and ideally there should be no additional services without the consent of the majority of the tenants in the centre, but the following is a possible starting (or ending) point:

PROVIDED THAT no additional services shall be implemented without prior consultation with the tenants in the Centre [or with the Tenants' Association][14]

## Part D—The Additional Items

### 23  Fees

**13.24**  23.1   The [proper] fees and disbursements (and any VAT payable on them) of:

23.1.1  the Surveyor the Accountant and any other individual firm or company employed or retained by the Landlord for (or in connection with) such surveying or accounting functions or the management of the Centre

23.1.2  the managing agents (whether or not the Surveyor) for or in connection with:

23.1.2.1  the management of the Centre

23.1.2.2  the collection of the rents and all other sums due to the Landlord from the tenants of the Centre

23.1.2.3  the performance of the Services and any other duties in and about the Centre or any part of it relating to (without prejudice to the generality of the above) the general management administration security maintenance protection and cleanliness of the Centre

23.1.3  any individual firm or company valuing the Centre for the purposes of assessing the full cost of rebuilding and reinstatement

23.1.4  any individual firm or company providing caretaking or security arrangements and services to the Centre

23.1.5  any other individual firm or company employed or retained by the Landlord to perform (or in connection with) any of the Services or any of the functions or duties referred to in this paragraph

23.2  The [reasonable] fees of the Landlord or a Group Company for any of the Services or the other functions and duties referred to in paragraph 23.1 above that shall be undertaken by the Landlord or a Group Company and not by a third party

The landlord will wish to ensure that all fees are properly recoverable and may be aware of the case of *Cleve House Properties Ltd v. Schildof*,[15] which held that management costs could only be recovered in respect of a commercial letting where there is specific provision for them in the lease. The problem so far as the tenant is concerned is to try to keep fees to a reasonable level and it will be a question of negotiation (and, indeed, the size of the centre) which determine which of the fees contained in this paragraph are unnecessary. Having said that, paragraph 23.1.2.2 should perhaps be deleted as being unreasonable to expect the tenants to pay for, and paragraph 23.1 should commence:

**The proper and reasonable fees and disbursements...**

As regards paragraph 23.2, this should make reference to proper as well as reasonable and is inserted by the landlord to enable its own staff to perform certain of the services or perform such services "in house". It is suggested that in order to ensure that these fees are recoverable by the landlord this provision should be specifically inserted, but if it is included the tenant should ensure that the words in square brackets at the end of paragraph 24 are included in order to avoid a charge being made in respect of both the fees under paragraph 23.2 and the employment of staff under paragraph 24.

Some service charge provisions attempt to charge the tenant a management fee, usually being a percentage of the service charge payable by the tenant. This obviously requires a good deal of consideration, and possibly negotiation, by the tenant to ensure that the resultant charge is reasonable. Perhaps it is obvious, but care should be taken to avoid the "fund" to which a percentage may be applied also including the management fee.

## 24    Staff, etc.

**The cost of employing (whether by the Landlord a Group Company the managing agents or any other individual firm or company) such staff as the Landlord may in [its] absolute discretion deem necessary for the performance of the Services and the other functions and duties referred to in paragraph 23.1 above and all other incidental expenditure in relation to such employment including but without prejudice to the generality of the above:** 13.25
24.1    **insurance pension and welfare contributions**
24.2    **transport facilities and benefits in kind**
24.3    **the provision of uniforms and working clothing**
24.4    **the provision of vehicles tools appliances cleaning and other materials fixtures fittings and other equipment for the proper performance of their duties and a store for housing the same and**

**24.5** a notional rent (not exceeding the current market rent such rent to be determined by the Surveyor acting as an expert and not as an arbitrator) for any premises in the Centre provided rent free for every such person's use occupancy or residence

[except that where the Services or the functions and duties referred to in paragraph 23.1 above (or any of them) are undertaken by the Landlord or a Group Company rather than by a third party nothing in this schedule shall permit the Landlord to include in the Annual Expenditure both a fee by virtue of paragraph 23.2 above for the performance of the same and also by virtue of this paragraph the cost of employing staff to perform them and in such circumstances the Landlord shall in [its] absolute discretion in respect of each Financial Year elect to include in the Annual Expenditure either a fee for any such items or the cost of employing staff to perform them]

The landlord's discretion in employing such staff should be reasonable and not absolute, and there must be a limitation on the other incidental expenditure. The words "including but without prejudice to the generality of the above" should therefore be deleted and the latter part of the first paragraph should be amended to read:

... and the following incidental expenditure in relation to such employment:

Nobody would deny the staff the various ancillary benefits detailed in this paragraph (although "benefits in kind" in paragraph 24.2 is a rather nebulous phrase), provided that "transport facilities" does not result in an expensive car being provided to every employee or even key persons employed in the centre. Similarly, the tenant would not expect paragraph 24.5 to result in free housing accommodation to all employees, and there may in fact be no necessity to provide residential accommodation at all. If there is residential accommodation, the tenant should again ensure that a limitation be placed on the persons entitled to enjoy it and that it should be reasonably necessary for the proper performance of the employee's duties. The tenant should consider deleting paragraph 24.5 on the basis that if the centre is such that it is necessary to provide residential accommodation to an employee or employees, the landlord should not expect to receive compensation for that accommodation by way of a notional rent. The accommodation should be treated as no different to other ancillary structures within the centre and being necessary as part of the overall development. Paragraph 24.2 could be amended as follows:

**24.2** **transport facilities (where reasonably necessary) for the proper performance of the Services by such staff as aforesaid**

and paragraph 24.4 should commence:

**24.4** **the provision of necessary and reasonable vehicles (not for personal use) tools appliances . . .**

although the tenant may object to paying for the initial provision of vehicles and contend that the landlord should pay for that expense.

**25   Contracts for Services**

**The cost of entering into any contracts for the carrying out of all or any of the Services and other functions and duties that the Landlord may in [its] absolute discretion deem desirable or necessary**                                                                                13.26

This should refer to the reasonable and proper cost of entering into the contracts, and the landlord's discretion should be reasonable not absolute.

**26   Outgoings**

**All rates taxes assessments duties charges impositions and outgoings which are now or during the Term shall be charged assessed or imposed on:**                                                    13.27

**26.1**   **the whole of the Centre where there is no separate charge assessment or imposition on or in respect of an individual unit**

**26.2**   **the whole of the Retained Parts or any part of them including but without prejudice to the generality of the above residential accommodation for caretakers engineers and other staff employed in connection with the Centre**

The tenant may object to having to pay outgoings in respect of any unlet units and, should the landlord accept this as being a reasonable objection, paragraph 26.1 should either be deleted or amended to ensure that no liability falls on the tenant for them. The same point as above applies to the reference to residential accommodation in paragraph 26.2.[16] There is also the question as to whether the cost of rates (possibly) levied on the car park should pass through the service charge in circumstances where the landlord imposes car parking charges which it intends to retain, although it agrees to maintain the car park and pay other expenses. If so, the tenant should be wary of this and exclude the payment of rates, etc., from this provision.

### 27 Electricity gas, etc.

**13.28** The cost of the supply of electricity gas oil or other fuel for the provision of the Services and for all purposes in connection with the Retained Parts

This should commence with a reference to:

The reasonable and proper cost...

### 28 Road, etc., charges

**13.29** The amount which the Landlord shall be called upon to pay as a contribution towards the expense of making repairing maintaining rebuilding and cleansing any ways roads pavements or structures Pipes or anything which may belong to or be used for the Centre or any part of it exclusively or in common with other neighbouring or adjoining premises

This should be amended to commence:

The reasonable and proper amount which the Landlord shall be called upon to pay as a contribution towards the necessary expense of repairing maintaining rebuilding (where reasonable to do so) and cleansing...

### 29 Regulations

**13.30** The costs charges and expenses of preparing and supplying to the tenants copies of any regulations made by the Landlord relating to the Centre or the use of it

Continually changing regulations can be a bane to tenants and this paragraph should be amended to read:

The reasonable and proper costs charges and expenses of preparing and supplying to the tenants copies of any reasonable regulations made by the Landlord relating to the Centre or the use of it

or alternatively it should end:

... any reasonable regulations made by the Landlord relating to the Centre or the use of it after full consultation with the tenants in the Centre [or the Tenants' Association] although the tenant may query as to why it should be expected to pay for the preparation of something to which it may take exception.

### 30    Statutory, etc., requirements

**The cost of taking all steps deemed desirable or expedient by the Landlord for complying with making representations against or otherwise contesting the incidence of the provisions of any statute byelaw or notice concerning town planning public health highways streets drainage or other matters relating to or alleged to relate to the Centre or any part of it for which any tenant is not directly and exclusively liable**

**13.31**

Apart from the amendment of the opening words to refer to "proper and reasonable cost" the tenant may object to this provision as giving the landlord extensive rights to run up expenses at the cost of the tenants. The matters complained of may not even affect the tenant's premises and be in respect of another part of the centre. The tenant should attempt to delete the paragraph but, if that fails, it should consider the following amendments:

**The proper and reasonable cost of taking all reasonable steps for complying with making representations against or otherwise contesting the incidence of the provisions of any statute byelaw or notice concerning town planning public health highways streets drainage or other matters relating to or alleged to relate to the Centre or any part of it for which any tenant is not directly and exclusively liable and provided that any such part of the Centre includes the Premises or the matter in question is capable of being enjoyed by the Tenant or the occupier of the Premises [or otherwise affects the Premises]**

The notes to the precedent suggests the latter amendment (other than the words in square brackets), but it is highly unlikely that the landlord will accept it as the landlord will not generally agree to apportion costs in such a manner. The addition of the words in square brackets may make the amendment slightly more palatable to the landlord.

### 31    Nuisance

**The cost to the Landlord of abating a nuisance in respect of the Centre or any part of it in so far as the same is not the liability of any individual tenant**

**13.32**

The point in respect of apportionment applies as in paragraph 30 above.

## 32 Interest

**13.33** **Any interest and fees in respect of money borrowed to finance the provision of the Services or the Additional Items**

In the absence of a provision such as this, the landlord will not be able to recover interest on any borrowing.[17] The tenant may not be happy to accept this provision at all, arguing that the landlord should manage the services carefully to ensure that borrowing is unnecessary, but if this argument is unsuccessful the tenant will wish to contain the landlord's borrowing, and it may be as well to add the following words at the end of this paragraph:

> . . . where it is reasonable and proper for the Landlord to borrow money for this purpose

## 33 Anticipated expenditure

**13.34** **Such provision (if any) for anticipated expenditure in respect of any of the Services or the Additional Items as the Landlord shall in its absolute discretion consider appropriate**

This provision allows the establishment of what is known as a sinking fund and could give rise to all sorts of problems, quite frequently resulting in landlords preferring not to create sinking funds even where they have the right to do so. From the landlord's point of view, problems result from various taxation concerns, and from the tenant's standpoint it would be necessary to ensure that a sinking fund is held on trust to protect it from the landlord's creditors should the landlord subsequently get into difficulties. Also, see the case of *Secretary of State for the Environment v. Possfund*[18] where it was held that a sinking fund for the replacement of plant belonged to the landlord at the end of the term, who was entitled to use it towards the cost of depreciation and subsequent replacement of the plant in question. In this case, there was no reference to the fund being held on trust and one does not know if a similar conclusion would have been reached if there had been such a provision. The preference is to delete the provision, but if it must remain, it should be amended as follows:

> **Such reasonable provision (if any) for expenditure anticipated within the following three years (or such other period as may be reasonable) in respect of any of the Services or the**

Additional Items as the Landlord shall in its reasonable discretion consider appropriate provided that such provision shall until expended be held by the Landlord in a separate account on trust for the tenants in the Centre from time to time with interest thereon to accrue to the account and not to the Landlord

It is suggested that complications may arise by referring to the beneficiaries as being the tenants from time to time (in case they put an end to the trust and appropriate the trust fund) and that the beneficiaries should be the persons who would be the tenants of the centre at the expiration of the perpetuity period, but the risk is possibly worth taking.

Where there is no trust fund but service charge payments are merely paid on account, the tenant should include the statement set out as paragraph 7.5 of Part B of this schedule.

## SEVENTH SCHEDULE

### Particulars of matters to which the Premises are subject     13.35

(insert details)

## EIGHTH SCHEDULE

### Specification for the Tenant's fitting-out of the Premises    13.36

---

[1] See *Broomleigh Housing Association Ltd v. Hughes* 1999] E.G.C.S. 134.
[2] The full effects of the Environmental Protection Act 1990 are yet to be realised.
[3] See clause 2.14 of the agreement for lease.
[4] See *Finchbourne Ltd v. Rodrigues* [1976] 3 All E.R. 581.
[5] See *Britel Corporation v. Orbach* (1997) 29 H.L.R. 883, CA.
[6] *Re Davstone Estate Ltd's Leases, Re, Manprop Ltd v. O'Dell* [1969] 2 Ch. 378; [1969] 2 All E.R. 849 and *Jones v. Sherwood Computer Services plc* [1992] 2 All E.R. 170; [1992] 1 W.L.R. 277, CA.
[7] See *Concorde Graphics Ltd v. Andromeda Investments SA* (1982) 265 E.G. 386 in which the court held that a certificate given by managing agents, and who were also the landlord's surveyors, could not be final and binding where the tenant disputed the service charge.
[8] See also para. 33 of this schedule.
[9] See *Kleinwort Benson Ltd v. Lincoln City Council* [1998] 4 All E.R. 513 and *Universities Superannuation Scheme Ltd v. Marks & Spencer plc* [1999] 04 E.G. 158.
[10] [2001] E.G.C.S. 8.

[11] [1999] E.G.C.S. 43.
[12] *Finchbourne Ltd v. Rodrigues*, n. 2 above. This case is also authority for the fact that the landlord need not necessarily choose the cheapest tender available for the work.
[13] If there is a tenants' association it may be in both parties' best interests for the landlord to consult with it generally with regard to services and ancillary matters which may otherwise be disputed.
[14] See footnote under para. 14.
[15] [1980] C.L.Y. 1641.
[16] See para. 24.5.
[17] *Boldmark Ltd v. Cohen* [1986] 1 E.G.L.R. 47.
[18] [1990] N.P.C. 151.

*Chapter 14*

# Authorised Guarantee Agreement

## Introduction

Pursuant to clause 5.9.5.1 of the lease an assigning tenant will almost definitely be required to enter into an authorised guarantee agreement to guarantee the obligations of the assignee. The form of the authorised guarantee agreement must comply with the requirements of section 16 of the Landlord and Tenant (Covenants) Act 1995.

**NINTH SCHEDULE**

**Authorised Guarantee Agreement** 14.01

**THIS GUARANTEE is made the [ ] day of [ ]**

**BETWEEN:**
(1) (*name of outgoing tenant*) [of (*address*) (*or as appropriate*) **the registered office of which is at** (*address*)] [(**Company Registration no....**] ("the Guarantor") and
(2) (*name of landlord*) [of (*address*) (*or as appropriate*) **the registered office of which is at** (*address*)] [**Company Registration no....**] ("the Landlord")

**NOW THIS DEED WITNESSES as follows:**

1 **Definitions and interpretation**

    For all purposes of this guarantee the terms defined in this clause have the meanings specified 14.02

1.1 "The Assignee"

    "The Assignee" means (*insert name of incoming tenant*) 14.03

1.2 "The Lease"

**14.04** "The Lease" means the lease dated (*date*) and made between (*name of original landlord*) and (*name of original tenant*) [and (*name of original guarantor*)] for a term of (*number*) years commencing on and including (*commencement date*) [and varied by a deed dated (*date*) and made between (*names of parties*)]

1.3 "The Premises"

**14.05** "The Premises" means the premises demised by the Lease

1.4 "The Liability Period"

**14.06** "The Liability Period" means the period during which the term granted by the Lease shall be vested in the Assignee and until the Lease is assigned by the Assignee to a third party in accordance with the provisions of the Lease (or if such assignment is an excluded assignment within the meaning of section 11(1) of the Landlord and Tenant (Covenants) Act 1995 until the next subsequent assignment which is not an excluded assignment as aforesaid or until the date of the expiration of the contractual term of the Lease)

1.5 The Landlord and Tenant (Covenants) Act 1995

**14.07** The expression "authorised guarantee agreement" has the same meaning in this guarantee as in the Landlord and Tenant (Covenants) Act 1995 section 28(1)

1.6 References to clauses

**14.08** Any reference in this deed to a clause without further designation is to be construed as a reference to the clause of this deed so numbered

2 Recitals

2.1 Consent required

**14.09** By clause (*insert number*) of the Lease the Landlord's consent to an assignment of the Lease is required

## 2.2 Agreement to consent

The Landlord has agreed to give consent to the assignment to the Assignee on condition that the Guarantor enters into this guarantee  **14.10**

## 2.3 Effective time

This guarantee takes effect only when the Lease is assigned to the Assignee  **14.11**

## 3 Guarantor's covenants

In consideration of the Landlord's consent to the assignment the Guarantor convenants with the Landlord and without the need for any express assignment with all his successors in title as set out in this clause 3  **14.12**

### 3.1 Payment and performance

The Assignee shall punctually pay the rents reserved by the Lease and observe and perform the covenants and other terms of it throughout the Liability Period and if at any time during the Liability Period the Assignee shall make any default in payment of the rents or in observing or performing any of the covenants or other terms of the Lease the Guarantor will pay the rents and observe or perform the covenants or terms in respect of which the Assignee shall be in default and make good to the Landlord on demand and indemnify the Landlord against all losses damages costs and expenses as a result of such non-payment non-performance or non-observance notwithstanding:  **14.13**

**3.1.1** any time or indulgence granted by the Landlord to the Assignee or any neglect or forbearance of the Landlord in enforcing the payment of the rents or the observance or performance of the covenants or other terms of the Lease or any refusal by the Landlord to accept rents tendered by or on behalf of the Assignee at a time when the Landlord is entitled (or would after the service of a notice under the Law of Property Act 1925, section 146 have been entitled) to re-enter the Premises

**3.1.2** that the terms of the Lease may have been varied by agreement between the parties [provided such variation is not prejudicial to the Guarantor]

| | 3.1.3 | that the Assignee shall have surrendered part of the Premises in which event the liability of the Guarantor under the Lease shall continue in respect of the part of the Premises not so surrendered after making any necessary aportionments under the Law of Property Act 1925 section 140 and |
|---|---|---|
| | 3.1.4 | any other act or thing by which but for this clause 3.1 the Guarantor would have been released |

    3.2    New lease following disclaimer

**14.14** If during the Liability Period any trustee in bankruptcy or liquidator of the Assignee disclaims the Lease the Guarantor shall if required by notice served by the Landlord within (*state period, e.g. 60 days*) of the Landlord becoming aware of the disclaimer take from the Landlord forthwith a lease of the Premises for the residue of the contractual term of the Lease as at the date of the disclaimer at the rent then being paid under the Lease and subject to the same covenants and terms as in the Lease (except that the Guarantor shall not be required to procure that any other person is made a party to that lease as guarantor) such new lease to commence on the date of the disclaimer and in such case the Guarantor shall pay the costs of such new lease and execute and deliver to the Landlord a counterpart of it

    3.3    Payments following disclaimer

**14.15** If during the Liability Period the Lease is disclaimed and for any reason the Landlord does not require the Guarantor to accept a new lease of the Premises in accordance with clause 3.2 the Guarantor shall pay to the Landlord on demand an amount equal to [the difference between any money received by the Landlord for the use or occupation of the Premises and] the rents reserved by the Lease [in both cases] for the period commencing with the date of such disclaimer and ending on whichever is the earliest of the date (*state period, e.g. six months*) after such disclaimer the date if any on which the Premises are relet and the date of expiration of the contractual term of the Lease

    4    Landlord's covenant

**14.16** The Landlord covenants with the Guarantor that it will notify the Guarantor in writing within (*state period, e.g.*

*seven days*) of being informed of the facts bringing the Liability Period to an end

## 5 Severance

### 5.1 Severance of void provisions

Any provision of this deed rendered void by virtue of the Landlord and Tenant (Covenants) Act 1995 section 25 is to be severed from all remaining provisions and the remaining provisions are to be preserved    14.17

### 5.2 Limitation of provisions

If any provision in this deed extends beyond the limits permitted by the Landlord and Tenant (Covenants) Act 1995 section 25 that provision is to be varied so as not to extend beyond those limits    14.18

**IN WITNESS, etc.**

(*signatures (or common seals) of the guarantor and the landlord*)
(*signatures of witnesses*)

This form of authorised guarantee agreement ("AGA") is as set out in Form 217 from volume 22(3) of the *Encyclopaedia* (1997 Reissue), but has been adapted slightly by the author to bring it into line with the guarantors's covenants set out in clause 8 of the lease. Similar comments apply to the various provisions of the AGA as expressed in respect of the guarantor's covenants in chapter 7. The form of the AGA seems fair, as adapted, although the tenant should make certain that "the liability period" is carefully defined, to ensure that the outgoing tenant is not also expected to guarantee the assignee's obligations under an AGA to be entered into by the assignee on a subsequent assignment.

Clause 5 of the AGA endeavours to counter the provisions of section 25 of the 1995 Act which provides that any agreement (which would include an AGA) relating to a tenancy is void if it restricts the operation of the Act as detailed in that section. As a belt and braces exercise, the tenant may consider adding the following clause:

## 6 Exclusion of liability

**14.19**    Nothing in this deed shall:
- 6.1 make the Guarantor liable for the obligations of anyone other than the Assignee
- 6.2 impose any liabilities on the Guarantor which are more onerous than the Assignee's obligations under the Lease
- 6.3 impose any liability restriction or other requirement on the guarantor in relation to any period of time after the Assignee is released from liability under the Lease by virtue of the Landlord and Tenant (Covenants) Act 1995

The lease is concluded by the signatures and/or seals of all parties

*Chapter 15*

# Licence for Alterations

## Introduction

It has become fairly standard practice in agreements for lease for there to be a provision requiring the tenant to complete a licence for alterations to evidence the tenant's works. This can be seen to be beneficial for both the landlord and the tenant. From the landlord's point of view, the licence will contain various provisions to which the tenant will be subject, including, not least, a covenant to reinstate the premises at the expiration of the term granted by the lease. From the tenant's point of view, the licence will be evidence of the landlord's consent and should contain a provision specifically disregarding the tenant's works on rent reviews under the lease.

The drafting of the licence for alterations should therefore be carefully considered by the tenant's solicitor.

**15.01**

THIS LICENCE is made the _____ day of _____
BETWEEN:
(1) *(name of landlord)* [of *(address)* *(or as appropriate)* **the registered office of which is at** *(address)*] ("**the Landlord**")
(2) *(name of tenant)* [of *(address)* *(or as appropriate)* **the registered office of which is at** *(address)*] ("**the Tenant**")

NOW THIS DEED WITNESSES as follows

1  **Definitions and interpretation**  **15.02**

   In this deed the words and expressions defined in this clause 1 are to have the meanings specified

### 1.1 "Approval"

**15.03** **References to "approval by the Landlord" or words to similar effect are references to written approval [which may not be unreasonably withheld [or delayed]] whether conditional or unconditional**

It is obviously sensible for the tenant to include the wording in square brackets.

### 1.2 "Completed"

**15.04** **References to works being "completed" are references to them being completed to the [complete *(or as required)* reasonable] satisfaction of the Landlord's surveyors and certified to have been so completed such certification not to be unreasonably withheld [or delayed]**

It is preferable for the reference to be to the reasonable satisfaction of the landlord's surveyors. The words "or delayed" should be included.

### 1.3 "Consents"

**15.05** **References to "consents" are references to:**

**1.3.1 planning permission under the Town and Country Planning Act 1990**
**1.3.2 consent of the Insurers**
**1.3.3 any permissions licences certificates consents and approvals required under a statute and**
**1.3.4 any consents from the owners or occupiers of adjoining or neighbouring property or any other person**

**for to or in respect of the commencement execution or retention of any of the Permitted Works**

It is suggested that the landlord should ascertain what consents will be needed for the works, with all the consents needed to be referred to specifically. It is, of course, in the tenant's best interests to ensure that all necessary consents have been obtained.

### 1.4 "the Insurers"

**15.06** **"The Insurers" means the insurers with whom the Premises are for the time being insured**

The insurers will in all probability be the landlord's insurers.

## 1.5 Interpretation

In this licence:

**1.5.1** "the Landlord" includes the person in whom the reversion immediately expectant on the determination of the Term is for the time being vested

[**1.5.2** "the Tenant" includes its successors in title]

This definition is not appropriate in the case of a new tenancy as defined by the Landlord and Tenant (Covenants) Act 1995.

**1.5.3** "the Lease" includes all or any deeds and documents supplemental to the Lease whether or not expressed to be so

There may, for instance, have been a deed of variation entered into since the grant of the lease, though obviously not where the licence is in respect of initial fitting out works on the grant of a lease.

**1.5.4** "the Term" includes any continuation or extension of the Term and any holding over whether by statute at common law or otherwise

**1.5.5** references to "statute" are references to any statute or statutory provision for the time being in force and any regulations orders byelaws or other subordinate legislation made under any such statute or statutory provision from time to time

**1.5.6** unless expressly stated to the contrary any reference to a specific statute includes any statutory extension or modification amendment or re-enactment of that statute and any regulations or orders made under it and any general reference to a statute includes any regulations or orders made under that statute

**1.5.7** if any party at any time comprises two or more persons the obligations of that party are to be joint and several obligations of those persons

**1.5.8** words importing one gender include all other genders words importing the singular include the plural and vice versa and any reference to a person includes a reference to a company authority board department or other body

**1.5.9** the clause headings do not form part of this deed and are not to be taken into account for the purposes of its construction or interpretation

**1.5.10** any covenant by the Tenant not to do anything is to be construed as including a covenant by the Tenant not to permit or suffer the thing to be done

**15.07**

It may be advisable for the latter part of the clause to read:

> ... or knowingly suffer the thing to be done

**1.5.11** references to clauses and paragraphs without further designation are references to the clauses and paragraphs of this licence so numbered and references to this licence include references to the schedule to this licence

**1.6 "The Lease"**

**15.08** "The Lease" means a [lease *(or as appropriate) underlease*] dated *(date)* and made between (1) [the Landlord *(or as appropriate) (name of original landlord)*] and (2) [the Tenant *(or as appropriate) (name of original tenant)*]

The form of the licence is drafted on the basis for use either at the commencement of the lease or during the term granted by it.

**1.7 "The Permitted Works"**

**15.09** "The Permitted Works" means the *(specify works)* the nature and extent of which are detailed in the Plans or any different works and subject to clause 5.4 any additional works the execution of which is required under any approved consent or the Landlord's approval of any other matter relating to the works

It is suggested that a brief description of the works is helpful for estate management purposes. As stated under clause 5.4, it may not be advisable for the tenant to agree to that clause.

**1.8 "The Permitted Works Completion Date"**

**15.10** "The Permitted Works Completion Date" means *(date)* [or any later date that is agreed in writing between the Landlord and the Tenant from time to time]

This definition is referred to in clause 4.2 and is the date by which the tenant must complete the execution of the works in their entirety. The tenant may wish to avoid an obligation of this nature as various factors could delay the completion of the work. If the tenant has no choice but to agree this provision, the date should be sufficiently long to take into account unforeseen delays.

## 1.9 "The Plans"

"**The Plans**" **means the drawing[s] numbered** *(number(s))* **[and the specification dated** *(date)*] **annexed [or any varied or substitute drawings[s] [and/or specification] and any additional drawings[s] and/or specification that the Landlord may from time to time approve]**

15.11

The problem is that the tenant's drawings may be periodically updated, but it is obviously important from both parties' points of view that the latest available drawings are annexed to the licence. The landlord's approval should be qualified so that it is not to be unreasonably withheld or delayed.

## 1.10 "The Premises"

"**The Premises**" **means all that** *(describe the premises comprised in the lease)*

15.12

## [1.11 "The Reinstatement Plans"

"**The Reinstatement Plans**" **means the drawings[s] numbered** *(number(s)* **[and the specification dated** *(date)*] **annexed [or any varied or substitute drawings[s] [and/or specification] and any additional drawings[s] and/or specification that the Landlord may from time to time approve]]**

15.13

It is not usual to find a covenant by the tenant to reinstate the premises in accordance with reinstatement plans, but such a provision at least makes for certainty, and is unobjectionable. The tenant may, however, if possible, wish to avoid an obligation to reinstate. The landlord's approval should not be unreasonably withheld or delayed and an amendment in that regard is advised.

## 1.12 "The Reinstatement Works"

"**The Reinstatement Works**" **means [the [partial] restoration of the Premises to their present plan design state and condition] [as shown and described in the Reinstatement Plans] or any different works and any additional works that the Landlord reasonably requires or the execution of which is for the time being required under any approved consent or approval of the Landlord relating to such works**

15.14

This is too wide as it enables the landlord to require the tenant to carry out different or additional works, which could be expensive or inconvenient.

The reference to those works being such that the landlord "reasonably requires" is an inadequate qualification, although the tenant may try to avoid any reinstatement obligation. The Code of Practice for Commercial Leases may also be a factor in this regard.

### 1.13 "The Relevant Works"

**15.15** Until the date on which the Landlord serves notice pursuant to paragraph 1–4.1 or clause 5.6 that it requires the Premises to be reinstated "the Relevant Works" means the Permitted Works. Thereafter "the Relevant Works" means the Reinstatement Works

This is self-explanatory.

### 1.14 "The Restrictive Clauses"

**15.16** "The Restrictive Clauses" means clauses *(specify the clause(s) prohibiting alterations and applications for planning permission)* of the Lease

This also self-explanatory.

### 1.15 "The Term"

**15.17** "The Term" means *(state term as described in the lease)*

## 2 Recitals

### 2.1 The Lease

**15.18** This licence is supplemental to the Lease by which the Premises were demised for the Term subject to the payment of the rent[s] reserved by it and the performance and observance of the tenant's covenants and the conditions contained in it

### 2.2 Devolution of title

**15.19** The immediate reversion to the Lease [remains *(or as appropriate)* is now] vested in the Landlord and the unexpired residue of the Term [remains *(or as appropriate)* is now] vested in the Tenant

As mentioned above, the form of this licence can be used for works carried out at any time during the term granted by the lease and not just in respect of the initial fitting out works.

## 2.3 Agreement to permit the alterations

The Restrictive Clauses prohibit the Tenant from [carrying out [structural] alterations or additions to the Premises [and from applying for planning permission]] [*(where alterations are permitted with consent)* without the consent of the Landlord] and the Landlord has agreed to grant this licence on the terms set out below including the obligation to reinstate the Premises to enable the Tenant to carry out the Permitted Works

15.20

The footnote to this clause in the precedent draws attention to the fact that the landlord may be restrained from withholding consent to certain alterations sought to enable the tenant to comply with its obligations under the Disability Discrimination Act 1995.

It is suggested that, wherever possible, the tenant should in fact try to resist an obligation to reinstate.

## 3 Licence

Subject to the conditions set out below and to all rights of any person not a party to this licence the Landlord [*(where alterations permitted with consent)* grants to the Tenant consent pursuant to the Restrictive Clauses only to the extent that such consent is necessary to enable the Tenant *(or where the prohibition is absolute)* waives its rights in respect of any breach of the Restrictive Clauses that it is necessary for the Tenant to commit in order] to commence execute and complete the Relevant Works and any further works required under clause 4.2 or paragraph 1–3 in compliance with the provisions of this licence

15.21

This clause authorises the carrying out of the alterations, either where the lease permits alterations with the landlord's previous consent, or where it does not, but the landlord agrees that the alterations may be carried out.

## 4 Tenant's covenants

The Tenant covenants with the Landlord to observe and perform the requirements of this clause 4

15.22

### 4.1 Starting the Permitted Works

The Tenant must not start the Permitted Works until:

15.23

**[4.1.1 the Landlord has received from it the sum of £ plus VAT]**

This is rather an unusual provision to be found in a licence for alterations. The precedent justifies it by stating that in the case of a qualified restriction, section 19(2) of the Landlord and Tenant Act 1927 does not preclude the landlord from requiring, as a condition of its licence or consent, a reasonable sum in respect of damage to, or diminution in the value of, the premises or neighbouring premises belonging to the landlord. Where the landlord demands a particular sum as compensation, the onus is on the tenant to prove that in demanding that sum the landlord has unreasonably withheld its consent.[1]

**4.1.2 it has obtained all necessary or desirable consents relating to the Permitted Works that should be obtained before they are started and paid any charges for them and the consents referred to in clause 1.3.1 and 1.3.2 [those *(insert reference to any other specific consents about which the landlord is concerned)*] and any consents granted or given subject to any conditions have been approved by the Landlord**

The wording of this clause differs from the usual format, which quite frequently provides that the tenant will obtain all consents necessary for the works prior to commencing them. Some consents are obtained during the carrying out of the works and the wording of this clause is adequate to cover that position. The approval by the landlord should, of course, be qualified by adding that it should not be unreasonably withheld or delayed.

**4.1.3 it has complied with all conditions contained in an approved consent or any approval by the Landlord relating to the Permitted Works with which it is necessary or desirable to comply before starting the Permitted Works**

This is unobjectionable.

**4.1.4 it is otherwise lawful for it to do so and**
**4.1.5 it has given the Landlord and the Insurers at least *(state period, e.g. seven days')* prior written notice of the date on which it proposes to do so**

It should not be for the tenant to give the landlord's insurers notice and, in fact, many landlords would not wish the tenant to approach its insurers direct. The clause should be amended by deleting the words . . . **and the Insurers**

### 4.2 Execution of the Permitted Works

> **Without prejudice to clause 4.1 if the Permitted Works are started the Tenant must execute them in accordance with the Plans complete them in their entirety by the Permitted Works Completion Date start execute and complete any works referred to in clause 5.4 not forming part of the Permitted Works in accordance with the relevant approved consent and approval by the Landlord and in any event by the end or sooner determination of the Term and observe and perform the further covenants contained in the schedule**

**15.24**

This provision may seem reasonable from the landlord's point of view, but it is quite stringent so far as the tenant is concerned. There may be reasons such as force majeure why the tenant is unable to complete the works by the permitted works completion date and the tenant may not in fact be able to complete the works in their entirety, or indeed wish to do so. The tenant may not find clause 5.4 acceptable and therefore the tenant may decide to delete reference to that clause. The clause could be amended to read as follows:

> **Without prejudice to clause 4.1 if the Permitted Works are started the Tenant must execute them in accordance with the Plans and use reasonable endeavours to complete them by the Permitted Works Completion Date or by the end or sooner determination of the Term (whichever is the earlier) and observe and perform the further covenants contained in the schedule**

### 4.3 Entry to the Premises

> **The Tenant must permit the Landlord and its architects surveyors agents and workmen to enter the Premises at all times for any purpose in connection with this licence or any works permitted or required under this licence**

**15.25**

The tenant may object to a continual stream of visitors and may also object to the reference to the landlord requiring works to be carried out. The clause could therefore be amended to read:

> **The Tenant must permit the Landlord and its architects surveyors agents and workmen to enter the Premises at all reasonable times for any reasonable purpose in connection with this licence or any works permitted under this licence on reasonable prior notice being given**

### 4.4 Copies information and evidence

**15.26** The Tenant must produce to the Landlord on demand copies of all letters notices applications consents or other documents sent served received or made by or granted to the Tenant in connection with any works permitted or required under this licence and must supply to the Landlord on demand any information or evidence the Landlord [reasonably] requires in order to satisfy itself that the provisions of this licence have been complied with

The reference to "reasonably" in line six should most certainly be included.

### 4.5 Landlord's costs

**15.27** The Tenant must pay to the Landlord on demand and indemnify the Landlord against all costs charges fees disbursements and expenses including those of professional advisers and agents and including in each case any VAT incurred by the Landlord in connection with this licence or the Permitted Works including without limitation those arising from considering the application for and preparing negotiating and completing this licence considering and approving the consents and the Plans [the Reinstatement Plans] and any other plans and specifications submitted to the Landlord supervising any works permitted or required by this licence and obtaining the consent or approval of or information from any other person

The tenant should ensure that it is part of the heads of terms that the tenant should not have to pay the landlord's costs in connection with the tenant's initial fitting out works.

If the licence is granted during the term of the lease, however, it is not unreasonable for the tenant to have to pay the landlord's costs, although amendments should be made to this clause to try to ensure that they are kept to a reasonable level. As regards VAT, the general principle is that where a tenant is obliged to pay the landlord's solicitors' legal costs and the landlord is registered for VAT, the tenant pays only the legal costs and the VAT is recovered from the client by the landlord's solicitors. This principle applies where the liability of the tenant is one of indemnity only. The clause could be amended to read as follows:

> The Tenant must pay to the Landlord and indemnify the Landlord against all reasonable and proper costs charges

fees disbursements and expenses including those of necessary professional advisers including in each case any irrecoverable VAT incurred by the Landlord in connection with this licence or the Permitted Works including without limitation those arising from considering the application for (except where consent is unreasonably withheld) and preparing negotiating and completing this licence considering and approving the consents and the Plans [the Reinstatement Plans] and any other plans and specifications submitted to the Landlord and obtaining any necessary consent or approval of or information from any other person

## 5 General

The Landlord and the Tenant agree as set out in this clause 5     **15.28**

### 5.1 Sums recoverable as rent

All sums payable by the Tenant under this licence are to be recoverable as rent in arrear     **15.29**

It is not acceptable that sums payable under the licence are to be recoverable as rent in arrear and this clause should be deleted.

### 5.2 Waiver of existing breach excluded

Nothing contained in this licence waives or is to be deemed to waive any breach of the obligations on the tenant's part contained in the Lease that may have occurred before the date of this licence or authorises or is to be deemed to authorise the execution of further works [or application for any further planning permission] or anything that is not expressly authorised in clause 3     **15.30**

This provision is not unreasonable but the clause does little more than expound the provisions in respect of licences contained in section 143 of the Law of Property Act 1925.

### 5.3 Right to withhold approval of any consent

Approval of any consent may be withheld on the grounds that anything contained in it required or prohibited under it or omitted from it or its duration would or might [in the     **15.31** [reasonable] opinion of the Landlord's surveyor] adversely affect the Landlord's interest with regard to the Premises or adjoining or neighbouring property or otherwise whether during the Term or after the end or sooner determination of it and whether financially or otherwise]

This clause should be deleted. As the footnote to the precedent states, an objection by the landlord on the grounds of pecuniary damage only is not a reasonable ground for refusing consent absolutely under section 19(2) of the Landlord and Tenant Act 1927.[2]

### 5.4 Additional works

**15.32** If any approved consent relating to the Permitted Works requires the execution of additional works that are stipulated to be executed at some time after the Permitted Works Completion Date or ought reasonably to be so executed then those works are not to form part of the Permitted Works

It is safer for the tenant to delete this clause, particularly having regard to the reference that any such additional works are not to form part of the permitted works.

### 5.5 Liability and warranties excluded

**15.33** This licence and any approval consent instruction certification supervision or works granted given or carried out by or on behalf of the Landlord under this licence are granted given or carried out without any liability on the part of the Landlord or its surveyors agents or workmen and imply no responsibility for any of the works permitted or required by this licence or their design execution or existence nor do they imply warrant or constitute any representation that it is lawful to execute such works or limit or discharge any of the obligations of the Tenant under this licence

This is self-explanatory and requires no comment.

### 5.6 Landlord's remedies

**15.34** Without prejudice to any other remedy of the Landlord if the Tenant is in breach of any of its obligations under this licence the Landlord may serve notice on the Tenant specifying the breach and if the breach is not remedied within a reasonable time either serve a notice on the Tenant requiring him to reinstate the Premises or itself remedy the breach at the expense of the Tenant

This does not seem unreasonable although the reference in line three that the landlord ... **may serve** ... should be replaced with the words ... **must serve**.

## [5.7 Risk

> Notwithstanding the covenants on the Landlord's part and other provisions contained in the Lease all parts of the Relevant Works from time to time executed are to be at the sole risk of the Tenant until they are completed]

15.35

As the footnote to the precedent points out, particularly if the works are substantial, the landlord will probably wish to ensure that the relevant obligations of the landlord under the lease, *e.g.* with regard to insurance or repair, do not extend to the works until they are completed to the satisfaction of the landlord's surveyor. In certain circumstances the obligations may be passed to the tenant during execution of the works.[3]

## 5.8 Lease provisions

> Subject to any variation of them made by this licence the covenants and other provisions in the Lease are to extend to all works permitted or required by this licence from time to time executed and are to apply in full force and effect to the Premises as altered as they now apply to the Premises demised by the Lease

15.36

The problem with this clause is that unless the licence contains another provision specifically disregarding the permitted works on rent review, there is the risk that the works will be assumed to form part of the premises as originally granted and therefore not be disregarded on rent review.[4]

## 5.9 Amendment of rent review provisions

> If the Permitted Works are completed on any review of the [initial *or as appropriate)* rent reserved by the Lease *(insert amendments to the rent review provisions as appropriate)*]

15.37

As stated in the footnote, in the absence of a contrary indication, the premises will be valued in the state and condition in which they are on the review date. The usual rent review provisions contain a direction to disregard improvements carried out by the tenant otherwise than in pursuance of an obligation to the landlord. It is advisable for the licence to make it clear whether or not the works, or their effect on rent, are to be taken into account or disregarded on rent reviews under the lease. From the tenant's point of view, the clause could read as follows:

> **If the Permitted Works are completed on any review of the rent reserved by the Lease any effect on rent of the Permitted Works shall be disregarded**

### 5.10 Variation of the Lease

**15.38** **The Lease is to be varied to incorporate the covenants contained in clause 4 unless and until they determine and cease to have effect pursuant to clause 5.11 and the forfeiture provisions contained in the Lease are to be exercisable on any breach of those covenants during the subsistence of their incorporation as well as on the happening of any of the events mentioned in the forfeiture provisions**

This is self-explanatory and requires no comment, except that the parties may wish to endorse a memorandum of the licence on the lease and counterpart or, if the title is registered, register a notice of the variation at H.M. Land Registry.

### 5.11 Time Limit

**15.39** **If the Permitted Works are not commenced within** *(state period, e.g. three months)* **of the date of this licence the provisions of this licence except for clause 4.5 are to determine immediately and cease to have effect as of that date**

The time limit will depend upon the extent of the works and the tenant may find three months to be too short a period, having regard to the fact that it may take the tenant a month or two to commence the works once the licence has been granted.

### 5.12 Alterations not to be improvements

**15.40** **The alterations [and additions] comprised in the works permitted or required under this licence are not improvements for the purposes of the Landlord and Tenant Act 1927 Part 1 and are carried out by the Tenant to suit its own personal requirements and neither the Tenant nor any other person is to be entitled to compensation in respect of the alterations**

[and additions] at the end or sooner determination of the Term or at any other time]

By inserting this provision, the landlord is trying to avoid having to pay compensation for the works under the Landlord and Tenant Act 1927, Part 1. Compensation will be payable if the works add to the value of the holding at the end of the tenancy, as opposed to being merely fitting out works. There is a statutory procedure which the tenant must follow in order to be entitled to compensation, but it has been suggested that it is possible that applying for and obtaining a licence for the execution of the works may constitute compliance with that procedure.[5] As stated in the footnote to the precedent, clauses similar to this are frequently found in licences, but they will be of no effect if the declaration is incorrect, because contracting out of the Landlord and Tenant Act 1927 is prohibited, the position, however, is far from clear.

**IN WITNESS, etc.**

## SCHEDULE: TENANT'S FURTHER COVENANTS

**1–1 Execution of works**

**1–1.1** *Materials and workmanship*
The Tenant must execute all works required or permitted under this licence

**1–1.1.1** with all due diligence and speed and with new sound and proper materials in a good and workmanlike manner [under the supervision and] to the [complete *(or as required)* reasonable] satisfaction of the Landlord's surveyors and

**1–1.1.2** in strict compliance with all statutes and with the terms conditions and requirements of all approved consents and approvals of the Landlord

**15.41**

The tenant may consider replacing "new" with the words "good and suitable", as it is conceivable that the materials may not necessarily be new. The tenant may also wish to delete reference to the works being carried out under the supervision of the landlord's surveyors and should certainly amend 1–1.1.1 to refer to reasonable as opposed to complete satisfaction. The word "requirements" in line 2 of 1–1.1.2 should be qualified with the word "reasonable".

The landlord's approval should be qualified with the words "which should not be unreasonably withheld or delayed".

**1–1.2** *Approval of consents*

**15.42** The Tenant must submit any consent obtained pursuant to the provisions of this licence other than those referred to in clause 4.1.2 or paragraph 1.4.2.1 and granted or given subject to any condition to the Landlord for approval and must not implement that consent until the approval has been given

The landlord's approval should be qualified with the words "which should not be unreasonably withheld or delayed".

**1–1.3** *Hours of working*

**15.43** The Tenant must not execute any works *(state times when work prohibited, e.g. at weekends, during normal business hours or outside normal business hours)*

This is a question for negotiation, although, in order to meet a tight timetable, the tenant may wish to carry out the works 24 hours a day every day of the week.

**1–1.4** *Conduct of the work*

**15.44** During the execution of any works the Tenant must keep all materials and equipment stored inside the Premises. It must not cause any damage disturbance annoyance nuisance or inconvenience whether by noise dust vibration the emission of smoke fumes or effluvia or otherwise to the Landlord or to the owners or occupiers of any adjoining or neighbouring property or any plant or machinery at the Premises. The structure of the Premises or any adjoining or neighbouring property must not be weakened or rendered unsafe. The Tenant must not infringe interrupt or destroy any right easement or privilege or interrupt any service to or from adjoining or neighbouring property

These provisions seem reasonable, although it may be difficult for the tenant to comply with the requirement to keep all materials and equipment inside the premises. The tenant should also amend the second sentence by deleting the words . . . **disturbance annoyance nuisance or inconvenience** . . . as these may be unavoidable in undertaking fitting out works.

**[1–2 Insurance**

**[1–2.1** *The Relevant Works*

**15.45** The Tenant must insure all parts of the Relevant Works from time to time executed and all unfixed materials and goods at the Premises intended for the Relevant Works and keep them insured with the Insurers from the date of the commencement of the Relevant Works to the date of their completion in the joint names of the Landlord and the Tenant against loss and damage by fire lightning explosion storm tempest flood bursting or overflowing of water tanks apparatus or pipes earthquake aircraft and other aerial devices or articles dropped from aircraft and other aerial devices riot and civil commotion and any other risks the Landlord from time to time [reasonably] requires in the full reinstatement or replacement value. It is agreed that all money received under the insurance policy is to be applied in restoring reinstating and replacing the works materials and goods. The Tenant must make up any deficiency out of its own money]

1–2.2 *Liability*
Without prejudice to paragraph 1.5.2 the Tenant must insure the Landlord and the Tenant and keep them insured with the Insurers in a sufficient sum against all liability actions proceedings costs claims demands and expenses whatever resulting from personal injury to or the death of any person or any injury or damage to any real or personal property arising out of or in the course of or as a result of the execution of any works required or permitted by this licence

**15.46**

1–2.3 *Copies and receipts*
The Tenant must supply to the Landlord on demand a copy of every insurance policy effected by it pursuant to its obligations under this licence and the receipt or other evidence of payment of the current premium]

**15.47**

An insurance obligation of this nature is not acceptable and should be deleted, although the tenant may have to accept that, with regard to initial fitting out works, the landlord may not want its insurance obligations under the lease to extend to fitting out works until they have been completed to the landlord's surveyor's satisfaction. Quite often the tenant's contractor would be responsible for insuring the works under its own policy.

1–3 Completion of works

On completion of the Relevant Works and on completion of any works required under clause 4.2 the Tenant must remove all debris and equipment from the Premises make good any damage caused to the Premises or adjoining or

**15.48**

neighbouring property of the Landlord by the execution of the works [put the Premises into the same decorative state and condition as they were before the start of the works] and then notify the Landlord so that its surveyors may make their final inspection and certify that the works have been completed

Apart from the deletion of the words . . . **and on completion of any works required under clause 4.2** . . . as well as the words in square brackets, this covenant is not unreasonable, although the tenant may wish to add the following words at the end of this clause:

> **which inspection shall take place as soon as possible and the certificate issued as soon as practicable thereafter**

### 1–4 Reinstatement

#### 1–4.1 *Notice to reinstate*

**15.49** **If the Permitted Works are completed then unless the Landlord and Tenant have agreed on the grant of a new lease to the Tenant containing provisions for the reinstatement of the Premises before the end or sooner determination of the term of the new lease including any continuation or extension of it and any holding over whether by statute common law or otherwise to the same effect as those contained in this licence or the Court has ordered the grant of such a lease the Landlord may serve notice on the Tenant at any time during the last year of the Term requiring the Premises to be reinstated**

The reference to the possibility of the tenant having been granted a new lease is probably unnecessary as it seems that the tenant's reinstatement obligation would not be enforceable if the tenant has obtained a new lease, but this is inserted for the avoidance of any doubt. Most reinstatement provisions oblige the tenant to carry out reinstatement works unless the landlord states otherwise during the last six months or year of the term. This obliges the tenant to enquire of the landlord as to its intentions and therefore the wording of the last few lines of this clause are particularly welcome to the tenant.

#### 1–4.2 *Obligations to reinstate*

**15.50** **If the Landlord serves a notice on the Tenant pursuant to paragraph 1.4.1 or clause 5.6 that it requires the Premises to be reinstated the Tenant must**

**1–4.2.1 immediately obtain all consents relating to the Reinstatement Works that should be obtained before they are started and submit those consents granted or given subject to any condition to the Landlord for approval**

The landlord's approval should obviously not be unreasonably withheld or delayed.

**1–4.2.2 serve on the Landlord and the Insurers at least** *(state period, e.g. seven days')* **prior notice of the date on which it proposes to start the Reinstatement Works**

The tenant should not have to serve notice on the insurers, as it should be the landlord's obligation to notify them. Most landlords require a little longer than seven days prior notice.

**1–4.2.3 Start the Reinstatement Works as soon as the consents referred to in sub-paragraph 1–4.2.1 have been approved and it is otherwise lawful to do so [and execute them in accordance with the Reinstatement Plans]**

The tenant will obviously not wish to commence the reinstatement works several months before the end of its lease as it will be paying a market rent for the premises and will presumably wish to continue trading until the last possible moment. This sub-paragraph should therefore ideally be deleted with the landlord relying on sub-paragraph 1–4.2.4. The reference to reinstatement plans will, of course, only apply if there are any.

**1–4.2.4 complete the Reinstatement Works in their entirety by the end or sooner determination of the Term and**

There is no objection to this sub-paragraph.

**1–4.2.5 comply with any [reasonable] further or substitute requirements of the Landlord in connection with starting or executing the Reinstatement Works**

The tenant may, with good reason, object to this provision.

## 1–5 Indemnities

**[1–5.1** *Insurance premiums*
**[Without prejudice to clause 5.3 the** *(or as appropriate)* **The] Tenant must pay to the Landlord on demand and indemnify the Landlord against any increased or extra premium payable for insurance of the Premises or any adjoining or neighbouring property as a result of the execution or retention of any works required or permitted by this licence]**

15.51

See the comments under clause 5.3 above. As the precedent points out, a provision of this nature may already be contained in the lease and, if so, it should be deleted from this licence.

**15.52** 1–5.2 **Indemnity**

**The Tenant must indemnify the Landlord against all liability actions proceedings claims demands costs and expenses whatsoever including without limitation those for personal injury to or the death of any person or any injury or damage to any real or personal property however arising whether directly or indirectly as a result of the grant of this licence or any failure by the Tenant to comply with the covenants and conditions contained in it the commencement execution or retention of any works required or permitted by it the state and condition of the Premises whether during or after the execution of those works or the existence operation or use of any apparatus machinery substance or thing on the Premises in connection with those works**

Although one tries to avoid the tenant entering into too many indemnity covenants, this provision does not seem entirely unreasonable.

**[1–6 General**

**15.53** **Subject to any statutory direction to the contrary the Tenant must pay and satisfy any charge or levy that may be imposed under the Town and Country Planning Act 1990 or any other statute in respect of the commencement execution or retention of any works]**

Again, as the footnote to the precedent points out, such a provision may already be contained in the lease.

The license is concluded by the signatories and/or seals of all parties.

---

[1] *Lambert v. F.W. Woolworth & Co Ltd* (No. 2) [1938] Ch. 883; [1938] 2 All E.R. 664.
[2] See also *Lambert v. F. W. Woolworth & Co Ltd* (No. 2) [1938] Ch. 883; [1938] 2 All E.R. 664.
[3] See para. 1–2.1 below.
[4] *Ponsford v. H.M.S. Aerosols Ltd* [1979] A.C. 63; [1978] 2 All E.R. 837.
[5] See Hill and Redman's *Law of Landlord and Tenant* (18th ed.) B [28], [341] and *Deerfield Travel Services Ltd v. Leathersellers Co* (1983) 46 P. & C.R. 132.]

# Index

1954 Act
    definition, **2**.08
1995 Act
    definition, **2**.08
    new tenancy, and, **8**.25

Access to premises
    interpretation, and, **2**.11
    rights reserved, and, **10**.13
    shop covenants, and, **12**.06
    tenant's covenants, and, **4**.10–**4**.11
Access ramps
    common parts, and, **2**.05
Accidents
    provisos, and, **8**.08
Accountant
    definition, **2**.05
Actions, costs, claims, demands and liabilities
    tenant's works, and, **1**.13
Additional works
    licence for alterations, and, **15**.32
Additions to premises
    extent of premises, and, **10**.02
    shop covenants, and, **12**.04
Adjoining occupiers, disputes with
    provisos, and, **8**.05
Adjoining premises
    definition, **2**.05
    provisos, and, **8**.04
Advertisements
    shop covenants, and, **12**.07
    tenant's covenants, and, **4**.08
Aerial devices
    insured risks, and, **2**.07
Aerials
    planning applications, and, **4**.20
    tenant's covenants, and, **4**.08
Agents
    representations, and, **1**.22

Agreement for lease
    costs, **1**.25
    damage, **1**.19
    definitions, **1**.02–**1**.05
    entire understanding, **1**.28
    executory agreement, **1**.26
    form of lease, **1**.14
    grant of lease, **1**.17
    interpretation, **1**.02–**1**.05
    introduction, **1**.01
    non-assignment, **1**.23
    non-merger, **1**.27
    notices, **1**.24
    provisos, and, **8**.25
    rent commencement, **1**.18
    representations, **1**.22
    restrictions, **1**.21
    tenant's works, **1**.11–**1**.13
    termination, **1**.15–**1**.16
    title, **1**.20
    trading commencement, **1**.18
    works, **1**.06–**1**.10
Aircraft
    insured risks, and, **2**.07
Airspace
    extent of premises, and, **10**.02
Alienation
    tenant's covenants, and, **4**.12–**4**.16
Alterations to premises
    extent of premises, and, **10**.02
    licence for
        *and see* Licence for alterations
        additional works, **15**.32
        amendment of rent review provisions, **15**.37
        definitions, **15**.02–**15**.17
        improvements, **15**.40
        introduction, **15**.01
        landlord's remedies, **15**.34
        lease provisions, **15**.36

Alterations to premises—*contd.*
　licence for—*contd.*
　　licence, **15**.21
　　limitation of liability, **15**.33
　　recitals, **15**.18–**15**.20
　　risk, **15**.35
　　sums recoverable as rent, **15**.29
　　tenant's covenants, **15**.22–**15**.27, **15**.41–**15**.53
　　time limit, **15**.39
　　variation of lease, **15**.38
　　waiver of existing breach, **15**.30
　　withholding approval of consent, **15**.31
　shop covenants, and, **12**.04
Animals on premises
　tenant's covenants, and, **4**.17
Annoyance or disturbance
　tenant's covenants, and, **4**.17
Annual expenditure
　service charge, and, **13**.03
Anticipated expenditure
　service charge, and, 13.34
Application for approvals
　works, and, **1**.06
Apparatus, plant and machinery
　service charge, and, **13**.11
Approval
　licence for alterations, and, **15**.03
Architect
　definition, **1**.02
Architect's notice
　tenant's works, and, **1**.11
Approval of consents
　licence for alterations, and, **15**.42
Approval of plans
　tenant's works, and, **1**.11
Arbitrator
　definition, **11**.10
Arrangement with creditors
　re-entry, and, **8**.02
　termination of agreement for lease, and, **1**.15
Assessments
　tenant's works, and, **1**.13
Assignee
　authorised guarantee agreement, and, **14**.03
Assignment
　agreement for lease, and, **1**.23
　alienation, and, **4**.12–**4**.16
　guarantor's covenants, and, **7**.03
　opening hours, and, **12**.06
Assumptions
　rent review, and, **11**.02–**11**.03

Auction sales
　tenant's covenants, and, **4**.17
Authorised guarantee agreement
　definitions
　　assignee, **14**.03
　　generally, **14**.02
　　lease, **14**.04
　　liability period, **14**.06
　　premises, **14**.05
　exclusion of liability, **14**.19
　guarantor's covenants
　　generally, **14**.12
　　new lease following disclaimer, **14**.14
　　payment, **14**.13
　　payments following disclaimer, **14**.15
　　performance, **14**.13
　interpretation, **14**.07–**14**.08
　landlord's covenant, **14**.16
　limitation, **14**.18
　parties, **14**.01
　recitals
　　agreement to consent, **14**.10
　　effective time, **14**.11
　　requirement for consent, **14**.09
　severance, **14**.17

Banker's order
　rent, and, **4**.03
Bankruptcy
　re-entry, and, **8**.02
　termination of agreement for lease, and, **1**.15
Base lending rate
　interest, and, **2**.03
Break clauses
　provisos, and, **8**.24
Building contract
　definition, **1**.02
Building defects insurance
　defects in works, and, **1**.27
Building documents
　definition, **1**.06
　modification, **1**.07
Bursting pipes
　insured risks, and, **2**.07

Cables
　pipes, and, **2**.08
Cancellation of land charge
　termination of agreement for lease, and, **1**.15
Car park
　common parts, and, **2**.05
　definition, **2**.06
　landlord's covenants, and, **5**.09

CDM Regulations
   statutory obligations, and, **4**.09
   works, and, **1**.06
Ceiling
   extent of premises, and, **10**.02
Ceiling loading
   shop covenants, and, **12**.09
Certificate
   definition, **1**.02
Certificate date
   definition, **1**.02
Certificate of value
   provisos, and, **8**.26
Centre, the
   particulars of lease, and, **2**.02
Certificate of practical completion
   definition, **1**.02
   termination of agreement for lease, and, **1**.15
   works, and, **1**.09
Channels
   pipes, and, **2**.08
Charge certificate
   title, and, **1**.20
Charge on property
   agreement for lease, and, **1**.23
   alienation, and, **4**.12–**4**.16
Charges and payments
   statutory obligations, and, **4**.09
   tenant's covenants, and, **4**.04
   tenant's works, and, **1**.13
Circulation areas
   common parts, and, **2**.05
Civil commotion
   insured risks, and, **2**.07
Claims
   tenant's works, and, **1**.13
Cleaning
   service charge, and, **13**.14
   shop covenants, and, **12**.08
   tenant's covenants, and, **4**.06
Code of Practice for commercial leases
   generally, **2**.01
Collateral agreements
   entire understanding, and, **1**.28
Common parts
   clean and tidy, and, **12**.08
   definition, **2**.05
   landlord's covenants, and, **5**.08
   retained parts, and, **2**.08
   rights granted, and, **10**.04
Combustible material
   insurance, and, **6**.13–**6**.14
Compensation
   provisos, and, **8**.15

Compensation—*contd.*
   statutory obligations, and, **4**.09
Completed
   licence for alterations, and, **15**.04
Completion date
   definition, **1**.03
   grant of lease, and, **1**.17
   trading commencement, and, **1**.18
Completion of work
   licence for alterations, and, **15**.48
   tenant's works, and, **1**.12
Composition with creditors
   termination of agreement for lease, and, **1**.15
Computing date
   service charge, and, **13**.04
Concourses
   common parts, and, **2**.05
Conduct of work
   licence for alterations, and, **15**.44
Conduits
   pipes, and, **2**.08
Consent of landlord
   aerials, signs and advertisements, and, **4**.08
   alienation, and, **4**.12–**4**.16
   alterations, and, **12**.04
   costs, and, **4**.18–**4**.19
   interpretation, and, **2**.11
   licence for alterations, and
     *and see* Licence for alterations
     additional works, **15**.32
     amendment of rent review provisions, **15**.37
     definitions, **15**.02–**15**.17
     improvements, **15**.40
     introduction, **15**.01
     landlord's remedies, **15**.34
     lease provisions, **15**.36
     licence, **15**.21
     limitation of liability, **15**.33
     recitals, **15**.18–**15**.20
     risk, **15**.35
     sums recoverable as rent, **15**.29
     tenant's covenants, **15**.22–**15**.27, **15**.41–**15**.53
     time limit, **15**.39
     variation of lease, **15**.38
     waiver of existing breach, **15**.30
     withholding approval of consent, **15**.31
   planning applications, and, **4**.20
Construction (Design and Management) Regulations
   statutory obligations, and, **4**.09
   works, and, **1**.06

Construction of pipes
  rights reserved, and, **10**.12
Contracts for services
  service charge, and, **13**.26
Contractual term
  interpretation, and, **2**.10
  particulars of lease, and, **2**.02
Convictions
  insurance, and, **6**.02
Cooking food
  user, and, **12**.03
Cooling
  service charge, and, **13**.15
  shop covenants, and, **12**.12
Costs
  agreement for lease, and, **1**.25
  statutory obligations, and, **4**.09
  tenant's works, and, **1**.13
Counterpart
  grant of lease, and, **1**.17
Course of employment
  repairs, and, **4**.06
Covenants
  access to premises
    shop covenants, **12**.06
    tenant's covenants, **4**.10–**4**.11
  advertisements
    shop covenants, **12**.07
    tenant's covenants, **4**.08
  aerials, **4**.08
  alienation, **4**.12–**4**.16
  alterations, **12**.04
  car park, **5**.09
  ceiling loading, **12**.09
  cleaning
    shop covenants, **12**.08
    tenant's covenants, **4**.06
  common parts, **5**.08
  cooling, **12**.12
  decoration, **4**.07
  defective premises, **4**.30
  display, **12**.06
  electricity charges, **4**.05
  encroachments, **4**.24
  enforcement between adjoining
    occupiers, and, **8**.05
  environmental matters, **5**.07
  fire alarms, **12**.11
  fitting out, **12**.02
  floor loading, **12**.09
  gas charges, **4**.05
  guarantor, by
    *and see* **Guarantor's covenants**
    authorised guarantee agreement, in,
      **14**.01–**14**.19
    lease, in, **7**.01–**7**.05

Covenants—*contd.*
  heating, **12**.12
  hours of trading, **12**.06
  indemnities, **4**.22
  interest on arrears, **4**.26
  interpretation, and, **2**.11
  keyholders, **4**.28
  kiosks, **5**.10
  landlord, by
    *and see* **Landlord's covenants**
    generally, **5**.02–**5**.11
    introduction, **5**.01
  landlord's costs
    consents, licences, etc., **4**.18–**4**.19
    grant of lease, **4**.34
  landlord's regulations, **12**.14
  landlord's rights, **4**.32
  loading and unloading, **12**.10
  new guarantor, **4**.31
  non-competition, **5**.05
  notice to repair, **4**.10–**4**.11
  nuisance, **4**.17
  opening hours, **12**.06
  outgoings, **4**.04
  permitted user, **12**.03
  planning control, **4**.20
  plans, documents and information, **4**.21
  plate glass, **12**.13
  quiet enjoyment, **5**.02
  regulations, **12**.14
  re-letting boards, **4**.23
  rent, **4**.03
  repair, **4**.06
  residential restrictions, **4**.17
  sale of reversion, **4**.29
  security alarms, **12**.11
  services, provision of, **5**.03
  shop covenants
    *and see* **Shop covenants**
    generally, **12**.02–**12**.12
    introduction, **12**.01
    tenant's covenants, and, **4**.33
  signboards, **5**.11
  signs
    shop covenants, **12**.07
    tenant's covenants, **4**.08
  similar leases, provision of, **5**.06
  stalls, **5**.10
  statutory notices, **4**.27
  statutory obligations, **4**.09
  superior lease, compliance with, **5**.04
  take precautions, **12**.05
  tenant, by
    *and see* **Tenant's covenants**
    generally, **4**.02–**4**.34
    introduction, **4**.01

# Index

Covenants—*contd.*
  unloading, **12**.10
  user, **12**.03
  utility charges, **4**.05
  VAT, **4**.04
  ventilation, **12**.12
  yielding up, **4**.25
Credit transfer
  rent, and, **4**.03

Damage to premises
  agreement for lease, and, **1**.19
  insurance, and, **6**.04
  opening hours, and, **12**.06
  suspension of rent, and, **6**.08
Damages and costs
  statutory obligations, and, **4**.09
Dangerous trade or occupation
  tenant's covenants, and, **4**.17
Darkening windows
  encroachments, and, **4**.24
Decorating years
  particulars of lease, and, **2**.04
Decoration
  tenant's covenants, and, **4**.07
Defective premises
  tenant's covenants, and, **4**.30
Defects in title
  title, and, **1**.20
Defects in works
  agreement for lease, and, **1**.27
Defects notice
  works, and, **1**.08
Definitions
  agreement for lease, and, **1**.02–**1**.05
  lease, and, **2**.05–**2**.09
Delay
  works, and, **1**.09
Deleterious substances
  works, and, **1**.06
Demands and liabilities
  tenant's works, and, **1**.13
Demise
  generally, **3**.02–**3**.03
  introduction, **3**.01
  service charge, and, **3**.02
Deposit of land certificate
  title, and, **1**.20
Destruction of premises
  agreement for lease, and, **1**.19
  insurance, and, **6**.04
  opening hours, and, **12**.06
  reinstatement and termination, and, **6**.10–**6**.12
  suspension of rent, and, **6**.08

Development
  interpretation, and, **2**.11
Development of neighbouring property
  provisos, and, **8**.17
Disclaimer, guarantor's covenants following
  make payment, **7**.03
  take lease, **7**.04
Display
  shop covenants, and, **12**.06
Dispute resolution
  adjoining occupiers, and, **8**.05
  entire understanding, and, **1**.28
  provisos, and, **8**.05
  rent review, **11**.10
  suspension of rent, and, **6**.08
  variation of form of lease, and, **1**.14
Disregarded matters
  fitting out, and, **12**.02
  rent review, and, **11**.07–**11**.09
Distress for rent
  re-entry, and, **8**.02
  third party rights, and, **8**.26
Disturbance or inconvenience
  quiet enjoyment, and, **5**.02
  tenant's covenants, and, **4**.17
Doors
  cleaning, and
    shop covenants, **12**.08
    tenant's covenants, **4**.06
  extent of premises, and, **10**.02
Drains
  pipes, and, **2**.08
Ducts
  pipes, and, **2**.08
Duties and charges
  tenant's covenants, and, **4**.04
  tenant's works, and, **1**.13

Earthquake
  insured risks, and, **2**.07
Easements
  encroachments, and, **4**.24
  provisos, and, **8**.07
Electrical components, repair of
  landlord's covenants, and, **5**.07
Electricity charges
  service charge, and, **13**.28
  tenant's covenants, and, **4**.05
Encroachments
  tenant's covenants, and, **4**.24
Entire understanding
  agreement for lease, and, **1**.28
  lease, and, **8**.11

## Index

Entry to premises
  licence for alterations, and, **15**.25
  provisos, and, **8**.22
  rights granted, and, **10**.07
  tenant's works, and, **1**.12
Environmental matters
  landlord's covenants, and, **5**.07
  provisos, and, **8**.23
Escalators
  common parts, and, **2**.05
'Excepting and reserving'
  demise, and, **3**.02
Exclusion of liability
  authorised guarantee agreement, and, **14**.19
Exclusion of use warranty
  provisos, and, **8**.10
Exclusive possession
  tenant's works, and, **1**.12
Execution of deeds
  agreement for lease, and, **1**.28
  lease, and, **9**.01
Execution of permitted works
  licence for alterations, and, **15**.24
Executory agreement
  agreement for lease, and, **1**.26
Expenses
  statutory obligations, and, **4**.09
Explosion
  insured risks, and, **2**.07
Explosive material
  insurance, and, **6**.13–**6**.14
Extension of time
  works, and, **1**.09

Failure to comply with obligations
  termination of agreement for lease, and, **1**.15
Fair wear and tear
  repairs, and, **4**.06
Fees, charges and payments
  service charge, and, **13**.24
  tenant's works, and, **1**.13
Financial year
  service charge, and, **13**.05
Fire
  insured risks, and, **2**.07
Fire alarm
  service charge, and, **13**.13
  shop covenants, and, **12**.11
Fire escape
  rights granted, and, **10**.08
Fire-fighting equipment
  insurance, and, **6**.13–**6**.14
Fitting out
  generally, **12**.02

Fitting out—*contd.*
  specifications, **13**.36
Fixtures
  extent of premises, and, **10**.02
  service charge, and, **13**.19
  tenant's works, and, **1**.13
Flamable material
  insurance, and, **6**.13–**6**.14
Flashing lights
  user, and, **12**.03
Flood
  insured risks, and, **2**.07
Floor
  extent of premises, and, **10**.02
Floor loading
  shop covenants, and, **12**.09
Flues
  pipes, and, **2**.08
Food
  user, and, **12**.03
Forbearance
  guarantor's covenants, and, **7**.03
Forecourts
  common parts, and, **2**.05
Forfeiture, relief against
  re-entry, and, **8**.02
  termination of agreement for lease, and, **1**.15
Form of lease
  variation, and, **1**.14
Foundations
  extent of premises, and, **10**.02
  retained parts, and, **2**.08
Freehold reversion
  title, and, **1**.20
Frustration
  damage or destruction, and, **1**.19
  reinstatement, and, **8**.18
Future interests
  perpetuity period, and, **8**.09

Garden
  service charge, and, **13**.18
Gas charges
  service charge, and, **13**.28
  tenant's covenants, and, **4**.05
Gender
  interpretation, and, **2**.10
Good and workmanlike manner
  tenant's works, and, **1**.12
Grant of lease
  agreement for lease, and, **1**.17
Gross internal area, measurement of
  works, and, **1**.10
Group company
  definition, **2**.05

## Index

Guarantor
  covenants by
    *and see below*
    authorised guarantee agreement, in, **14**.01–**14**.19
    lease, in, **7**.01–**7**.05
    interpretation, and, **2**.10
    particulars of lease, and, **2**.02
    re-entry, and, **8**.02
    tenant's covenants, and, **4**.31
Guarantor's covenants
  authorised guarantee agreement, in
    generally, **14**.12
    new lease following disclaimer, **14**.14
    payment, **14**.13
    payments following disclaimer, **14**.15
    performance, **14**.13
  lease, in
    generally, **7**.02
    introduction, **7**.01
    new lease following disclaimer, **7**.04
    payment, **7**.03
    payments following disclaimer, **7**.05
    performance, **7**.03
Gutters
  pipes, and, **2**.08

Harmful substances
  works, and, **1**.06
Headings to clauses etc.
  interpretation, and, **2**.12
Heating
  service charge, and, **13**.15
  shop covenants, and, **12**.12
Heave
  insured risks, and, **2**.07
'Hold the premises'
  demise, and, **3**.02
Hours of trading
  common parts, and, **2**.05
  particulars of lease, and, **2**.04
  shop covenants, and, **12**.06
Hours of working
  licence for alterations, and, **15**.43

Illegal acts or purpose
  tenant's covenants, and, **4**.17
Immaterial error, etc.
  representations, and, **1**.22
Immoral acts or purpose
  tenant's covenants, and, **4**.17
Impact by vehicle
  insured risks, and, **2**.07
Impositions and outgoings
  tenant's covenants, and, **4**.04
  tenant's works, and, **1**.13
Improvements to premises
  extent of premises, and, **10**.02
  licence for alterations, and, **15**.40
Inconvenience or injury
  tenant's covenants, and, **4**.17
Indemnification of landlord
    tenant's works, and, **1**.13
  Indemnities
    licence for alterations, and, **15**.51–**15**.52
    tenant's covenants, and, **4**.22
Indulgence by landlord
  guarantor's covenants, and, **7**.03
Inflammable material
  insurance, and, **6**.13–**6**.14
Inherent defects
  repairs, and, **4**.06
Initial provisional service charge
  particulars of lease, and, **2**.04
Initial rent
  particulars of lease, and, **2**.03
Initial yearly rent
  works, and, **1**.10
Injury to premises
  tenant's covenants, and, **4**.17
Insolvency
  re-entry, and, **8**.02
  termination of agreement for lease, and, **1**.15
Inspection
  architect's notice, and, **1**.09
  surveyors' rights, and, **1**.08
Insurance
  amount, **6**.04
  cover, **6**.05–**6**.06
  defects in works, and, **1**.27
  insurance rent
    payment, **6**.07
    suspension, **6**.08–**6**.09
    variation, **6**.15
  insurer's identity, **6**.04
  introduction, **6**.01
  landlord's covenants
    further, **6**.12
    generally, **6**.03
    licence for alterations, and
      generally, **15**.45–**15**.47
      premiums, **15**.51
    reinstatement and termination, **6**.10–**6**.12
  repairs, and, **4**.06
  tenant's covenants, **6**.13–**6**.14
  warranty re-convictions, **6**.02
Insurance cost
  definition, **2**.06
Insurance rent
  definition, **2**.06

Insurance rent—*contd.*
  demise, and, **3**.02
  payment, **6**.07
  suspension, **6**.08–**6**.09
  variation, **6**.15
Insurance rent percentage
  particulars of lease, and, **2**.04
Insured risks
  definition, **2**.07
  generally, **6**.05
Insurer's identity
  insurance, and, **6**.04
Insurers
  licence for alterations, and, **15**.06
Intended possession date
  tenant's works, and, **1**.11
Interest
  definition, **2**.07
  service charge, and, **13**.33
Interest on arrears
  tenant's covenants, and, **4**.26
Interest rate
  particulars of lease, and, **2**.03
Interference with carrying of works
  tenant's works, and, **1**.12
Internal walls
  party walls, and, **8**.03
Interpretation
  agreement for lease, of, **1**.02–**1**.05
  lease, of, **2**.10–**2**.12
Interruption
  quiet enjoyment, and, **5**.02
Investigation of title
  generally, **1**.20

"Keep in repair"
  repairs, and, **4**.06
"Keep open" covenants
  opening hours, and, **2**.04
Keyholders
  tenant's covenants, and, **4**.28
Kiosks
  landlord's covenants, and, **5**.10

Land certificate
  title, and, **1**.20
Landlord
  definition
    agreement for lease, in, **1**.03
    lease, in, **2**.10
    licence for alterations, in. **15**.07
    particulars of lease, and, **2**.02
Landlord approvals
  definition, **1**.06
  tenant's works, and, **1**.11

Landlord's address
  definition, **1**.24
Landlord's consent
  aerials, signs and advertisements, and, **4**.08
  alienation, and, **4**.12–**4**.16
  alterations, and, **12**.04
  costs, and, **4**.18–**4**.19
  interpretation, and, **2**.11
  licence for alterations, and
    *and see* Licence for alterations
    additional works, **15**.32
    amendment of rent review provisions, **15**.37
    definitions, **15**.02–**15**.17
    improvements, **15**.40
    introduction, **15**.01
    landlord's remedies, **15**.34
    lease provisions, **15**.36
    licence, **15**.21
    limitation of liability, **15**.33
    recitals, **15**.18–**15**.20
    risk, **15**.35
    sums recoverable as rent, **15**.29
    tenant's covenants, **15**.22–**15**.27, **15**.41–**15**.53
    time limit, **15**.39
    variation of lease, **15**.38
    waiver of existing breach, **15**.30
    withholding approval of consent, **15**.31
  planning applications, and, **4**.20
Landlord's costs
  consents, licences, etc., **4**.18–**4**.19
  grant of lease, **4**.34
  licence for alterations, and, **15**.27
Landlord's covenants
  authorised guarantee agreement, and, **14**.16
  car park, **5**.09
  common parts, **5**.08
  environmental matters, **5**.07
  insurance, and
    further, **6**.12
    generally, **6**.03
  introduction, **5**.01
  kiosks, **5**.10
  non-competition, **5**.05
  quiet enjoyment, **5**.02
  services, provision of, **5**.03
  signboards, **5**.11
  similar leases, provision of, **5**.06
  stalls, **5**.10
  superior lease, compliance with, **5**.04
Landlord's fixtures and fittings
  extent of premises, and, **10**.02

# Index

Landlord's notice
  tenant's works, and, **1**.11
Landlord's regulations
  shop covenants, and, **12**.14
Landlord's remedies
  licence for alterations, and, **15**.34
Landlord's rights
  tenant's covenants, and, **4**.32
Landlord's solicitors
  definition, **1**.03
Landslip
  insured risks, and, **2**.07
Last year of the term
  interpretation, and, **2**.10
Latent defects insurance
  defects in works, and, **1**.27
Lease
  *and see under individual headings*
  authorised guarantee agreement, and, **14**.04
  definition
    agreement for lease, in, **1**.03
    lease, in, **2**.08
    licence for alterations, in, **15**.07–**15**.08
  definitions, **2**.05–**2**.09
  demise, **3**.01–**3**.03
  execution, **9**.01
  guarantor's covenants, **7**.01–**7**.05
  insurance, **6**.01–**6**.12
  interpretation, **2**.10–**2**.12
  introduction, **2**.01
  landlord's covenants, **5**.01–**5**.11
  particulars, **2**.02–**2**.04
  premises, **10**.01–**10**.16
  provisos, **8**.01–**8**.26
  rent review, **11**.01–**11**.16
  service charges, **13**.01–**13**.35
  shop covenants, **12**.01–**12**.13
  tenant's covenants, **4**.02–**4**.34
Leasehold reversion
  title, and, **1**.20
Letting boards
  tenant's covenants, and, **4**.23
Levying execution
  re-entry, and, **8**.02
Liabilities
  tenant's works, and, **1**.13
Liability, limitations on
  provisos, and, **8**.21
Liability period
  authorised guarantee agreement, and, **14**.06
  guarantor's covenants, and, **7**.03
Licence for alterations
  additional works, **15**.32

Licence for alterations—*contd.*
  amendment of rent review provisions, **15**.37
  definitions
    approval, **15**.03
    completed, **15**.04
    consents, **15**.05
    generally, **15**.02
    insurers, **15**.06
    landlord. **15**.07
    lease, **15**.07–**15**.08
    permitted works, **15**.09
    permitted works completion date, **15**.10
    plans, **15**.11
    premises, **15**.12
    reinstatement plans, **15**.13
    reinstatement works, **15**.14
    relevant works, **15**.15
    restrictive clauses, **15**.16
    tenant, **15**.07
    term, **15**.07, **15**.17
  improvements, **15**.40
  interpretation, **15**.07–**15**.15
  introduction, **15**.01
  landlord's remedies, **15**.34
  lease provisions, **15**.36
  licence, **15**.21
  limitation of liability, **15**.33
  recitals
    agreement to permit alterations, **15**.20
    devolution of title, **15**.19
    purpose of lease, **15**.18
  risk, **15**.35
  sums recoverable as rent, **15**.29
  tenant's covenants
    approval of consents, **15**.42
    completion of works, **15**.48
    conduct of work, **15**.44
    copies, information and evidence, **15**.26
    entry to premises, **15**.25
    execution of permitted works, **15**.24
    generally, **15**.22
    hours of working, **15**.43
    indemnities, **15**.51–**15**.52
    insurance, **15**.45–**15**.47
    insurance premiums, **15**.51
    landlord's costs, **15**.27
    materials and workmanship, **15**.41
    planning fees, **15**.53
    reinstatement, **15**.49–**15**.50
    starting permitted works, **15**.23
    VAT, **15**.27
  time limit, **15**.39
  variation of lease, **15**.38

Licence for alterations—*contd.*
  waiver of existing breach, **15**.30
  withholding approval of consent,
    **15**.31
Licences, etc., under hand
  provisos, and, **8**.13
Lifts
  common parts, and, **2**.05
Light
  provisos, and, **8**.20
  rights reserved, and, **10**.16
Lightning
  insured risks, and, **2**.07
Limitations on liability
  authorised guarantee agreement, and,
    **14**.18
  licence for alterations, and, **15**.33
  provisos, and, **8**.21
Liquidation
  re-entry, and, **8**.02
  termination of agreement for lease, and,
    **1**.15
Loading and unloading
  shop covenants, and, **12**.10
Loading bays
  common parts, and, **2**.05
Loudspeakers
  user, and, **12**.03

Malicious damage
  insured risks, and, **2**.07
Materials and workmanship
  licence for alterations, and, **15**.41
Measurement of gross internal area
  works, and, **1**.10
Misdescription
  generally, **1**.22
  title, and, **1**.20
Misrepresentation
  generally, **1**.22
  title, and, **1**.20
Misstatements
  representations, and, **1**.22
Modification to building documents
  works, and, **1**.07
Music
  user, and, **12**.03

Neglect of enforcement
  guarantor's covenants, and, **7**.03
Neighbouring property, development of
  provisos, and, **8**.17
New guarantor
  tenant's covenants, and, **4**.31
New tenancy
  provisos, and, **8**.25

1954 Act
  definition, **2**.08
1995 Act
  definition, **2**.08
Noisy trade or occupation
  tenant's covenants, and, **4**.17
  user, and, **12**.03
Non-assignment
  agreement for lease, and, **1**.23
  alienation, and, **4**.12
Non-competition
  landlord's covenants, and, **5**.05
Non-compliance with obligations
  termination of agreement for lease, and,
    **1**.15
Non-disclosure
  representations, and, **1**.22
Non-merger
  agreement for lease, and, **1**.27
Note of tenant's interest
  insurance, and, **6**.12
Notice to repair
  tenant's covenants, and,
    **4**.10–**4**.11
Notices
  agreement for lease, and, **1**.24
  break clause, and, **8**.24
  insurance, and, **6**.13–**6**.14
  service
    agreement for lease, **1**.24
    lease, **8**.16
  tenant's covenants, and, **4**.27
Noxious trade or occupation
  tenant's covenants, and, **4**.17
Nuisance
  service charge, and, **13**.32
  tenant's covenants, and, **4**.17
Nursery premises
  retained parts, and, **2**.08

Obligations of parties
  damage or destruction, and, **1**.19
  restrictions, and, **1**.21
  termination of agreement for lease, and,
    **1**.15
Obstruction of access
  insurance, and, **6**.13–**6**.14
  user, and, **12**.03
Obstruction of windows
  encroachments, and, **4**.24
Obstruction to carrying of works
  tenant's works, and, **1**.12
Occupation of premises
  executory agreement, and, **1**.26
  termination of agreement for lease, and,
    **1**.15

Offensive trade or occupation
  tenant's covenants, and, **4**.17
Oil charges
  service charge, and, **13**.28
Omissions
  representations, and, **1**.22
Opening hours
  common parts, and, **2**.05
  particulars of lease, and, **2**.04
  shop covenants, and, **12**.06
Ornamental features
  service charge, and, **13**.18
Outgoings
  service charge, and, **13**.27
  tenant's covenants, and, **4**.04
  tenant's works, and, **1**.13
Overflowing of pipes
  insured risks, and, **2**.07

Particulars of lease
  Centre, the, **2**.02
  contractual term, **2**.02
  decorating years, **2**.04
  guarantor, **2**.02
  initial provisional service charge, **2**.04
  initial rent, **2**.03
  insurance rent percentage, **2**.04
  interest rate, **2**.03
  landlord, **2**.02
  opening hours, **2**.04
  permitted user, **2**.03
  premises, **2**.02
  prohibited users, **2**.03
  rent commencement date, **2**.03
  review dates, **2**.03
  service charge percentage, **2**.04
  shop opening hours, **2**.04
  tenant, **2**.02
Parties, the
  authorised guarantee agreement, and, **14**.01
  lease, and, **2**.11
Party walls
  provisos, and, **8**.03
Peaceful enjoyment
  landlord's covenants, and, **5**.02
Permitted use
  restrictions, and, **1**.21
Permitted user
  common parts, and, **2**.05
  particulars of lease, and, **2**.03
  shop covenants, and, **12**.03
Permitted works
  licence for alterations, and, **15**.09
Permitted works completion date
  licence for alterations, and, **15**.10

Perpetuity period
  provisos, and, **8**.09
Pipes
  definition, **2**.08
  extent of premises, and, **10**.02
  retained parts, and, **2**.08
  rights granted, and, **10**.05
  rights reserved, and construction, **10**.12
  use, **10**.11
  service charge, and, **13**.12
  user, and, **12**.03
Plan, the
  definition, **2**.08
Planning Acts
  definition, **2**.08
  tenant's covenants, and, **4**.20
Planning fees
  licence for alterations, and, **15**.53
Planning permission
  tenant's covenants, and, **4**.20
Plans
  definition
    agreement for lease, in, **1**.11
    licence for alterations, in, **15**.11
  extent of premises, and, **10**.02
  tenant's covenants, and, **4**.21
Plant and machinery
  service charge, and, **13**.11
Plant rooms
  retained parts, and, **2**.08
Plate glass
  insurance, and, **6**.03
  shop covenants, and, **12**.13
Pool Re
  insured risks, and, **2**.07
Possession date
  definition, **1**.03
  tenant's works, and, **1**.11
  termination of agreement for lease, and, **1**.16
Possession of premises
  executory agreement, and, **1**.26
  termination of agreement for lease, and, **1**.15
Premises, the
  authorised guarantee agreement, and, **14**.05
  definition
    agreement for lease, in, **1**.03
    lease, in, **2**.10
    licence for alterations, in, **15**.12
  extent, **10**.02
  interpretation, and, **2**.10
  introduction, **10**.01
  particulars of lease, and, **2**.02

Premises, the—*contd.*
  rights granted
    common parts, **10**.04
    entry, **10**.07
    fire escape, **10**.08
    introduction, **10**.03
    other, **10**.09
    pipes, **10**.05
    support, **10**.06
  rights reserved
    access, **10**.13
    construction of pipes, **10**.12
    introduction, **10**.10
    light, **10**.16
    scaffolding, **10**.14
    support, **10**.15
    use of pipes, **10**.11
Premium rates
  insured risks, and, **2**.07
Premium renewal receipt
  insurance, and, **6**.12
President
  definition, **11**.09
Prohibited users
  particulars of lease, and, **2**.03
Provisos
  accidents, **8**.08
  adjoining occupiers, **8**.05
  adjoining premises, **8**.04
  agreement for lease, **8**.25
  break clause, **8**.24
  certificate of value, **8**.26
  compensation on vacation, **8**.15
  development of neighbouring property, **8**.17
  easements, **8**.07
  entire understanding, **8**.11
  entry, **8**.22
  environment, **8**.23
  exclusion of use warranty, **8**.10
  frustration of reinstatement, **8**.18
  introduction, **8**.01
  licences, etc., under hand, **8**.13
  light, rights of, **8**.20
  limitations on liability, **8**.21
  new tenancy, **8**.25
  party walls, **8**.03
  perpetuity period, **8**.09
  re-entry, **8**.02
  representations, **8**.12
  service of notices, **8**.16
  tenant's property, **8**.14
  third party rights, **8**.26
  VAT, **8**.19
  waiver, **8**.06

Public lavatories
  retained parts, and, **2**.08
'Put in repair'
  repairs, and, **4**.06

Quarterly payment of rent
  demise, and, **3**.02
Quiet enjoyment
  landlord's covenants, and, **5**.02

Radio aerials, poles or masts
  tenant's covenants, and, **4**.08
Ramps
  common parts, and, **2**.05
Rates and taxes
  tenant's covenants, and, **4**.04
  tenant's works, and, **1**.13
Reasonable endeavours of landlord
  works, and, **1**.08
Re-convictions, warranty
  insurance, and, **6**.02
Re-entry
  provisos, and, **8**.02
Refuse
  service charge, and, **13**.21
Regulations
  service charge, and, **13**.30
  shop covenants, and, **12**.14
Reinstatement
  frustration, and, **8**.18
  licence for alterations, and, **15**.49–**15**.50
Reinstatement and termination
  insurance, and, **6**.10–**6**.12
Reinstatement plans
  licence for alterations, and, **15**.13
Reinstatement works
  licence for alterations, and, **15**.14
Re-letting boards
  tenant's covenants, and, **4**.23
Relevant review date
  particulars of lease, and, **2**.03
Relief against forfeiture
  termination of agreement for lease, and, **1**.15
Removal from premises
  termination of agreement for lease, and, **1**.15
Rent
  definition, **2**.08
  demise, and, **3**.02
  guarantor's covenants, and
    authorised guarantee agreement, **14**.13
    lease, **7**.03
  insurance, and, **6**.04
  interest on arrears, and, **4**.26
  quiet enjoyment, and, **5**.02

Rent—*contd.*
  re-entry, and, **8**.02
rent review
  *and see* **Rent review**
  generally, **11**.02–**11**.16
  introduction, **11**.01
  superior lease, and, **5**.04
  suspension of rent, and
    insurance, **6**.08
    toxic materials, **8**.23
  tenant's covenants, and, **4**.03
Rent commencement
  generally, **1**.18
Rent commencement date
  definition, **1**.03
  demise, and, **3**.02
  generally, **1**.18
  particulars of lease, and, **2**.03
Rent review
  alienation, and, **4**.15
  ascertainment
    arrangements on prevention of
      increase, **11**.16
    arrangements pending review, **11**.13
    generally, **11**.11–**11**.12
  assumptions, **11**.03–**11**.06
  definitions
    Arbitrator, **11**.10
    generally, **11**.02–**11**.09
    President, **11**.09
  disregarded matters, **11**.07–**11**.09
  dispute resolution, **11**.10
  introduction, **11**.01
  licence for alterations, and, **15**.37
  payment of revised sum, **11**.14–**11**.15
Rent-free periods
  demise, and, **3**.02
Repair
  opening hours, and, **12**.06
  tenant's covenants, and
    access by landlord, **4**.10
    generally, **4**.06
Representations
  agreement for lease, and
    generally, **1**.22
    restrictions, **1**.21
  lease, and, **8**.12
Reservation of rent
  demise, and, **3**.02–**3**.03
Reserve fund
  service charge, and, **13**.08
Residential restrictions
  tenant's covenants, and, **4**.17
Restrictions
  definition, **1**.04
  generally, **1**.21

Restrictions—*contd.*
  tenant's covenants, and, **4**.17
Restrictive clauses
  licence for alterations, and, **15**.16
Retained parts
  definition, **2**.08
  insurance, and, **6**.03
  party walls, and, **8**.03
  service charge, and
    cleaning, **13**.14
    maintenance, **13**.10
  suspension of rent, and, **6**.08
Reversion, sale of
  tenant's covenants, and, **4**.29
Review dates
  particulars of lease, and, **2**.03
Review period
  definition, **11**.02
Rights granted
  common parts, **10**.04
  entry, **10**.07
  fire escape, **10**.08
  introduction, **10**.03
  other, **10**.09
  pipes, **10**.05
  support, **10**.06
Rights reserved
  access, **10**.13
  construction of pipes, **10**.12
  introduction, **10**.10
  light, **10**.16
  scaffolding, **10**.14
  support, **10**.15
  use of pipes, **10**.11
Riot
  insured risks, and, **2**.07
Risk
  licence for alterations, and, **15**.35
Road charges
  service charge, and, **13**.29
Roof
  retained parts, and, **2**.08

Sale of reversion
  tenant's covenants, and, **4**.29
Satisfaction of architect
  tenant's works, and, **1**.12
Security alarms
  shop covenants, and, **12**.11
Security control centre
  retained parts, and, **2**.08
Service charge
  additional items
    anticipated expenditure, **13**.34
    contracts for services, **13**.26
    electricity charges, **13**.28

Service charge—*contd.*
  additional items—*contd.*
    fees, **13**.24
    gas charges, **13**.28
    interest, **13**.33
    nuisance, **13**.32
    oil charges, **13**.28
    outgoings, **13**.27
    regulations, **13**.30
    road charges, **13**.29
    staff, **13**.25
    statutory requirements, **13**.31
  anticipated expenditure, **13**.34
  apparatus, plant and machinery, **13**.11
  cleaning, **13**.14
  composition of services
    cleaning, **13**.14
    fixtures and fittings, **13**.19
    heating, **13**.15
    introduction, **13**.09
    maintenance, **13**.10–**13**.13
    opening malls, **13**.16
    ornamental features, **13**.18
    other, **13**.23
    refuse, **13**.21
    speakers, **13**.17
    traffic, **13**.22
    windows, **13**.20
  contracts for services, **13**.26
  definitions
    annual expenditure, **13**.03
    computing date, **13**.04
    financial year, **13**.05
    service charge percentage, **13**.06
    services, **13**.02
  demise, and, **3**.02
  electricity charges, **13**.28
  fees, **13**.24
  fire alarms, **13**.13
  fixtures and fittings, **13**.19
  gas charges, **13**.28
  heating, **13**.15
  insurance, and, **6**.04
  interest, **13**.33
  introduction, **13**.01
  maintenance services
    apparatus, plant and machinery, **13**.11
    fire alarms, **13**.13
    pipes, **13**.12
    retained parts, **13**.10
  nuisance, **13**.32
  oil charges, **13**.28
  ornamental features, **13**.18
  outgoings, **13**.27
  payment, **13**.08
  performance of the services, **13**.07

Service charge—*contd.*
  pipes, **13**.12
  refuse, **13**.21
  regulations, **13**.30
  road charges, **13**.29
  retained parts
    cleaning, **13**.14
    maintenance, **13**.10
  service provision by landlord, and, **5**.03
  speakers, **13**.17
  staff, **13**.25
  statutory requirements, **13**.31
  suspension of rent, and, **6**.08
  traffic, **13**.22
  variations, **13**.09
  windows, **13**.20
Service charge percentage
  particulars of lease, and, **2**.04
  service charge, and, **13**.06
Service of notices
  agreement for lease, and, **1**.24
  lease, and, **8**.16
Service roads
  common parts, and, **2**.05
Services, provision of
  landlord's covenants, and, **5**.03
Set-off
  demise, and, **3**.02
  rent, and, **4**.03
Severance
  authorised guarantee agreement, and, **14**.17
Sewers
  pipes, and, **2**.08
Shop covenants
  access, **12**.06
  advertisements, **12**.07
  alterations, **12**.04
  ceiling loading, **12**.09
  clean and tidy, **12**.08
  cooling, **12**.12
  definition, **2**.09
  display, **12**.06
  fire alarms, **12**.11
  fitting out, **12**.02
  floor loading, **12**.09
  heating, **12**.12
  hours of trading, **12**.06
  introduction, **12**.01
  landlord's regulations, **12**.14
  loading and unloading, **12**.10
  opening hours, **12**.06
  permitted user, **12**.03
  plate glass, **12**.13
  regulations, **12**.14
  security alarms, **12**.11

Shop covenants—*contd.*
　signs, **12.**07
　take precautions, **12.**05
　tenant's covenants, and, **4.**33
　unloading, **12.**10
　user, **12.**03
　ventilation, **12.**12
Shop front
　extent of premises, and, **10.**02
Shop opening hours
　common parts, and, **2.**05
　particulars of lease, and, **2.**04
　shop covenants, and, **12.**06
Side letters
　entire understanding, and, **1.**28
Signboards
　landlord's covenants, and, **5.**11
Signs
　landlord's covenants, and, **5.**11
　planning applications, and, **4.**20
　shop covenants, and, **12.**07
　tenant's covenants, and, **4.**08
　yielding up, and, **4.**25
Similar leases, provision of
　landlord's covenants, and, **5.**06
Sinking fund
　service charge, and, **13.**08
Site, the
　definition, **1.**04
Sleeping accommodation, use as
　tenant's covenants, and, **4.**17
Sound materials
　tenant's works, and, **1.**12
Speakers
　service charge, and, **13.**17
Sprinkler system
　insured risks, and, **2.**07
　statutory obligations, and, **4.**09
Staff
　service charge, and,. **13.**25
Staircases
　common parts, and, **2.**05
Stalls
　landlord's covenants, and, **5.**10
Stamp duty
　demise, and, **3.**03
Statutory notices
　tenant's covenants, and, **4.**23
Statutory obligations
　tenant's covenants, and, **4.**09
Statutory requirements
　service charge, and, **13.**31
Storm
　insured risks, and, **2.**07
Structural defects
　repairs, and, **4.**06

"Subject to"
　demise, and, **3.**02
Subrogation
　insurance, and, **6.**12
Subsidence
　insured risks, and, **2.**07
Substitution of materials
　works, and, **1.**07
Sunday trading
　opening hours, and, **2.**04
Superior lease, compliance with
　landlord's covenants, and, **5.**04
Support
　rights granted, and, **10.**06
　rights reserved, and, **10.**15
Supplemental agreements
　entire understanding, and, **1.**28
Surrender-back
　alienation, and, **4.**14
Surrender of part of premises
　guarantor's covenants, and, **7.**03
Surveyors
　application for approvals, **1.**06
　definition
　　agreement for lease, in, **1.**06
　　lease, in, **2.**09
　entry rights, **1.**08
　inspection rights, **1.**08
Suspension of rent
　insurance, and, **6.**08–**6.**09
　service charge, and, **6.**08
　toxic materials, and, **8.**23

Take precautions
　shop covenants, and, **12.**05
Taxes and assessments
　tenant's covenants, and, **4.**04
　tenant's works, and, **1.**13
Telegraphic aerials, poles or masts
　extent of premises, and, **10.**09
　planning applications, and, **4.**20
　tenant's covenants, and, **4.**08
Tempest
　insured risks, and, **2.**07
Tenancy at will
　tenant's works, and, **1.**12
Tenant, the
　definition
　　agreement for lease, in, **1.**04
　　lease, in, **2.**10
　　licence for alterations, in, **15.**07
　interpretation, and, **2.**10
　particulars of lease, and, **2.**02
Tenant's address
　definition, **1.**24

Tenant's approvals
  definition, **1.**11
  generally, **1.**12
Tenant's certificate
  tenant's works, and, **1.**13
  termination of agreement for lease, and, **1.**15
Tenant's covenants
  access of landlord, **4.**10–**4.**11
  advertisements, **4.**08
  aerials, **4.**08
  alienation, **4.**12–**4.**16
  cleaning, **4.**06
  decoration, **4.**07
  defective premises, **4.**30
  electricity charges, **4.**05
  encroachments, **4.**24
  gas charges, **4.**05
  indemnities, **4.**22
  insurance, and, **6.**13–**6.**14
  interest on arrears, **4.**26
  interpretation, and, **2.**11
  introduction, **4.**01
  keyholders, **4.**28
  landlord's costs
    consents, licences, etc., **4.**18–**4.**19
    grant of lease, **4.**34
  landlord's rights, **4.**32
  licence for alterations, and
    approval of consents, **15.**42
    completion of works, **15.**48
    conduct of work, **15.**44
    copies, information and evidence, **15.**26
    entry to premises, **15.**25
    execution of permitted works, **15.**24
    generally, **15.**22
    hours of working, **15.**43
    indemnities, **15.**51–**15.**52
    insurance, **15.**45–**15.**47
    insurance premiums, **15.**51
    landlord's costs, **15.**27
    materials and workmanship, **15.**41
    planning fees, **15.**53
    reinstatement, **15.**49–**15.**50
    starting permitted works, **15.**23
    VAT, **15.**27
  new guarantor, **4.**31
  notice to repair, **4.**10–**4.**11
  nuisance, **4.**17
  outgoings, **4.**04
  planning control, **4.**20
  plans, documents and information, **4.**21
  re-letting boards, **4.**23
  rent, **4.**03
  repair, **4.**06

Tenant's covenants—*contd.*
  residential restrictions, **4.**17
  sale of reversion, **4.**29
  shop covenants, **4.**33
  signs, **4.**08
  statutory notices, **4.**27
  statutory obligations, **4.**09
  utility charges, **4.**05
  VAT, **4.**04
  yielding up, **4.**25
Tenant's fixtures
  tenant's works, and, **1.**13
Tenant's property
  provisos, and, **8.**14
Tenant's solicitors
  definition, **1.**04
Tenant's works
  definitions, **1.**11
  fitting out, and, **12.**02
  generally, **1.**11–**1.**13
  termination of agreement for lease, and, **1.**16
Term, the
  interpretation, and, **2.**10
  licence for alterations, and, **15.**07, **15.**17
  particulars of lease, and, **2.**02
Term commencement date
  definition, **1.**05
Termination
  agreement for lease, and, **1.**15–**1.**16
Terrorism
  insured risks, and, **2.**07
  repairs, and, **4.**06
  suspension of rent, and, **6.**08–**6.**09
Testimonium
  agreement for lease, and, **1.**28
  lease, and, **9.**01
Third party rights
  provisos, and, **8.**26
Time limits
  licence for alterations, and, **15.**39
Title of landlord
  generally, **1.**20
Title paramount
  quiet enjoyment, and, **5.**02
"Together with"
  demise, and, **3.**02
Trading, commencement of
  generally, **1.**18
Traffic
  service charge, and, **13.**22

*Uberrimae fidei*
  insurance, and, **6.**02
Underletting premises
  agreement for lease, and, **1.**23

Underletting premises—*contd.*
  alienation, and, **4**.12–**4**.16
  opening hours, and, **12**.06
Unloading
  shop covenants, and, **12**.10
Use of pipes
  rights reserved, and, **10**.11
Use of site
  restrictions, and, **1**.21
User
  common parts, and, **2**.05
  particulars of lease, and, **2**.03
  shop covenants, and, **12**.03
Utility charges
  tenant's covenants, and, **4**.05

Vacation of premises
  compensation, and, **8**.15
  termination of agreement for lease, and, **1**.15
Variation of lease
  agreement for lease, and, **1**.14
  guarantor's covenants, and, **7**.03
  landlord's entitlement, and, **1**.14
  licence for alterations, and, **15**.38
Variation of service charge
  generally, **13**.09
VAT
  assumptions on rent review, and, **11**.06
  costs of agreement for lease, and, **1**.25
  definition, **2**.09
  demise, and, **3**.03
  licence for alterations, and, **15**.27
  provisos, and, **8**.19
  tenant's covenants, and, **4**.04
  variation of form of lease, and, **1**.14
Ventilation
  service charge, and, **13**.15
  shop covenants, and, **12**.12
Vitiation
  insurance, and, **6**.03

Waiver
  licence for alterations, and, **15**.30
  provisos, and, **8**.06
Walls
  retained parts, and, **2**.08
Warranties
  exclusion of use, and, **8**.10
  insurance, and, **6**.02
  restrictions, and, **1**.21
  works, and, **1**.10
Warranty re-convictions
  insurance, and, **6**.02

Watercourses
  pipes, and, **2**.08
Watertight premises
  works, and, **1**.08
Wear and tear
  repairs, and, **4**.06
Weatherproof premises
  works, and, **1**.08
Winding up
  re-entry, and, **8**.02
  termination of agreement for lease, and, **1**.15
Window
  cleaning, and
    shop covenants, **12**.08
    tenant's covenants, **4**.06
  extent of premises, and, **10**.02
  insurance, and, **6**.03
  service charge, and, **13**.20
Wires
  pipes, and, **2**.08
Working day, definition of
  agreement for lease, and, **1**.05
  lease, and, **8**.16
Workmanlike manner
  tenant's works, and, **1**.12
Works
  application for approvals, **1**.06
  building documents
    definition, **1**.06
    modification, **1**.07
  certificate of practical completion, **1**.09
  compliance with CDM Regulations, **1**.06
  defects notice, **1**.08
  definition, **1**.05
  delay, **1**.09
  deleterious substances, **1**.06
  extension of time, **1**.09
  harmful substances, **1**.06
  initial yearly rent, **1**.10
  inspection
    architect's notice, **1**.09
    surveyors' rights, **1**.08
  landlord's approvals, **1**.06
  measurement of gross yearly rent, **1**.10
  modification to building documents, **1**.07
  reasonable endeavours of landlord, **1**.08
  substitution of materials, **1**.07
  surveyors
    application for approvals, **1**.06
    definition, **1**.06

Works—*contd.*
  surveyors—*contd.*
    entry rights, **1**.08
    inspection rights, **1**.08
  tenant, by
    *and see* **Tenant's works**
    generally, **1**.11–**1**.13
  warranties, **1**.10

Works—*contd.*
  weatherproof premises, **1**.08

"Yielding and paying"
  demise, and, **3**.02
Yielding up
  tenant's covenants, and, **4**.25